CHESHIRE
ACADEMY

CHESHIRE ACADEMY
FOUNDED 1794

EX LIBRIS

HENRY ADAMS

AND

HENRY JAMES

The Emergence of a
Modern Consciousness

HENRY ADAMS

AND

HENRY JAMES

The Emergence of a Modern Consciousness

JOHN CARLOS ROWE

Cornell University Press Ithaca and London

First published 1976 by Cornell University Press.
Published in the United Kingdom by Cornell University Press Ltd., 2-4 Brook Street, London W1Y 1AA.

International Standard Book Number 0-8014-0954-3
Library of Congress Catalog Card Number 75-16928
Printed in the United States of America by York Composition Co., Inc.

For Kristin and Sean

Contents

Contents

Preface

Henry Adams and Henry James invite obvious comparisons. Exact contemporaries on the American literary scene, both were beguiled by European culture, both were distressed by American ills. Philosophically and aesthetically they also had much in common. But these two writers arrived at logically opposite extremes in struggling with the historical, political, economic, and social problems of their age. Adams came to view the basic impulse toward unity as the force that could give coherence to the multiplicity of experience; he viewed philosophies of history as aesthetic systems that made it possible to organize the incoherence of historical and natural events. James, on the other hand, felt that art and history were inextricably related, and that history could be viewed in terms of the differing interpretations man designs to relate himself to the social or natural world.

Yet both these writers reflect and embody a fundamental shift in American literature, from an earlier transcendental and logocentric vision to an increasingly speculative and experimental emphasis on methodology. Re-evaluated together in a study of the literary imagination, they illuminate the unfolding, self-conscious position that has characterized modern literature since the turn of the century. And James is a most appropriate counterpart for Adams in a study concerned with changing concepts of meaning, for in his criticism and fiction James described a creative imagination fundamental to both artistic expression and historical order.

This book began as an attempt to clarify the intellectual and aesthetic problems that confronted American imaginative writers at the end of the nineteenth century. The rapid changes that took place in science, technology, and economics from the end of the Civil War to the first decade of the twentieth century clearly had an enormous impact on traditional American values. Confronted with swift and uncontrolled industrialization, many Americans found untenable the accepted beliefs of an older agrarian society. American writers were faced with a task of reconciliation: man's desire for secure moral values and for spiritual direction seemed at odds with a society increasingly at the mercy of random and undirected forces. Science and industry harnessed natural energies to effect material changes, but the individual felt even less capable of finding meaning in a world lacking spiritual intention. Mark Twain attacked modern America for its failure to use science to create a community supporting individual worth and human dignity. Stephen Crane and Frank Norris condemned an urban America that increasingly alienated man from his own nature. The literature of the period expresses the failure of the American dream to establish a society in which the individual would find his significance through communication with others.

In attempting to understand this critical period in American thought, I found that the breakdown of older American values went far beyond their conflict with contemporary science and technology. American history after the Civil War merely made explicit the gradual deterioration of man's confidence in his own rational faculties and an inherent order in nature. The American writer at the end of the nineteenth century is especially skeptical of the idea that human inquiry could reveal man's place in a universal design. These writers recognize the illusory quality of man's truths and reject any transcendental level for human thought. This skepticism may reflect merely cultural disaffection in a time of marked upheaval and confusion, but it has been the foundation for a still emerging consciousness that has detached itself from a venerable humanist heritage. Imaginative writing at the end of the nineteenth century in America reflects a general need for new definitions of basic philosophical concepts of meaning and truth, existence and being, unity and multiplicity.

Thus the crisis in modern thought that I viewed initially in terms of social and historical factors led me inevitably to questions of epistemology and ontology. In their obsessive concern with cosmic and metaphysical problems, the writers of the period were in effect trying to abstract a general structure for the transformation of values that was occurring on all levels of American society. No American writer at this time struggled more determinedly than Henry Adams to define the infrastructure of modern history. Adams's attempt to extract a general pattern of similarities and oppositions from the varied and apparently unrelated forces that determine historical periods suggested both a subject and method for my study. I decided to focus the crisis of the period in terms of a basic shift in attitudes toward signification.

Henry Adams began writing in quest of a far-reaching historical unity, but found himself forced to deal with the philosophical assumptions fundamental to any history. Instead of claiming that the works of Adams and James are representative of the literature of the period, I prefer to maintain that they deal more explicitly than others with a phenomenology of knowing that characterizes much turn-of-the-century thought and literature. Similarly, I have selected texts by Adams and James for close analysis that clarify crucial questions about aesthetic and historical meaning basic to all their writing. Thus the emerging modern consciousness described by Adams and James is not limited to their later works, even though the possibilities of the modern imagination are given their fullest treatment in Adams's *Mont-Saint-Michel and Chartres* and *The Education of Henry Adams* and in James's *The Wings of the Dove* and *The Golden Bowl*.

The genesis of this book should clarify the purposes of a selective process that are implicit in my general argument. I have made critical choices that contribute to a structure of ideas as "unreal" in its abstraction as Adams's own historical theories or James's fictional forms. I have tried, moreover, to organize basic concepts in Adams and James that reflect the general crisis in thought at the turn of the century. I emphasize the contrivances of the critical act, because I recognize how heavily this study depends on the interplay of its critical metalanguage with its historical subjects. In short, I have tried to write a literary history that gives structure to the past in the language of the present. As Roland Barthes writes in "What Is Criticism?": "One can say that the critical task . . . is purely formal: not to 'discover' in the work or the author something 'hidden,' 'profound,' 'secret' which hitherto passed unnoticed (by what miracle? Are we more perspicacious than our predecessors?), but only to adjust the language his period affords him (existentialism, Marxism, psychoanalysis) to the language, i.e., the formal system of logical constraints elaborated by the author according to his own period" (*Critical Essays*, pp. 258–9).

One important subject of this book is the critical methodology that underlies it. The notion of critical activity itself as the subject matter of criticism emerges from Adams's and James's own conceptions of signification and interpretation. The unfulfilled meaning, the suspended question, and the incomplete sentence are more than mere rhetorical techniques in their works. My attempt to analyze signification as a relational process fundamental to Adams's and James's art must involve a commentary on criticism itself.

This study was first made possible by a grant from the State University of New York at Buffalo for the academic year 1970–1971. My greatest thanks belong to Joseph Riddel, who spent much time and effort helping me to organize and compose the book. His work and thought have greatly sustained me, and I only hope that some trace of his inspiration remains. Edgar Dryden invariably caught inconsistencies in thought and lapses in style. Joseph Fradin's confidence in my ideas helped me to complete the first draft. Among the many people at Buffalo who contributed to this study, I owe special thanks to Frederick See, Royal Roussel, Jerome Mazzaro, R. E. Johnson, Jr., and Gary Davis.

The final version of this study is the result of the financing and encouragement of the Department of English at the University of Maryland. John Howard and Molly Emler assisted me with the mechanics of revision, frequently saving me needless worry or labor. Milne Holton, Gerald Tyson, Robert Kolker, Marjorie Perloff, Robert Moore, and Shirley Kenny all showed special interest in my project and offered aid whenever it was needed. The libraries of the State University of New York at Buffalo, The Johns Hopkins University, the University of Maryland, the Library of Congress, and the University of California at Los Angeles were most helpful in my research.

I wish to thank the editors of *ELH* for permission to republish as Chapter 6 an extensive revision of an essay that first appeared in their pages. I would also like to thank Professors J. Hillis Miller and Roy Harvey Pearce for their encouraging readings of that early essay. I owe a special debt of gratitude to the editors and staff at Cornell University Press, especially Jeanne Duell. Their insistence on clarity and precision resulted in major improvements throughout the manuscript. Their editorial judgment and good sense encouraged me to try to meet their high standards.

My gratitude and devotion to my wife, Kristin, clearly belong elsewhere than at the end of a list of personal acknowledgments.

J. C. R.

College Park, Maryland

HENRY ADAMS

AND

HENRY JAMES

The Emergence of a
Modern Consciousness

I   Henry Adams and Henry James in the American Literary Tradition

> There are thus two interpretations of interpretation, of structure, of sign, of freeplay. The one seeks to decipher, dreams of deciphering a truth or an origin which is free from freeplay and from the order of the sign, and lives like an exile the necessity of interpretation. The other, which is no longer turned toward the origin, affirms freeplay and tries to pass beyond man and humanism, the name man being the name of that being who, throughout the history of metaphysics or of ontotheology—in other words, through the history of all his history—has dreamed of full presence, the reassuring foundation, the origin and the end of the game.
>
> —Jacques Derrida, "Structure, Sign, and Play in the Discourse of the Human Sciences"

Any study of nineteenth- and twentieth-century American thought must confront the breakdown of metaphysical values that had been fundamental to Western thought since the seventeenth century. Nineteenth-century American history dramatically expresses the discontinuity of an emerging modern consciousness from more traditional views relying on an inherent order in nature. As we read the texts of American literature and history, we are reminded constantly that two conflicting conceptions of America are at work: progress and revolution. The progressive spirit in America is founded upon a general sense of historical continuity. Puritan thought relied primarily on the methods and texts of a seventeenth-century European philosophic tradition. On the other hand, the quest for an American identity and philosophy involved a repudiation of those aspects of the Puritan heritage that limited the range of the creative mind. Thus the rebellion of the nineteenth-century writer against European culture resulted in alienating him from the primary tradition of eighteenth-century American thought as well.

The documents that so consciously express the need for an American literature in the latter half of the eighteenth century and first half of the nineteenth century demand an affirmation of American independence in a rejection of European subjects and forms. They demand a literature that will reflect the indigenous American condition. William Ellery Channing's definition of a national literature in 1830 is representative: "We begin with stating what we mean by national literature. We mean the expression of a nation's mind in writing. We mean the production among a people of important works in philosophy and in the department of imagination and taste."[1] Repeatedly, the word "creation" is used in connection with this literary development. It is conceived of not as furthering the continuity of Western literature, but as a radical newness which to "foretell" would be to "create."[2] Channing further emphasizes the dependence of our literary originality upon cultural detachment:

A people in whose minds the thoughts of foreigners are poured perpetually needs an energy within itself to resist, to modify this mighty influence, and without it, will inevitably sink under the worst bondage, will become intellectually tame and enslaved. . . . Better have no literature than form ourselves unresistingly on a foreign one. The true sovereigns of a country are those who determine its mind, its mode of thinking, its tastes, its principles; and we cannot consent to lodge this sovereignty in the hands of strangers.[3]

1. William Ellery Channing, "Remarks on National Literature," in *The Christian Examiner* (January 1830), quoted in *The American Literary Revolution: 1783–1837*, ed. Robert E. Spiller, p. 343.

2. Edward Everett said in his Phi Beta Kappa address at Harvard in 1824: "To foretell our literature would be to create it." Quoted in *American Literary Revolution*, p. 296.

3. Channing, in *American Literary Revolution*, p. 357. Compare with Melville's remarks twenty years later in "Hawthorne and His Mosses" (1850): "Let America then prize and cherish her writers; yea let her glorify them. They are not so many in number as to exhaust her good will. And while she has good kith and kin of her own, to take to her

Channing's political and judicial rhetoric is the rule rather than the exception in contemporary documents. For writers of the period the liberation of the American mind through the vital forms of its own literature is a necessary concomitant of a political and social revolution. The optimism and bravado of Channing's remarks emphasize his confidence that the American mind could discover its own cultural sovereignty. Channing nevertheless rejoices in an "increasing intellectual connexion" between America and Europe. The future movement of American thought *toward* a reciprocal relation with European culture was to be a further affirmation of its very independence from that tradition. Implicit in the insistence that an independent American literature might be created is the conscious sense of a "new beginning" that dominates early American thought. All the myths of an American Adam, a new Garden, and the American Dream depend upon an idea of historical and intellectual discontinuity.

This apparent discontinuity informs the genesis of the American literary renaissance. Emerson, Thoreau, Poe, Hawthorne, Melville, and Whitman recognized the need for new forms in a literature that would define the American consciousness. In a more sophisticated manner than Channing, they set about the task of redefining the nature and aims of American thought. They realized that the mere infusion of an American "subject" into European forms was not sufficient. Brockden Brown and Franklin had demonstrated the inadequacy of such an approach in the quest for an autonomous American literature, although for this very reason their works succeeded in reflecting the eighteenth-century American consciousness. But the American Renaissance writers began in the trap of the paradoxical nature of the American mind, which was defined by the European

---

bosom, let her not lavish her embraces on the household of an alien. For believe it or not, England, after all, is, in many things, an alien to us. China has more bowels of real love for us than she." *The Portable Melville,* ed. Jay Leyda, pp. 411–12.

philosophical heritage and yet was to be constituted by a repudiation of that tradition. As Charles Feidelson has pointed out, the "revolution" of the writers of the American Renaissance was primarily *methodological:*

The intellectual stance of the conscious artist in American literature has been determined very largely by *problems inherent in the method of the Puritans.* The isolation of the American artist in society, so often lamented, is actually parallel to the furtive and unacknowledged role of artistic method in the American mind; both factors began in the seventeenth century with the establishment of Puritan philosophy and of a society that tried to live by it. Hence the crudity or conventionality of a great part of American literature from 1620 through the third quarter of the nineteenth century may be attributed no more surely to frontier conditions, provinciality, and industrialism than to inherited mental habits which proscribed a functional artistic form. *And the symbolism of Emerson, Thoreau, Melville, Hawthorne, and Whitman was an attempt to hew out such a form in defiance of intellectual methods that denied its validity.*[4]

The attempt to "hew out" a form that might validate the epistemological methods of the nineteenth-century American writer implied also a movement toward the establishment of a center for metaphysics as well as for literature. Despite the call for a new history and a new culture, American literature began by interpreting the texts of its Puritan heritage and seeking a more appropriate methodology for dealing with the basic problems of that tradition. The American Renaissance confirmed the essential Cartesian dualism of reason and madness, subject and object, phenomenon and noumenon. The historical texts from Shakespeare and Milton to Cotton Mather and the records of the Salem Witch Trials were reread with an eye to finding an appropriate center for American philosophy. It is quite appropriate that the history of philosophy and the history of literature in the first half of the nineteenth century in America should be so nearly synonymous.

4. Charles Feidelson, Jr., *Symbolism and American Literature,* pp. 89–90; italics mine.

The symbolism of the American Renaissance depends upon a movement toward a transcendental center for the structures of thought which at the same time governs their internal order. Jacques Derrida has abstracted the classical conception of structural unity in similar terms: "It has always been thought that the center, which is by definition unique, constituted that very thing within a structure which governs the structure, while escaping structurality. This is why classical thought concerning structure could say that the center is, paradoxically, *within* the structure and *outside* it."[5] The symbolic mode of the American Renaissance writers is an attempt to provide new signs by which to approach a center for consciousness that is evasive and inscrutable. Although the literary symbolism of the period is founded on man's subjectivity, the symbolic function intends the relation of individual consciousness to a unifying origin and end. There is an impulse to resolve the conflict between temporal discourse and the "silence" that is the language of Poe's "Unity," Melville's "Whiteness," Thoreau's "cry of the loon," or Whitman's "word final, superior to all."[6] Thus Whitman expresses the longing of the poet to unite in his rhythms life and death, his names and the word. As the poet of "Out of the Cradle Endlessly Rocking" struggles to resurrect his origins, he tries to relate subject and object. The poetic "I" claims to "fuse the song of my dusky demon and brother, / That he sang to me in the moonlight on Paumanok's gray beach," until at last "the sea whisper'd me."[7] The symbolism of the American Renaissance expresses man's existence in an ultimately teleological manner. The quest of the poet or hero is an attempt to resolve the dualism of his condition. Like Ahab's doubloon or Whitman's poetic ego,

5. Jacques Derrida, "Structure, Sign, and Play in the Discourse of the Human Sciences," in *The Languages of Criticism and the Sciences of Man*, ed. Macksey and Donato, p. 248.

6. See Henry David Thoreau, "Brute Neighbors," in *The Variorum Walden*, ed. Walter Harding.

7. Walt Whitman, "Out of the Cradle Endlessly Rocking," ll. 175–6, 183, in *Leaves of Grass*, ed. Scully Bradley and Harold Blodgett, p. 253.

the symbol becomes a center for subjectivity which ought to embody a direction and intention for such a quest, search, or hunt.

If the symbolism of this period may be interpreted as intentional, it is equally reductive. As a center for subjectivity, the symbol suggests a point of reference for "the reduction of life to its lowest terms."[8] Fundamental to the conception of the literary *isolato*—such an archetypal figure in the literature of this period —is a process of historical and social reduction that enables him to define his own *cogito* in a spiritual wilderness. The goal of that reduction is the possibility of a viable contract between the self and its social other. The "I" of *Walden* does not find withdrawal and isolation ends in themselves. He must return to Concord every few weeks to reaffirm the disjunction between his little world and the society that he has repudiated. His oscillation between those two worlds prefigures the ultimate need to return from the woods, once he has developed an ego capable of some independence. Ishmael may echo the Book of Job, " 'And I only am escaped alone to tell thee,' " in the context of a literary vocation that aims at relating his reductive journey through an ocean wilderness to the discourse of social man. Hester Prynne's process of withdrawal moves toward its ultimate fulfillment in Pearl's marriage into a foreign aristocracy and in Hester's own works as an "angel of mercy." Implicit in this process of philosophical reduction and ultimate social relation is the possibility of approaching an essential center for the structures of thought and language.

The reading of cultural and historical texts by the authors of this period and their characters also has a reductive aim. In the simplest sense, the accumulation of texts in *Moby-Dick* is mythopoeic in its attempt to suggest patterns for human or natural behavior. Mythopoeia is primarily a reductive process because it attempts to produce general archetypes and models for dealing with a vast and unmanageable tangle of human thought and

8. The phrase is Thoreau's in *Walden*.

experience. The volumes in the narrator's library in *Walden* or the extensive quotations and analyses that counterpoint the account of the journey in *A Week on the Concord and Merrimack Rivers* are alternate means of "honing the senses" into more perceptive instruments. Thoreau's readings, as well as his experiments in the woods, contribute to that process of discovery which is the transcendentalist's *cogito:* "The process of discovery is very simple. An unwearied and systematic application of known laws to nature causes the unknown to reveal themselves. Almost any *mode* of observation will be successful at last, for what is most wanted is method. Only let something be determined and fixed around which observation may rally. . . . Where there is an observatory and a telescope, we expect that any eyes will see new worlds at once."[9] The epistemological quest is reductive in its determination of a center "around which observation" by the subjective consciousness "may rally."

The intentional and reductive symbolism of the American Renaissance attempts to reconcile the differences of human subjectivity. The symbol achieves meaning as it relates the individual to the universal, the temporal to the eternal. The symbol is necessitated by the distance that separates man from the meaning he calls being. The more inaccessible such a metaphysical center becomes, the more the symbol ought to offer direction for the quest itself. In *Moby-Dick* Ahab tacks the doubloon to the mainmast in hopes of inspiring his crew with his own singleness of purpose. Given monetary value, it ought to serve as an incentive for a questionable journey. As "the white whale's talisman" it becomes a symbolic representation of the process of symbolization itself. Pip's summary of the readings defines the real function of the doubloon: " 'I look, you look, he looks, we look, ye look, they look.' " The text of the coin is appropriately "foreign" in its iconography, and it must be read to clarify the various attitudes toward the voyage. As Pip reads it, it is the ship's *navel*

9. Thoreau, *A Week on the Concord and Merrimack Rivers,* p. 310.

without the promise of Delphic revelations concerning their purpose and fate. Pip's conjugation of the verb "to look" exposes the distance separating his divine madness from the Pequod's world of ambiguity and perspectivism. Ultimately, the doubloon dramatizes human multiplicity as well as metaphysical dualism, foreshadowing the dark, shifting worlds of *The Confidence-Man*.

The American Renaissance is a period of radical transformation in the patterns of American thought, despite its initial dependence upon the philosophical dualism of its seventeenth-century heritage. In attempting to come to terms with that dualism, Emerson, Thoreau, Hawthorne, Poe, Whitman, and Melville increasingly find the metaphysical and ontological structures vague and indefinable. In the context of the period's symbolism the expression of a metaphysical center more and more intends toward a formless Energy, which in its very ebb and flow denies any conception of center. Melville's "Whiteness" is as early as *Mardi* the "visible absence of color," and Poe's "Unity" in *Eureka* involves its own decentralization and fragmentation. Increasingly, the human condition is defined as a lie and a masquerade. The metaphysical blankness in the later works of Melville repudiates the forms and structures of thought that define our human reality. Melville's cosmic energy denies the possibility of an authentic human ontology. His formless center appears to be defined by the creation of structures out of it—its potentiality for coming-into-being. Yet "meaning" in the fragmentary language of human discourse can be only a lie, an essential condition of "no trust," in which violence is done to the conception of the human process as a quest, discovery, or real-ization. The human masquerade is defined by its alienation from the truth. What Melville develops out of a tradition of philosophical dualism is a conflict between the polarities of human and metaphysical realities, which threatens to empty both of all meaning. Confronted with the disjunction between what conventionally would be termed the "center" and its conscious forms, Melville must repudiate the possibility of any metaphysical meaning or essential human nature. The rupture between the governing center and man's creations reduces both to the level of lies and fictions. As the structures of thought float aimlessly, language can never hope to approach any substantive reality.

The symbolism of the American Renaissance cannot reconcile its intentional and reductive impulses. Melville in particular moves toward an ultimate repudiation of the possibility of that *telos* the writers of the period try to define. Melville in *The Confidence-Man* provides an appropriate, albeit somewhat arbitrary, point for marking the real rupture in American thought. He is able no longer to affirm his own "sovereign nature" or cry "No! in thunder." After completing *The Confidence-Man*, he travels to England where he visits Hawthorne. In Hawthorne's description, one sees how Melville's private crisis reflects the conflict of values in American thought at mid-century:

Melville, as he always does, began to reason of Providence and futurity, and of everything that lies beyond human ken, and informed me that he had "pretty much made up his mind to be annihilated;" but still he does not seem to rest in that anticipation; and, I think, will never rest until he gets hold of a definite belief. It is strange how he persists—and has persisted ever since I knew him, and probably long before—in wandering to-and-fro over these deserts, as dismal and monotonous as the sand hills amid which we were sitting. He can neither believe, nor be comfortable in his unbelief; and he is too honest and courageous not to try to do one or the other.[10]

In Whitman's poetry as well there is a failure to sustain that center which would reconcile the intentional and reductive thrust of consciousness. The expanding range of the poetic imagination in "Song of Myself" is equally the reduction of a pluralistic world to the control of the poetic voice. Whitman's ego knows itself through its names, the poet appropriating nature as

10. Nathaniel Hawthorne, *The English Notebooks*, ed. Randall Stewart, pp. 432–3.

he reaches out toward it.[11] The aesthetic taxonomies of "Song of Myself" reveal little at last but the phenomenology of the poet's mind. "All goes onward and outward, nothing collapses," but only as the poet concentrates the diversity of life in himself:

> In me the caresser of life wherever moving, backward as well
> as forward sluing,
> To niches aside and junior bending, not a person or object
> missing,
> Absorbing all to myself and for this song.[12]

Whitman's poetic ego increasingly loses definition and cannot sustain its prophetic integrity. As Roy Harvey Pearce has argued, the protagonist of "Passage to India" lacks an authentic identity "because the protagonist in this poem is that of cosmic man, who, because he is everywhere, is nowhere; who, because he can be everything, is nothing."[13]

The aesthetic difficulties of Melville and Whitman suggest a philosophical crisis in the middle of the nineteenth century involving an essential decentralization of the structures for thought and language. Three important texts in the American literary tradition help to clarify the nature of this crisis and its effect on changing concepts of self, identity, and knowledge. In these selections, Herman Melville, Henry Adams, and Henry James indirectly reread the text of Carlyle's *Sartor Resartus* and formulate different versions of Herr Teufelsdröckh's "clothes philosophy" and the "Everlasting Yea." *Sartor Resartus* is Carlyle's attempt to define a spiritual unity for human existence. Teufelsdröckh's massive work, "Die Kleider, ihr Werden und Wirken," reveals the intentional symbols that signify a divine presence in the world. It is that very presence which repudiates the symbols as things in themselves and posits their meaning in their ability

11. Roy Harvey Pearce, *The Continuity of American Poetry*, p. 166.
12. Whitman, "Song of Myself," ll. 232–4, in *Leaves of Grass*, p. 40.
13. Pearce, "Whitman: The Poet in 1860," in *Historicism Once More*, p. 207.

to suggest a transcendental reality. Carlyle's process of reduction begins with the "disillusioned negation" of the "Everlasting No," passes to the "Centre of Indifference," and finds meaning in the mystical revelation of the relation of God to man in the "Everlasting Yea." The spiritual rebirth of the individual through such a process is the denial of independent selfhood and a submission to divine purpose.[14]

As Lawrance Thompson shows, Melville strongly reacts against Carlyle's concept of spiritual identity.[15] His letter to Hawthorne affirms the self as an essential center for human consciousness and the goal of any reductive method: "There is a grand truth about Nathaniel Hawthorne. He says No! in thunder; but the Devil himself cannot make him say *yes*. For all men who say *yes*, lie; and all men who say *no*,—why, they are in the happy condition of judicious, unincumbered travellers in Europe; they cross the frontiers into Eternity with nothing but a carpet-bag,—that is to say, the Ego. Whereas those *yes*-gentry, they travel with heaps of baggage, and, damn them! they will never get through the Custom House."[16] To Melville Carlyle's "Everlasting Yea" is a comfortable delusion. Carlyle's spiritual rebirth really depends upon a mystical leap of faith, which leads to a blind acceptance and accumulation of the very dogmas it seeks to discard. Self-renunciation, for Melville, only compels the individual to multiply his "baggage," with no basis for selection or discrimination. What Melville is suggesting is that the "garments" have no symbolic power or meaning without the defining ego. Carlyle suggests that we look intently at clothes "till they become transparent" and their essential relation to a spiritual source is revealed. In Melville's passage, the central ego is a carpetbag containing the few rags necessary for the journey. The very form

14. W. H. Hudson, "Introduction" to *Sartor Resartus*, p. xv.
15. Lawrance Thompson, *Melville's Quarrel with God*, p. 131.
16. Herman Melville to Nathaniel Hawthorne, 16? April? 1851, in *The Letters of Herman Melville*, ed. Merrell R. Davis and William H. Gilman, p. 125.

of the carpetbag ego makes these few symbols, or beliefs, necessary and meaningful. Appropriately, Melville's center is at once
the bag literally *outside* the traveler and the principle that
governs from *within* his perceptions of the journey. In another
reading, the carpetbag is the enclosing shape for the garments
within it, and the structural principle that gives them meaning
for the traveler. In this way, the carpetbag ego defines the varying
movements of the traveler in time and space. Melville writes
earlier in the same letter:

By visible truth, we mean the apprehension of the absolute condition of present things as they strike the eye of the man who fears
them not, though they do their worst to him,—the man who, like
Russia or the British Empire, declares himself a sovereign nature
(in himself) amid the powers of heaven, hell, and earth. He may
perish; but so long as he exists he insists upon treating with all
Powers upon an equal basis. If any of those other Powers choose to
withhold certain secrets, let them; that does not impair my sovereignty in myself; that does not make me tributary. And perhaps,
after all there is *no* secret.[17]

His thunderous Nay is an essential affirmation of the self-reliant
American *isolato* in transit. In *Moby-Dick,* Ishmael's "Call me
Ishmael" of the first chapter leads directly to the possibility of
Chapter 2, "The Carpet-Bag," wherein he packs his bag with
the necessities for the journey: "I stuffed a shirt or two into my
old carpet-bag, tucked it under my arm, and started for Cape
Horn and the Pacific."[18]

In an analogous, though more complex, sense, the narrator of
White-Jacket wears a jacket that he makes protective by folding,
slitting, and then stuffing: "So, with many odds and ends of
patches—old socks, old trowser-legs, and the like—I bedarned
and bequilted the inside of my jacket till it became, all over,
stiff and padded, as King James's cotton-stuffed and dagger-
proof doublet; and no buckram or steel hauberk stood up more

17. Ibid., p. 124.
18. *Moby-Dick,* ed. Luther S. Mansfield and Howard P. Vincent, p. 6.

stoutly."[19] Here the narrator transforms a garment, the light linen duck frock, into a container. Melville combines the garments and their container in the figure of the jacket to form a protective shell as a shield for the narrator against the threats of the man-of-war world in which he finds himself. The whiteness of the jacket ("It was not a *very* white jacket, but white enough") provides a protective blankness that belies the motley of its interior, the persona laid bare. The conventional design of any carpetbag's exterior might be assumed as an alternative mode of protection: the intricacy of the superficial pattern leads the threatening other away from any plunge into its vulnerable contents. This very protective form of the ego is essential for Melville's earlier *isolatos*. The Melvillean "No! in thunder" is a rational act of survival, shielding the individual from the brutal and meaningless glare of reality. It is the absolutely necessary center without which consciousness cannot begin to assume a form. It is the goal of the reductive and intentional symbolism of the American Renaissance in the face of an increasingly veiled metaphysical center. Yet the very need to protect the self betrays the tenuous ontological foundation for the symbolism. Melville's struggle with the familiar polarities of subject and object, self and other, appropriately marks the crisis in form that demanded new languages. The ultimate ambiguity of the doubloon and the inadequacy of the duck frock to protect White-Jacket completely suggest the philosophical and aesthetic questions that Adams and James had to confront.[20]

In the preface to *The Education of Henry Adams,* Adams revises the text of Carlyle's Teufelsdröckh in a remarkably different fashion, although the tone and imagery seem to echo

19. *White-Jacket,* pp. 17–18.
20. See Howard P. Vincent, *The Tailoring of Melville's "White-Jacket,"* p. 23: "White-Jacket's isolation, however, results not from any deep desire to know himself through contemplation but rather from his refusal to participate in the ordinary life of humanity. Though he achieves a delusory protection from the cold and the storm, he finds his jacket inadequate and must, in time, abandon it or be destroyed by it."

Melville's letter. Like Melville in *The Confidence-Man*, Adams repudiates the possibility of any center for the structures of thought and language: "As educator, Jean Jacques was, in one respect, easily first; he erected a monument of warning against the Ego. Since his time, and largely thanks to him, the Ego has steadily tended to efface itself, and, for purposes of model, to become a manikin on which the toilet of education is to be draped in order to show the fit or misfit of the clothes. The object of study is the garment, not the figure."[21] For Adams the "transparency" of the garments reveals only the wood and wire of the manikin itself. Education becomes the successive activities of draping, cutting, and fitting garments and studying their "fit or misfit." Of course, there are three distinct, but related, meanings for Adams's manikin. For the purposes of a model, it is an anatomical figure. In another sense, we may read "manikin" in its etymological significance as "homunculus" or "little man." On a third level, it is a wooden puppet manipulated by an unseen hand to act out a succession of roles. All three senses are affirmed in the ironic historical process of the "effacement of the Ego," which Adams traces back to the romantic apotheosis of the subject. The effacement of the ego is the absolute decentralization of that subject. All three meanings for Adams's manikin confirm the conception of an essentially hollow, emptied self. Whether we read the manikin as the anonymous and obscure figure of "homunculus," as the wooden hulk of the store window dummy, or as the dancing puppet that collapses in a heap at the end of a show, we are face to face with a repudiation of education as a process of self-discovery.

In the editor's preface, which Adams wrote for Henry Cabot Lodge's signature, he refers to St. Augustine's *Confessions* as one of the possible models for the *Education*.[22] Adams rejected Augustine, however, precisely because "St. Augustine, like a great

21. Henry Adams, *The Education of Henry Adams*, p. x. Hereafter cited in the text as *EHA*.
22. J. C. Levenson, *The Mind and Art of Henry Adams*, p. 306.

artist, had worked from multiplicity to unity, while he, like a small one, had to reverse the method and work back from unity to multiplicity" (*EHA*, vii-viii). Augustine offers his readers such *exempla* as Alypius's experience at the Colosseum and Victorinus's conversion to complement a general pattern of self-renunciation and humiliation. The primary impulse of the *Confessions* is to transform the sins of self-consciousness into the virtue of a conscious immersion in God. The manikin of Adams's *Education* lacks the firm intention of Augustine and his faith. Adams cannot lay claim to the hindsight and illumination that Augustine's conversion and baptism bring to him. The mature author can offer little insight into the false turnings of youth.

As ironic as the appeal of the effaced author in the editor's preface to the self-renunciation of Augustine is the opening of his self-conscious preface with a quotation from Rousseau's *Confessions*. Certainly Jean-Jacques Rousseau's romantic ego is as remote for the student of modern multiplicity as the abnegation of Augustine. In the two prefaces, the pronoun "I" is used *only* in the quotation from Rousseau, where it is used to an extreme. The technique and form of the preface confirm the historical effacement of the ego. Self-consciousness in its conventional sense is a lie and a fiction for the author of the *Education*. Yet study and education still require a model on which to drape the garments. As Adams writes at the end of Chapter 21 and repeats in the editor's preface: "Any schoolboy could see that man as a force must be measured by motion from a fixed point" (*EHA*, xxi and 435). This very lack of a fixed point for the structure of thought is a primary problem in the *Education*. It is the essential emptiness and blankness of the manikin that make the "object of study . . . the garment, not the figure." From the beginning of the *Education*, the classical concept of a center as a principle of structurality for human discourse is absent. The center becomes a contrived fiction enabling us to "measure . . . man as a force": "Eight of ten years of study had led Adams to think he might use the century 1150-1250, expressed in Amiens

Cathedral and the works of Thomas Aquinas, as the unit from which he might measure motion down to his own time, without assuming anything as true or untrue except relation" (*EHA*, xxi)'. The conception that only relation could be assumed as true transforms the center from a principle governing structurality into a *function* describing structurality.

The "very metaphysical" discussion between Madame Merle and Isabel Archer in Chapter 19 of *The Portrait of a Lady* offers a third view of the problem. The dialectical movement of their conversation might be viewed as an ironic dramatization of the whole question of individual identity in the modern age. All three writers focus on the difficulty of discovering any authentic identity without the reassuring foundation of a transcendental *telos*. Madame Merle's analysis of man's intimate relation to his possessions and society attacks the very foundation of Carlyle's spiritual idealism. The ultimate *reductio ad absurdum* of the argument between Isabel and Madame Merle emphasizes the necessity for the modern American writer to generate new and vital languages to free himself from inadequate conventions and traditions.

Isabel's youthful dreams require a totally self-reliant ego, a sense of one's own being that might transcend the strict confines of social mores and habitual values. She clearly longs for some new and shining meaning, some vague disembodied hero who might take her away. Relying on her own varied experience of the world, Madame Merle can easily ridicule Isabel's romanticism by associating in two breaths " 'a pink sash and a doll that could close her eyes' " with " 'a young man with a fine moustache going down on his knees to you.' "[23] Isabel's defense is a simple denial of Madame Merle's sarcasm, her seriousness repeatedly conflicting with Madame Merle's irony. " 'No, I don't mean that' " and the repetition of " 'no, nor that either' " finally

23. Henry James, *The Portrait of a Lady*, I, 286. Hereafter cited in the text as *PL*.

expose Isabel's inability to articulate the dreams she is fighting to preserve. If Isabel's "hero" is a projection to a higher plane of her own desire for identity, for Madame Merle he is simply " 'the inevitable young man; he doesn't count.' " Isabel can only blush, " 'There are young men and young men' " (*PL,* I, 287). Despite the prodding tone of Madam Merle, she is incapable of expressing her own ideal, whether it be an adventurous hero or a vision of beauty and truth.

Isabel's repeated denials force the conversation to ultimate absurdity. Madame Merle pushes her ironic notion of Isabel's dreams to its limit by associating the "young man" with a stereotyped "castle in the Apennines." Again Isabel dramatically contends, " 'He has no castle in the Apennines.' " Driven to an understandable exasperation, Madame Merle queries, " 'What has he? An ugly brick house in Fortieth Street? Don't tell me that; I refuse to recognise that as an ideal,' " only to evoke one more negation: " 'I don't care anything about his house' " (287). For Madame Merle the entire problem surfaces, Isabel's vulnerable romanticism is fully exposed. Her denials reveal a shapeless dream with no relation to any necessary world of language or action.

Isabel has been caught in the fiction of a self complete in its own right, remote from the destructive elements of time, change, and social relation. For her, knowledge is a means of going beyond the ambiguity of this world to a realm full of meaning and truth. It is the conventional form of a romantic outlook, as artificial as Isabel's secluded world in the office with the green-papered windows and locked doors in the Albany house. Throughout the novel Isabel's ideas suggest a blind innocence. Earlier she had responded to Henrietta Stackpole's question, " 'Do you know where you're drifting?' " characteristically: " 'No, I haven't the least idea, and I find it very pleasant not to know. A swift carriage, of a dark night, rattling with four horses over roads that one can't see—that's my idea of happiness' " (235). James's own use of the image of the coach in motion as a metaphor for the novel and its form always affirms the wide prospect the ride affords.

Madame Merle's response in the conversation with Isabel affirms man's social condition, just as Isabel retreats from the ambiguity of the wide world. Madame Merle is, of course, an ironic spokesman for social order in the scene. As Laurence Holland has suggested, "Madame Merle seems to be deeply conventional in a world where the conventional touches upon everything, including, as Isabel recognizes, language itself."[24] Yet her "philosophy of things" is more than a simple defense of the status quo. In a more general sense it exposes the hollowness of the philosophical dualism of both Isabel and Carlyle:

"When you've lived as long as I you'll see that every human being has his shell and that you must take the shell into account. *By the shell I mean the whole envelope of circumstances.* There's no such thing as an isolated man or woman; we're each of us made up of some cluster of appurtenances. *What shall we call our 'self'? Where does it begin? Where does it end? It overflows into everything that belongs to us—and then it flows back again.* I know a large part of myself is in the clothes I choose to wear. I've a great respect for things. One's self—for other people—is one's expression of one's self; and one's house, one's furniture, one's garments, the books one reads, the company one keeps—these things are all expressive." [*PL,* I, 287–8; italics mine]

Madame Merle defines the self in its flow, in the constant effort of consciousness to express itself. Melville's "carpet-bag Ego" has become "the whole envelope of circumstances." Those circumstances have meaning for James only as they are given form and shape for the composition of life. The self is a constant process of drawing and redrawing that incomplete circle whereby the aesthetic consciousness expresses its shifting locus. This dialogue prefigures his brother's formulation of consciousness as a function and relation rather than a substance. William James

24. Laurence Holland, *The Expense of Vision: Essays on the Craft of Henry James,* p. 33.

would write in "Does 'Consciousness' Exist?": "Consciousness connotes a kind of external relation, and does not denote a special stuff or way of being. *The peculiarity of our experiences, that they not only are, but are known, which their 'conscious' quality is invoked to explain, is better explained by their relations—these relations themselves being experiences—to one another.*"[25] William's denial of consciousness as an entity perhaps helps to explain Henry's insistent reference to the "ado" of consciousness. The Jamesian novel is fundamentally one of relation, the character's self defined as he sees himself and as others see him.[26]

Isabel, of course, cannot accept Madame Merle's analysis. Her own sacred dreams are threatened by such an empirical approach to identity: " 'I don't agree with you. I think just the other way. I don't know whether I succeed in expressing myself, but I know that nothing else expresses me. Nothing that belongs to me is any measure of me; everything's on the contrary a limit, a barrier, and a perfectly arbitrary one. Certainly the clothes which, as you say, I choose to wear, don't express me; and heaven forbid they should!' " (*PL*, I, 288). At the heart of Isabel's declaration is that essential "me" to which things "belong." Madame Merle's very style of address moves from the "I" of her own view to a common "we" and finally to the abstract "one" in her philosophical outburst. Isabel, however, is incapable of grasping that interpretation of existence which translates the ego from a hidden essence into a fluid expression. Madame Merle's irony dissolves into a lighter wit when she remarks, " 'You dress very well.' " Isabel replies with youthful assurance: " 'Possibly, but I don't care to be judged by that. My clothes may express

25. In William James, *Essays in Radical Empiricism and A Pluralistic Universe*, ed. Ralph Barton Perry, p. 25.

26. See *Essays in Radical Empiricism*, p. 132: "The paradox of the same experience figuring in two consciousnesses seems thus no paradox at all. To be 'conscious' means not simply to be, but to be reported, known, to have awareness of one's being added to that being; and this is just what happens when the appropriative experience supervenes."

the dressmaker, but they don't express me. To begin with it's not my own choice that I wear them; they're imposed upon me by society' " (288).

Isabel's entire education is an attempt to understand the "fit or misfit" of her complex "envelope of circumstances." James's remarks in his Preface to *Portrait* echo Adams's statement in the *Education* that the "object of study is the garment, not the figure": "Millions of presumptuous girls, intelligent or not intelligent, daily affront their destiny, and what is it open to their destiny to *be*, at the most, that we should make an ado about it? The novel is of its very nature an 'ado,' an ado about something, and the larger the form it takes the greater of course the ado. Therefore, consciously, that was what one was in for—positively organising an ado about Isabel Archer."[27] Isabel is that very "ado" organized around her. Thus the new Isabel, who emerges from the fireside contemplation in Chapter 42, recognizes that social responsibility, unlike blind duty or romantic escapism, is the expression of one's self in relation to others. Without such an engagement of the world, there can be only the most illusory freedom.

Madame Merle's final remark reflects something of the tone of all three texts studied above. Isabel objects to her social clothes, but: " 'Should you prefer to go without them?' Madame Merle enquired in a tone which virtually terminated the discussion" (288). Isabel's youth has been fully exposed by Madame Merle's sophisticated wit. The distance separating the two women from any mutual understanding gapes even wider. They can end only with the absurdity of Madame Merle's final question.

In one sense, Adams and James begin where Melville's letter ends. Their attitudes suggest an incomplete self repeatedly transformed by the effort of consciousness to know itself. In spite of some clear differences in outlook and form of expression, Henry Adams and Henry James define the basic problems of the liter-

27. James, *The Art of the Novel*, ed. R. P. Blackmur, p. 48. Hereafter cited in the text as *AN*.

ary imagination at the turn of the century. In philosophy William James formulates his radical empiricism in response to analogous difficulties with conventional conceptions of epistemology and ontology. What Henry James called the "spreading human scene," his brother termed the "field of consciousness"; both recognize that the self which emerges in such a world comes to know itself only through the relations of its experience. William struggles to sustain the centrality of the "individualized self" in determining experience:

The individualized self, which I believe to be the only thing properly called self, is a part of the content of the world experienced. The world experienced (otherwise called the "field of consciousness") comes at all times with our body as its centre, centre of vision, centre of action, centre of interest. Where the body is is "here"; when the body acts is "now"; what the body touches is "this"; all other things are "there" and "then" and "that."[28]

William James is not entirely successful in overcoming the dualism of subject and object. His own ideas at times seem to work against the authority of the "individualized self." He does, however, begin to show how man's meaning comes into being through the functional interchange of the self and its perceptual other. John Wild argues that William James's *Essays in Radical Empiricism* (1912) and *A Pluralistic Universe* (1909) show clear affinities with the development of the phenomenology and existential philosophy of Husserl and Heidegger.[29] Henry Adams and Henry James also belong in that loose group of philosophers, artists, and thinkers at the beginning of the twentieth century who recognized the need for new methods to deal with an increasingly pluralistic world. In their own ways Henry Adams and Henry James struggle to define attitudes toward self, consciousness, and history which are complemented by the late writings of William James and developed and refined by such twentieth-

28. William James, *Essays in Radical Empiricism*, p. 170n.
29. John Wild, *The Radical Empiricism of William James*, p. 408.

century philosophers as Edmund Husserl, Martin Heidegger, Maurice Merleau-Ponty, and Jean-Paul Sartre.

The many various forms, methods, styles, and techniques that make up the works of Henry Adams and Henry James describe two related attempts to come to terms with a radical cultural discontinuity at the end of the century. Their works express the speculative qualities of a culture in transition. Without a transcendental *logos*, without a readable social text, they are faced with the need to generate their own phenomenological texts to provide a livable context. They both experiment with different literary forms in an attempt to give symbolic shape and meaning to a reality and a self. They explore scientific, literary, philosophical, and sociopolitical realms trying to find a relation between public and private, to formulate a nexus between the language of consciousness and the names of society.

Henry James approaches the philosophic problems of the latter half of the nineteenth century from a primarily aesthetic point of view, whereas Henry Adams begins by attempting to formulate an appropriate historical consciousness. Nonetheless, both authors increasingly move toward a phenomenology of mind at the very time when the possibility of a viable ontology appears to be unthinkable. In the later and major phases of both authors' careers, two words characterize their studies of consciousness: *process and relation*. As Adams does suggest at the end of chapter 29 of the *Education*, the only *thing* that might be assumed true is *relation*. In different manners, both authors come to define the center, or principle of structurality, as a *function* rather than a metaphoric *thing*. Both appear to agree basically with William James's repudiation of consciousness as an entity, although neither acknowledges the pluralistic continuity and unity of experience that William struggles to define:

To deny plumply that "consciousness" exists seems so absurd on the face of it—for undeniably "thoughts" do exist—that I fear some readers will follow me no farther. Let me then immediately explain that I mean only to deny that the word stands for an entity, but to insist emphatically that it does stand for a function. There is, I mean, no aboriginal stuff or quality of being, contrasted with that of which material objects are made, out of which our thoughts of them are made; but there is a function in experience which thoughts perform, and for the performance of which this quality of being is invoked. That function is *knowing*.[30]

For the author of *The Sacred Fount* relation itself becomes a principle of knowledge and meaning when properly understood. Selected "points of reference" in the history of the West for Adams and "points of view" in the Jamesian novel are principles of order only insofar as they permit us to examine the function of relation in itself.

A conception of structure as functional and relational seems fundamental to the intersubjective mode of modern literature. In his analysis of Victorian literature, J. Hillis Miller has argued that "when God vanishes, man turns to interpersonal relations as the only remaining arena for the search for authentic selfhood. Only in his fellow men can he find any longer a presence in the world which might replace the lost divine presence."[31] It is precisely the emphasis on interpersonal relations in Henry James's novels that often misleads us into taking him for the last of the Victorians. Yet it is James's most social characters who blindly accept the systematic rigidity of social forms, rejecting the responsibilities of more vital relations. Intersubjectivity denies the possibility of any external justification, but relies upon the interrelation of self and other.

Henry Adams turns to history when God vanishes and seeks there to define the function of relations between the individual and a history that everywhere transcends him. In such a context the illusion of continuity is founded upon the essential difference characteristic of a decentered cosmos. As Ortega y Gasset has expressed the problem in "History as a System," man's history is the dialectical process of his "being" and "unbeing":

30. William James, *Essays in Radical Empiricism*, p. 3.
31. J. Hillis Miller, *The Form of Victorian Fiction*, p. 33.

Man invents for himself a program of life, a static form of being, that gives a satisfactory answer to the difficulties posed for him by circumstance. He essays this form of life, attempts to realize this imaginary character he has resolved to be. He embarks on the essay full of illusions and prosecutes the experiment with thoroughness. This means that he comes to believe deeply that this character is his real being. But meanwhile the experience has made apparent the shortcomings and limitations of the said program of life. It does not solve all the difficulties, and it creates new ones of its own. . . . Man thinks out another program of life. But this second program is drawn up in the light, not only of circumstance, but also of the first. One aims at avoiding in the new project the drawbacks of the old. In the second, therefore, the first is still active; it is preserved in order to be avoided. Inexorably man shrinks from being what he was. On the second project of being, the second thorough experiment, there follows a third, forged in the light of the second and the first, and so on. Man "goes on being" and "unbeing"— living. He goes on accumulating being—the past; he goes on making for himself a being through his dialectical series of experiments. This is a dialectic not of logical but precisely of historical reason— the "Realdialektik" dreamt of somewhere in his papers by Dilthey.[32]

Such a method never affirms any given program or structure as essential, but defines the individual in the very dialectical function of his experiments.

The pattern of deconstructive creation described by Ortega is essential to the later works of James and Adams. For James the systematizing imagination of the analytic narrator of *The Sacred Fount* is a kind of fine madness. Any closed world is fatal for the Jamesian character, whether it be Isabel Archer's romantic isolation in the Albany office or the "temple of love" that Kate Croy and Merton Densher attempt to construct in *The Wings of the Dove*. Meaning depends upon the openness of the structures of thought. Whereas the characters of the fiction of the American Renaissance are presented in the midst of withdrawal and ontological reduction, the Jamesian central consciousness must come-

32. José Ortega y Gasset, "History as a System," in *History as a System and Other Essays toward a Philosophy of History*, pp. 215–16.

to-be in the midst of a social world. Withdrawal for James is an integral part of acting and living, not a distinct process. Consciousness comes to form precisely to be shattered and dislocated, to become the text for its own analysis and reformation. That perceptive consciousness, the focus of James's fiction, is a combination of critical and creative imaginations. Creation becomes an act of interpretation and criticism. Repeatedly, James's characters provide social, literary, or critical "pre-texts" as the bases of their movement and relation. The very organization of Jamesian society depends upon such presuppositions. Social communication relies on human, linguistic, and formal relations, which by their very interchange, transformation, and translation invest society with meaning. The closure of social worlds and the tendency of language to degenerate into convention restrict individual freedom and thus the vitality of social relations. In *What Maisie Knew,* Maisie's rites of passage depend upon the reading and interpretation of various social relations. Born into a world where mothers and fathers are mere names, constantly changing, Maisie ultimately must become a social manipulator and a maker of meaning in order to survive. Like the literary imagination, the social consciousness constantly seeks forms and finds them tentatively in the salon, the weekend party, the dance, the card game, and the tea ritual. The primary content of such forms is linguistic, and the language so formed becomes the referential text of social relations, which repeatedly must be broken down and reformed. The conversations of the salon, the interpersonal confidences, the public and private contrivances of deception and manipulation all contribute to restructuring the social form—nowhere more evident than in *The Sacred Fount, The Wings of the Dove,* and *The Golden Bowl.* This constant interchange of fictions, lies, actual experiences invests society with its changing meaning. Ethical judgments in James's fiction are curiously dependent upon the affirmation or denial of this essentially intersubjective mode. The dehumanization of others is the immorality of the various parents in *What Maisie Knew,* of Mrs. Brookenham in *The Awkward Age,* Grace Brissenden in *The Sacred Fount,* Kate Croy in *The Wings of the Dove,* and Maggie Verver in *The Golden Bowl.*

When the critical consciousness comes to read an explicitly literary or imaginative text, the method is not essentially different for James than the reading of a social or historical one. In the volumes of his own criticism from *French Poets and Novelists* to *Partial Portraits* James did not present an anecdotal picture of the writer's life or simply pass judgment on the basis of certain aesthetic rules. He attempted to reconstitute each author's consciousness by moving from his critical subjectivity *through* the given text to the creative process itself. In his criticism and in the later tales of the artistic and literary life James developed an attitude toward interpretation essential to the creative consciousness. In "The Figure in the Carpet" (1896) the critical task that George Corvick assumes in the quest for a basic design in the novels of Hugh Vereker becomes a life for him. That which gives order to the aesthetic carpet is precisely the quest of the critical eye for such a figure. It is the process of observation as part of the creative process that *makes* a pattern in the carpet at all. The quest is the goal and Corvick transforms his critical search into a creative one of impressive dimensions.

The monumental work of the New York Edition's revisions and Prefaces is the supreme example in American letters of a creative act of interpretation. James's rereadings of his own texts aim at a fundamental revision of the creative process itself. Such a new vision can only describe a different path. In the Preface to *The Golden Bowl,* James explicitly discusses the activity of reseeing his life's work:

It was, all sensibly, as if the clear matter being still there, even as a shining expanse of snow spread over a plain, my exploring tread, for application to it, had quite unlearned the old pace and found itself naturally falling into another, which might sometimes indeed more or less agree with the original tracks, but might most often, or very nearly, break the surface in other places. What was thus

predominantly interesting to note, at all events, was the high spon-
taneity of these deviations and differences, which became thus things
not of choice, but of immediate and perfect necessity.   [*AN*, 336]

As he reviews his life's work, James does not find a reassuring
continuity. Instead he is struck with the repeated transformations
in style and form that characterize his works. This quality of
experimentation itself informs his effort to reappropriate his
works in the Prefaces:

No march, accordingly, I was soon enough aware, could possibly
be more confident and free than this infinitely interesting and amusing *act* of re-appropriation; shaking off all shackles of theory, un-
attended, as was speedily to appear, with humiliating uncertainties,
and almost as enlivening, or at least as momentous, as, to a philosophic mind, a sudden large apprehension of the Absolute. What
indeed could be more delightful than to enjoy a sense of the absolute
in such easy conditions? The deviations and differences might of
course not have broken out at all, but from the moment they began
so naturally to multiply they became, as I say, my very terms of
cognition.   [336–7]

Here it is the "deviations and differences" in James's collected
works that provide his very mode of critical cognition. The
functional relation of his various forms and methods is itself the
"Absolute" for his critical imagination. The Prefaces themselves
describe the act of revision as an affirmation of the discontinuity
and "lapse of harmony" in his works. The "*act* of re-appropriation" is a fundamental attempt to see the basic processes of the
creative mind. It is not an attempt to reorder that disharmony:
"To revise is to see, or to look over, again—which means in the
case of a written thing neither more nor less than to re-read it.
I had attached to it, in a brooding spirit, the idea of a re-writing
—with which it was to have in the event, for my *conscious* play
of mind, almost nothing in common" (338–9). To rewrite would
be to approach his works from his *present* perspective and somehow define it as essential and final. James recognizes clearly
enough that his literary development depends upon the essential

differences among his works. For the critic in the Prefaces, the
varied methods suggest a general metaphor for the process of
human consciousness itself, which "goes on being and unbeing."
James's artistic process denies any ultimate end other than its
own play. Henry James, Sr., had taught his children to "be"
rather than to "do," but the aesthetic development of Henry
James could only assure him that "being" has no significance outside of "doing": "When it is a question of an artistic process,
we must always mistrust very sharp distinctions, for there is
surely in every method a little of every other method. . . . Our
history and our fiction are what we do; but it surely is not more
easy to determine where what we do begins than to determine
where it ends—notoriously a hopeless task."[33]

James's novels, novellas, tales, criticism, biography, autobiography, and travel sketches demonstrate in a monumental way the
manner in which he tried out forms, built houses of cards, and
then reshuffled the deck to deal again. The development of
the symbolic mode of the later novels—from *The Sacred Fount*
to the unfinished *Ivory Tower*—embodies a primary attempt to
come to terms with such a process in itself. In the literature of the
American Renaissance the intentional and reductive thrust of the
symbol made it an objective focus for subjectivity. The symbol
in its tangible form was operative in the education of the subject. But those symbols that provide the titles for James's later
novels repudiate the idea of an essential center. The Jamesian
symbol is defined by its genetic and processive nature. The
golden bowl, the wings of the dove, the ivory tower are from the
beginning flawed, absent, or empty. The symbolic process itself
is an accumulation of meaning, a shaping of form through
variant interpretations. Enclosed in its leather case in the chaos
of the antique shop, the golden bowl is a meaningless object.
When the shopkeeper carefully places it on a square satin mat,
it glints into a vital form with the magical " 'My golden Bowl

33. Henry James, *Partial Portraits*, p. 256.

. . .—' and it sounded on his lips, as if it said everything."[34] From that moment the golden bowl initiates a process of successive compositions and recompositions. From the beginning it is the rejected cup of communion between Charlotte and the Prince. By the end the golden bowl has become a text that must be read and interpreted to uncover its multiple layers of meaning: "The golden bowl put on, under consideration, a sturdy, a conscious perversity; as a document, somehow, it was ugly, though it might have a decorative grace" (*GB*, II, 165). Symbols are made by being talked about and around. The symbolic construct is the successive interrelation and interpenetration of consciousnesses. In its objective form the Jamesian symbol provides an arbitrary point of reference for "measuring motion" in social relations. In its linguistic significance the symbol embodies the function of relations, the defining and incarnating process that is at the basis of our human reality. As an artifact the golden bowl "might have a decorative grace"; yet as a "document" of the subjective interpretations that define the relations in the novel it can only be "ugly." The symbol neither mediates between the subjective and universal nor helps resolve the conflict of varying interpretations. The Jamesian symbol achieves its meaning as a reflection of the process of symbolization itself.

Dissatisfied with the positivism of his *History of the United States,* Henry Adams moved toward a similar mode of symbolic expression in his later writings. As a philosophical travel guide, *Mont-Saint-Michel and Chartres* is a quest for an historical and ontological origin in the thirteenth century. The uncle takes his niece on a journey into the medieval consciousness in order that they may find some relation to that imagined age of unity. But, if only on the evidence of the niece's Kodak, the journey is an affirmation of twentieth-century multiplicity and the disappearance of the Virgin's harmony. Those "two hundred and fifty million arithmetical ancestors living in the middle of the eleventh century" must remain merely ciphers, not relatives, for the

34. James, *The Golden Bowl,* I, 112. Hereafter cited in the text as *GB.*

traveling uncle and his photo-snapping niece.[35] The uncle's reading of the text of medieval unity aims at a revelation of an essential principle for cosmic order. For a moment of history the Virgin of Chartres managed to reconcile the multiplicity of human society and the longing for a divine unity. Yet the scholastic tradition that emerged from and affirmed the unified universe of thirteenth-century man nonetheless moved man away from his understanding of its order. For the uncle, unity is to be understood in the fact and symbol of architecture: "The old habit of centralizing a strain at one point, and then dividing and subdividing it, and distributing it on visible lines of support to a visible foundation, disappeared in architecture soon after 1500, but lingered in theology two centuries longer, and even, in very old-fashioned communities, far down to our own time, but its values were forgotten" (*MSM,* 382). The decentralization of metaphysics, to him, is the rupture leading to a modern universe of infinite multiplicity from "the sense of unity in art" (382).

The very concept of unity bore within it the necessity of its own critique, its own successive decentralization and fragmentation: "The fault, then, was not in man, if he no longer looked at science or art as an organic whole or as the expression of unity. Unity turned itself into complexity, multiplicity, variety, and even contradiction" (381). The measurement of man in motion requires the determination of points of relation, which embody their own disappearance. Ultimately, our historical interest in these reference points must be found in their revelation of the function and movement of human consciousness itself, not in the archaeology of its separate structures. For this reason *Mont-Saint-Michel and Chartres* reveals the twentieth-century relation to medieval unity as it emphasizes our discontinuity from that unity. As such it is no history but an imaginative and symbolic *act* that fills the empty choir of Chartres and relives the "dead faith" of the Virgin.

35. Adams, *Mont-Saint-Michel and Chartres,* p. 3. Hereafter cited in the text as *MSM.*

The text of *Mont-Saint-Michel* provides a pre-text for the imaginative history of the *Education*. The decentralization of metaphysics paves the way for the "effaced Ego" and the hollow manikin. In *Chartres* the Virgin is defined in the medieval context as an immediate presence, the simultaneity of word and thing. In the multiplicity of the twentieth century the Virgin is merely a nostalgic symbol. The absence of the Virgin is dramatized in relation to the figure of the Dynamo. In the *Education* symbolic meaning is expressed by the relation of difference. The study of history, whether public or private, could be only the study of such relations and conflicts: "Past history is only a value of relation to the future, and this value is wholly one of convenience" (*EHA*, 488). Almost every chapter in the *Education* ends with a repudiation of education gained. The last lines of "Harvard College" provide a leitmotiv for the whole work: "As yet he knew nothing. Education had not begun" (140).

Although Chartres may suggest a convenient relation for the modern mind, it provides no origin for that mind. The manikin of the *Education* moves back ever farther into history in quest of a point of departure. In "Rome" he finds a source without which "the Western world was pointless and fragmentary." Yet the text of Rome is unreadable, as is the modern condition of multiplicity: "A bewildering complex of ideas, experiments, ambitions, energies" (93). The manikin searches beyond history in natural science and geology, in an infinite regress, for a point that may be said to be determinate. Such a process ends with *Pteraspis,* the ganoid fish, his first existing vertebrate relative. Behind *Pteraspis* stretches the Cambrian Age and the millennia of nonorganic emptiness—the "crystalline cliffs" (229). Pteraspis is a tangible denial of evolution and development. The failure of the ganoid fish to evolve, its apparently stubborn resistance to evolution, repudiates the classical concept of origins and ends. The philosophical unity made scientific in Darwinian evolution becomes impossible in the "horrible grin" of *Pteraspis:* "He could detect no more evolution in life since the *Pteraspis* than he could detect it in architecture since the Abbey. All he could prove was change" (230). The quest for origins in either evolutionary or historical theory compels Adams to repudiate any point of origin. The discontinuity evidenced by the first vertebrate *Pteraspis*—from both its past and its future—denies the possibility of finding any continuity in man's movement in relation to nature, unless it were in that very movement itself: "Henry Adams was the first in an infinite series to discover and admit to himself that he really did not care whether truth was, or was not, true. He did not even care that it should be proved true, unless that process were new and amusing" (231–2). The quest for order, origin, and unity transforms itself into a game of relationships, by which the figure in the carpet itself is transcribed.

The symbolic imagination in *Chartres* and the *Education* is the result of Adams's efforts to establish tentative points of relation in the thirteenth century of the Virgin and St. Thomas, the eighteenth century of his family heritage, and the *fin-de-siècle* mood of his later years. Such a "measurement of motion" tells us less of history than of Adams himself. He could never affirm the accelerating multiplicity of the modern age with confidence or even with the qualified meliorism of William James. But it is clear enough that in both *Chartres* and the *Education* Adams acknowledges the impossibility of any monistic concept of unity. In his own way Adams achieves a pluralistic equilibrium in the literary relations of *Chartres* and the *Education*. Insofar as they rely on each other, these works dramatize the phenomenology of Adams's own consciousness under the pretense of establishing an historical sequence and theory. *Chartres* is certainly as "autobiographical" as the *Education*. Both works describe a modern figure who learns to use the failure of his own efforts and the chaos and discontinuity of his experiences as the means for surviving a maddening modern world.

2 The Quest for a Concept of Historical Order in *Democracy* and *Esther*

> A man said to the universe:
> "Sir, I exist!"
> "However," replied the universe,
> "the fact has not created in me
> A sense of obligation."
>
> —Stephen Crane, *War is Kind,* 1899

All his life Henry Adams was in quest of a language adequate to deal with the modern age. The expression of his historical vision was limited by a fundamentally eighteenth-century lexicon, revised and expanded by the science and philosophy of the nineteenth century. The positivism of his monumental *History of the United States During the Administrations of Jefferson and Madison* reflects a general empirical impulse. The avowed attempt "to state facts in their sequence" and "to give a running commentary on the documents to explain their relation" betrays an initial faith in the possibility of historical truth.[1] Adams's own sense of the failure of this work illustrates the inadequacy of the traditional languages for the student of the twentieth century. Adams saw modern man radically disengaged from his own history, spun into a new universe that denied conventional categories and habitual methods of thought. From Comte and Ranke to Darwin, Spencer, and even Marx, such notions as "progress" and "evolution," "fact" and "objectivity," "value"

1. Henry Adams to Sarah Hewitt, January 7, 1904; in Harold Cater, *Henry Adams and His Friends,* p. 548.

and "truth" depended upon an inherent sense of unity and order. The intention of thought and language had always been directed toward an ideal origin or end which is definition itself.

Adams's later writings are radical attacks on such conceptions of unity and meaning. The twentieth century requires an entirely new system of values, an original interpretation of man and consciousness. Yet, in affirming the death of the old order, Adams, like Nietzsche, recognizes how intimately his own language is tied to the subject of his critique. "A Dynamic Theory of History," "The Tendency of History" (1894), "A Letter to American Teachers of History" (1910), and "The Rule of Phase Applied to History" (1909) reveal a desperate search for new terms and appropriate metaphors for describing twentieth-century forces.[2] Only the scientific language of Mach, Faraday, Gibbs, and Haeckel seems to approximate the particular method Adams needs to express the new complexities. The scientific theorizing of his later works is often attacked as inaccurate and inconsistent.[3] The later essays, however, confirm Adams's continuing need for new terms and different perspectives on old problems. His systematic generalizations are not simply ironic commentaries on the inadequacies of modern science.[4] Adams is suggesting the need for an immense shift in the consciousness of modern man, a new awareness of the implications of a constantly shifting universe. If modern science teaches Adams anything, it is that the energy and movement of the universe could be described only in terms of "vibration," not of "direction."[5]

2. The latter three essays collected in *The Degradation of the Democratic Dogma*. References will be made to the specific essay.

3. William Jordy, *Henry Adams, Scientific Historian*, provides the most comprehensive and systematic evaluation of Adams's later "scientism." He recognizes, however, the varieties of interpretation possible for the significance of these theories in Adams's thought.

4. Melvin Lyon, *Symbol and Idea in Henry Adams*, suggests that the late essays are simply convenient fictions for Adams's questing mind. His treatment seems more useful than the analyses that attack the authority or accuracy of Adams's scientific knowledge.

5. "The Rule of Phase Applied to History," *Degradation of Democratic*

For the author of the *Education* it is a small step to argue the failure of human history as an intentional process; repudiating at once notions of sequence, continuity, and unity as conventionally defined. As Adams became increasingly convinced of such a view in the years leading up to the first World War, the question of how man was to live in such a "sea of supersensual chaos" became more pressing.

Throughout Adams's public and private writings we find the singularly pervasive idea that unity is the primitive instinct of man. As a guiding principle for reason and logic, unity has always been subject to an interpretation as a final and fixed point—the ultimate meaning. Man tends to conceive of unity in terms of centralization, the intention of all things toward their origin and end. Henry agrees with his often intractable brother Brooks on one fundamental point:

On your wording of your Law, it seemed to me to come out, in its first equation thus, in the fewest possible words:
All Civilisation is Centralisation
All Centralisation is Economy.
Therefore all Civilisation is the survival of the most economical (cheapest)
Darwin called it the fittest, and in one sense fittest is the fittest word. Unfortunately it is always relative, and therefore liable to misunderstanding.[6]

For Henry the implications of such an idea are far more complex and philosophical than the economic synthesis of Brooks's *Law of Civilization and Decay*. Brooks interprets economy quite literally, but Henry's conception of the economy of forces in-

---

Dogma, p. 279: "Possibly, in the chances of infinite time and space, the law of probabilities might assert that, sooner or later, some volume of kinetic motion must end in the accident of Direction, but no such accident has yet affected the gases, or imposed a general law on the visible universe. Down to our day Vibration and Direction remain as different as Matter and Mind."

6. Henry Adams to Brooks Adams, 2 April 1898, in *Letters of Henry Adams (1892–1918)*, ed. Worthington Chauncey Ford, p. 163.

volves much more than mere money, coinage, and labor. "All Centralisation is Economy," even metaphysical centralization, traditionally interpreted as the ultimate reconciliation of forces in an eschatological economy of energy. Darwin's revolutionary theories seem to confirm such a general intention as they revise it in the language of the "perfectibility of the species" and uniform evolution. In a similar manner, Marx would argue that class conflict is the result of an inevitable historical development.

History is, for Adams, the record of man's failure to define adequately the idea of unity. As the governing principle of structurality, the center ordering language and thought must transcend those structures. Paradoxically, man's own rational expression of unity is the source of philosophical dualism, the birth of multiplicity, and the ambiguity of human discourse. Both *Chartres* and the *Education* trace the degradation of man's primitive instinct for unity to the proliferation of his human orders. Repeatedly, Adams echoes Pascal's distrust of rational epistemology. In response to the Cartesian *cogito*, "Pascal wearily replied that it was not God he doubted, but logic." Nevertheless, Adams's Pascal recognizes the limitations of his own skepticism: he "was tortured by the impossibility of rejecting man's reason by reason; unconsciously skeptical, he forced himself to disbelieve in himself rather than admit a doubt of God. Man had tried to prove God, and had failed" (*MSM,* 323–4). Such an awareness seems to condemn modern man to the prison of his consciousness and his incomplete knowledge.

Adams's writings reflect this historical discontinuity. The *History* ends by questioning the very ideals of democratic order that had motivated the writing of the early volumes. Writing the history of America's independence from its European tradition, Adams ultimately must confront the dangers of a modern tendency aptly symbolized by the current American scene. The optimism of a consolidated United States in 1817 is highly problematic for the author of the ninth and final volume. The triumph of American ingenuity and intelligence was made possible only at the expense of aesthetic vitality: "Such literature and art as they produced, showed qualities akin to those which produced the swift-sailing schooner, the triumph of naval architecture. If the artistic instinct weakened, the quickness of intelligence increased."[7] With the foundations and character of the American people "fixed" in 1815, a new chapter in history must begin, separate and distinct from the diverse forces of Europe or Asia. Even in its different form, however, the direction of the new democracy is as problematic as the history of the Old World: "The American continent was happier in its conditions and easier in its resources than the regions of Europe and Asia, where Nature revelled in diversity and conflict. If at any time American character should change, it might as probably become sluggish as revert to the violence and extravagance of Old-World development. The inertia of several hundred million people, all formed in a similar social mould, was as likely to stifle energy as to stimulate evolution."[8]

Adams's *History* ultimately turns against its own methods and themes, suggesting in a final multiplication of questions the immense cost of American revolution and independence. The philosophical upheaval implicit in the consolidation of the Republic weighs heavily on the commentator of the final volume:

The traits of American character were fixed; the rate of physical and economical growth was established; and history . . . became thenceforward concerned to know what kind of people these millions were to be. They were intelligent, but what paths would their intelligence select? They were quick, but what solution of insoluble problems would quickness hurry? They were scientific, and what control would their science exercise over their destiny? They were mild, but what corruption would their relaxations bring? They were peaceful, but by what machinery were their corruptions to be purged? What interests were to vivify a society so vast and uniform? What ideals were to ennoble it? What object, besides physical con-

7. Adams, *History of the United States of America*, IX, 218. References to the nine-volume *History* hereafter cited in the notes as *History*.
8. Ibid., p. 241.

tent, must a democratic continent aspire to attain? For the treatment of such questions, history required another century of experience.[9]

Adams's dialectical tone suggests the acceleration of tensions rather than a new synthesis or vital unity. The last question summarizes his anxiety about the order and coherence of modern societies. In discovering the failure of Jefferson's ideal republicanism, the *History* suggests the need for a new interpretation of social change and relation that might invest this "vast and uniform" democracy with a vital order and direction.[10]

This final note in the *History* criticizes the original impulses of the first volume and marks Adams's break with his own heritage. It sets the stage for a radically modern Henry Adams, glaring into the void separating the nineteenth and twentieth centuries. Adams experiences the breakdown of his own eighteenth-century ancestry in the act of composing the *History*. He wrote to Elizabeth Cameron in 1891 concerning a recent review of his *History:* "I feel that the history is not what I care now to write, or want to say, if I say anything. It belongs to the *me* of 1870; a strangely different being from the *me* of 1890. There are not nine pages in the nine volumes that now express anything of my interests or feeling; unless perhaps some of my disillusionments. So you must not blame me if I feel, or seem to feel, morbid on the subject of the history."[11] The *Education* echoes these sentiments: "Education had ended in 1871; life was complete in 1890; the rest mattered so little!" (*EHA,* 316)'. Henry Adams in 1870 was still the son of the American Adams family. As one more factor in an eighteenth-century sequence,

9. Ibid., pp. 241–2.
10. See Levenson, *Mind and Art,* p. 153: "Adams remarked on the Jeffersonian utopia, 'The possibility of foreign war alone disturbed this dream.' The dream which was a practically effective vision might also be a delusion that Americans were exempt from the historic conditions of human life."
11. Henry Adams to Elizabeth Cameron, 6 February 1891, in *Letters of Henry Adams (1858–1891),* ed. Ford, p. 468. References to Ford's two-volume *Letters* hereafter cited in the notes as *Letters.*

the young Adams found his ancestry tied to a rapidly crumbling New England sense of justice and moral value. The *"me* of 1890" is restless and afloat, pushing history back ever farther, hoping to disclose a spiritual father that might guide him through an unfathomable future. The *History* led its author ultimately to questions of metaphysics and ontology.[12] For Adams history finally had to confront the fundamental questions of philosophy. The historian's accuracy becomes less a matter of data than of consistent and logical method.

In *Democracy* (1880) and *Esther* (1884) Adams investigates the directions American society and thought had taken at the end of the nineteenth century. The two novels, written in the midst of the researches and composition of the *History*, may be considered imaginative replies to the questions posed in the sections "American Ideals" of the first volume and "American Character" of the final volume of the *History*. Madeleine Lee grapples unsuccessfully with Adams's last series of questions, and Esther attempts to deal with the problems of American idealism:

These were in effect the problems that lay before American society: Could it transmute its social power into the higher forms of thought? Could it provide for the moral and intellectual needs of mankind? Could it take permanent political shape? Could it give new life to religion and art? Could it create and maintain in the mass of mankind those habits of mind which had hitherto belonged to men of science alone? Could it physically develop the convolutions of the human brain? Could it produce, or was it compatible with, the differentiation of a higher variety of the human race? Nothing less than this was necessary for its complete success.[13]

The failure of Jefferson's social vision to fulfill these rigorous demands is dramatized in the pilgrimages of Esther Dudley and

12. See George Hochfield, *Henry Adams,* p. 9: "Thus Adams's quest for the meaning of history, touched off, though certainly not wholly sustained, by the failure of his youthful assumptions in Washington, ended in a kind of conversion of history and metaphysics in which the laws of matter ironically replaced the moral law transcending human legislation."
13. *History*, I, 184.

Madeleine Lee. Both characters are in quest of a principle, implicit in Adams's own questions, that might order their historical and intellectual milieux.

Like *Chartres* and the *Education* or Volumes I and IX of the *History*, *Democracy* and *Esther* complement each other as two aspects of the modern crisis. Each novel suggests what has happened to the dreams of a younger America. Although Esther's youthful idealism contrasts sharply with Madeleine's experience and maturity, both women ask similar questions concerning the future of American society. Madeleine Lee's quest, however, seems initially more desperate than Esther's. She has the world-weariness of a woman who has been buffeted by the mindless forces of an alien universe. She has lost both her husband and her child, and she finds herself disrelated, alone, and "tortured by *ennui*."[14] She is hardly as impressionable as the young Esther, and thus she rejects the abstract theories of philosophy and science from the beginning: "In her despair she had resorted to desperate measures. She had read philosophy in the original German, and the more she read, the more she was disheartened that so much culture should lead to nothing—nothing" (*D*, 1–2). Unlike her literary contemporary, Isabel Archer, Madeleine has no confidence in the abstractions of German metaphysics. Experience seems to have taught her the inadequacy of mere words. She demands an active engagement of her world. Like that of the manikin in the *Education*, Madeleine's varied knowledge seems to count for nothing because it lacks some sense of the source of energy that motivates man's thought and behavior. Her quest for the power behind American politics is an archetypal tale of America in search of its own father, its own energy. Adams describes Madeleine's object in her "pilgrimage" to Washington in epic terms: "What she wished to see, she thought, was the clash of interests, the interests of forty millions of people and a whole continent, centering at Washington; guided, re-

14. [Henry Adams], *Democracy: An American Novel*, p. 1. Hereafter cited in the text as *D*.

strained, controlled, or unrestrained and uncontrollable, by men of ordinary mould; the tremendous forces of government, and the machinery of society, at work. What she wanted, was POWER" (9).

Madeleine's quest suggests a kind of determinism, but the narrator is quick to qualify her real goal: "Perhaps the force of the engine was a little confused in her mind with that of the engineer, the power with the man who wielded it. Perhaps the human interest of politics was after all what really attracted her, and, however strongly she might deny it, the passion for exercising power, for its own sake, might dazzle and mislead a woman who had exhausted all the ordinary feminine resources" (9). Power is expressly related to that engineer who wields and directs it, as if American democracy might have successfully substituted politics for the metaphysics of Aquinas. Implicit in Madeleine's notion of the political engineer is a theological ideal, comparable to Esther's dream of order. This peculiar connection of politics and metaphysics is made explicit in Madeleine's final renunciation of a disordered American scene for the mystic peace of Egypt: " 'I want to go to Egypt,' said Madeleine, still smiling faintly; 'democracy has shaken my nerves to pieces. Oh, what rest it would be to live in the Great Pyramid and look out for ever at the polar star!' " (277). The absence of a central figure or principle directing the diverse forces of American life drives her into the timeless space of the pyramids. Adams once wrote to his niece, Mabel Hooper LaFarge: "Egypt is an education, but is a sort of education that, for Americans, is worse than useless."[15] The pyramids offer only escape for a woman in quest of a vital social order.

15. Adams, *Letters to a Niece and Prayer to the Virgin of Chartres*, p. 102. Madeleine's flight to Egypt is related to a unique theme in American literature. The American myth of the New World often results in an attempt to leap the corruptions of European history and find a direct relation with the venerable antiquity of the Middle East, the Fertile Crescent, and the Holy Lands. This impulse may be parodied by Twain

In the capital Madeleine finds little trace of her sense of careful statesmanship and selfless diplomacy. Political expedience and social fashion have replaced right reason and dispassionate judgment. The manipulations of power in the modern capital and the idealism of Madeleine's vision can find no common ground. The Virginia lawyer Carrington best fits Madeleine's own idea of George Washington at thirty, but significantly he has no hand in the modern power struggles waged by men like Senator Ratcliffe. Carrington is an anachronism, as Henry Aiken recognizes: "The eighteenth-century world which he represents is, as he realizes, done for."[16] In the modern age any controlling principle, any myth or symbol of unity, must be out of time, remote from the exigencies of history. The bucolic retreat of Mount Vernon and the nirvanic calm of the Great Pyramid have little relevance for one caught in the multiplicity of forces at the end of the nineteenth century. The mystery Madeleine hoped to discover at the heart of the Republic is reduced to the inevitable fallibility of any agent of power. When Carrington reveals to Madeleine that Ratcliffe had accepted a bribe of $100,000 for his support of a subsidy bill for the "Inter-Oceanic Mail Steamship Company," she reads into this single act the general tendency of modern politics. Her quest for the source of political and social power ends in recognition of the failure of an American dream for order and unity: "Had she not come to Washington in search of men who cast a shadow, and was not Ratcliffe's shadow strong enough to satisfy her? Had she not penetrated the deepest recesses of politics, and learned how easily the mere possession of power could convert the shadow of a hobby-horse existing only in the brain of a foolish country farmer, into a lurid nightmare that convulsed the sleep of nations?" (255).

---

in *The Innocents Abroad,* but it plays an important part in the mythic structure of *Moby-Dick* and is the subject of Melville's *Journal of a Visit to Europe and the Levant* (1856–1857) and the subsequent *Clarel* (1876).

16. Henry Aiken, "Foreword," *Democracy,* p. vi.

Democracy describes an increasingly chaotic American scene, subject to random forces. Leadership becomes a question of individual psychology, a lesson the manikin of the *Education* would learn during Anglo-American diplomacy in the Civil War. Almost a century earlier, Franklin had suggested that although few men act for the good of their country, "fewer still, in public affairs, act with a view to the good of mankind."[17] The failure of Madeleine's dream of an engineer of power suggests a dehumanized state driven blindly into space. As J. C. Levenson has written, the dominant image of the machine in the novel "implies that mechanization has taken command and human reality has departed from politics. Public life becomes a dehumanized charade."[18] Yet corruption rests with man alone in his various interpretations of moral value. In *Democracy* Adams views the modern machine age as the product of man's failure to accept responsibility for his social situation.

Esther Dudley's quest for a principle of metaphysical order reveals the same fragmentation of American life that Madeleine Lee experiences in the play of Washington politics. American independence in 1815 involved a philosophical as well as a political revolution. Adams's final questions in the *History* imply the need for Americans to fill the gap left by the destruction of old dogmas and orthodoxies. In the final chapter of the *History*, Adams points to the enormous difference between the "theology of Jonathan Edwards and that of William Ellery Channing." The rigor of Edwards's and Hopkins's "reasoning," like Aquinas's architectural logic in the *Summa Theologiae*, provided a firm ground for metaphysics. As life in America became easier and "the struggle for existence . . . mitigated," the severity of Puritan justice was relaxed in the "spread of popular sects like the Universalists and Campbellites." Explicitly relating man's religious vision to his political and social conditions, Adams interprets the breakdown of Puritan orthodoxy: "The Unitarian and Uni-

17. *Benjamin Franklin's Autobiography and Selected Writings*, p. 95.
18. Levenson, *Mind and Art*, pp. 87–8.

versalist movements marked the beginning of an epoch when ethical and humanitarian ideas took the place of metaphysics, and even New England turned from contemplating the omnipotence of the Deity in order to praise the perfection of his creatures."[19] Adams sees the self-reliance of the Emersonian American as a radical self-consciousness. The nineteenth-century American turned away from "old religion," and he "rejected necessary conclusions of theology because they were inconsistent with human self-esteem."[20]

It is precisely this kind of self-consciousness that Esther Dudley rejects. In *Esther* Adams relentlessly attacks the nineteenth-century confidence in human perfectibility and the unlimited powers of reason. The Reverend Stephen Hazard fervently attempts to reconcile science and religion by founding his church on a fundamental *cogito:* " 'The Church now knows with the certainty of science what she once knew only by the certainty of faith, that you will find enthroned behind all thought and matter only one central idea—that idea which the church has never ceased to embody—I AM! Science like religion kneels before this mystery.' "[21] For all his skeptical detachment, the geologist George Strong confirms this faith in divine Reason.[22]

19. *History,* IX, 239.
20. *Ibid.,* p. 240.
21. Adams, *Esther,* p. 8. Hereafter cited in the text as *E.* Ernest Samuels, *Henry Adams: The Middle Years,* relates Hazard's theology, particularly as expressed in this sermon, to that of the Yale theologian George P. Fisher. In his article "Personality of God and Man" Fisher attempts to prove the existence of God within the individual consciousness. As Samuels quotes Fisher (pp. 234–5): "Belief in the personality of man and belief in the personality of God . . . stand or fall together. Recent philosophical theories which substitute matter or an 'Unknowable,' for the self-conscius Deity . . . cast away the personality of man as ordinarily conceived."
22. Although Strong is based on Adams's friend the geologist Clarence King, he frequently poses Adams's own questions concerning the validity of modern scientific attitudes. For biographical backgrounds on the characters in the novel, see Samuels, *The Middle Years,* pp. 236 ff.; Levenson, *Mind and Art,* pp. 199–204.

In spite of his awareness of the fictive language of science, Strong repeatedly affirms the possibility of scientific discovery as a key to the order of the universe. Like Josiah Royce, Strong believes in the ultimate accessibility of truth: " 'If our minds could get hold of one abstract truth, they would be immortal so far as that truth is concerned. My trouble is to find out how we can get hold of the truth at all' " (*E*, 271).

In *Esther* Adams moves toward an aesthetic sense of harmony and order that prefigures the symbolic centrality of the Virgin in *Chartres*. Absent though such a principle of order is in the modern world of this novel, it remains the only alternative to the restrictive *cogito* of Hazard's church or Strong's post-Darwinian hope for human evolution. Esther herself instinctively yearns for an order that might encompass both mind and matter without turning one into a manifestation of the other. Only the painter Wharton understands the limits of human reason and accepts his paradoxical condition. Whereas Hazard's faith is explicitly "thirteenth-century" in tone, and Strong stands for the nineteenth-century scientific mind (104), Wharton is the figure of the Renaissance artist. His sense of aesthetic harmony involves a relation of differences in a precarious balance. " 'An artist must be man, woman, and demigod,' " Wharton declares (76).[23] His art involves a truly religious passion and struggle: " 'To reach heaven you must go through hell, and carry its marks on your face and figure. I can't paint innocence without suggesting sin' " (128–9). Wharton understands that he can express only man's *desire* for the divine—as Petrarch longs for Laura—and the impossibility of fulfilling such a desire.

With the death of her father, Esther is forced to confront a similar sense of alienation. Her soul begins to experience the emptiness of infinite space. Her journey on the night train to

23. Millicent Bell, "Adams's *Esther:* The Morality of Taste," compares Esther to the Virgin of Chartres. Although this is the conventional interpretation, Wharton's aesthetic ideals seem closer to the Virgin's true anarchic power.

Buffalo provides an appropriate landscape for a world bereft of human significance. At first she longs for the protection society seems to offer against this cosmic blankness:

> She raised the curtain of her window and stared into the black void outside. Nothing in nature could be more mysterious and melancholy than this dark, polar world, beside which a winter storm on the Atlantic was at least exciting. On the ocean the forces of nature have it their own way; nothing comes between man and the elements; but as Esther gazed out into the night, it was not the darkness . . . that, by contrast, made the grave seem cheerful; it was rather the twinkling lights from distant and invisible farm-houses, the vague outlines of barn-yards and fences along doubtful roads, the sudden flash of lamps as the train hurried through unknown stations. . . . These signs of life behind the veil were like the steady lights of shore to the drowning fisherman off the reef outside. [247]

But in the dim light of dawn, Esther recognizes the futility of man's efforts to protect himself from his fundamental isolation. The romantic struggle of man against nature is reduced in the gray morning light to the dreary toil of daily life: "The world became real, prosaic, practical, mechanical, not worth struggling about; a mere colorless, passionless, pleasureless grayness" (249).

Niagara, however, provides Esther with a workable symbol for cosmic energy. The Falls suggest that unified direction for natural energy that she fails to find in the self-consciousness of Hazard's faith.[24] Esther's rejection of Hazard's confidence in the "resurrection of the body" summarizes Adams's sense of the modern failure of a religious instinct: " 'Why must the church always appeal to my weakness and never to my strength! I ask for spiritual life and you send me back to my flesh and blood as though I were a tigress you were sending back to her cubs' " (299). Self-consciousness is the fall of man, the source of the ambiguity of his condition. The principle of unity for

24. See Lyon, *Symbol and Idea in Adams,* p. 50.

which Esther longs must transcend the limits of human thought and reason. Only an energy as primal as that of the Falls might confirm Esther's instinctive faith in some central order. Like Melville's or Camus's sun, Niagara is at once a destructive and vital force, complete and significant in its presence.

In *Democracy* and *Esther* man appears to be ensnared by the unalterable forces of his historical and natural situations. Adams's apocalyptic tone is most frequently related to this sense of the physical determinism of actions and events. His interpretation of little man swirled against his will through an unintelligible universe must be distinguished from the philosophical naturalism of the turn of the century.[25] Esther interprets the unity of natural energy " 'as a sort of great reservoir of truth, and that what is true in us just pours into it like rain-drops' " (*E*, 273). The divorce of mind from matter, however, is not to be resolved so simply. Science attempts to express the mysterious through the operative fictions of mathematical signs, theology bridges the discontinuity between man and his universe by an act of faith. Both deal in illusions that give multiple forms to the essentially formless. As Robert Hume interprets the alienation of Adams's man from the knowledge he desires: "Any description of the cosmos and any definition of the part in it played by man, has to be fiction; for it comes from man, whose inquiries can be directed only toward that illusion of reality provided by his own senses and his own thought; and the utmost effort of the mind unveils not absolute truth but the mind's wavering reflection."[26] Man's drive to interpret his world reveals a primal desire that

25. Recent studies of many examples of American naturalism have placed such writers as Stephen Crane in a much more modern context. Milne Holton's attempt in *Cylinder of Vision* to relate Crane to the development of existential thought suggests possible reinterpretations of a good deal of turn-of-the-century fiction, especially those works loosely tagged "naturalistic" or "realistic."

26. Robert Hume, *Runaway Star: An Appreciation of Henry Adams*, p. 238.

can never be fulfilled. Knowledge of our condition always involves the ambiguity of our variant interpretations. The mind inevitably stumbles on itself in its effort to transcend its limits.

History can express only the repeated failures of man's desire to find significance. Meaning is precisely the activity of bringing to conscious form what otherwise must remain simple change and motion. Although modern science seems to teach Adams that man is controlled by arbitrary natural forces, man defines himself in his insistent efforts to find order and pattern in this random motion. If the scientists' discoveries deny the possibility of any *logos* beyond the structures of human thought and language, then meaning must reside in man alone. Subject to the vagaries of his world of time and change, man dreams of that full presence that is the end of interpretation. This desire functions as a point of reference for measuring man's motion and change. History is a discontinuous process that gives its own directions to the arbitrary vibration of cosmic force. For Adams history does not record as much as it expresses the frustration and renewal of man's insatiable demand for order and identity.

As in the architecture of the medieval cathedral, consciousness gives form to the formless. Any approach to the inexpressible must acknowledge the limitations of the metaphors and symbols of language itself. By the time Adams wrote *Chartres*, he recognized that language intends its own violation and revision. The constant transformations built into language, which reflect the failure of imagination to capture the evasive presence of truth, seem to deny the idea of a fixed and final center for human signification. Although Adams affirms Esther's vision of the vast and total energy reflected in the sun and Niagara, he ultimately denies the idea that they symbolize "a great reservoir of truth." Nirvana is only a denial of meaning, the dissolution of consciousness, "ecstatic suicide." Man in the world is compelled to find his values in the process of definition itself, in the vital act of renewing his own exhausted language.

Adams significantly reinterprets the idea of unity in *Chartres* and the *Education*. The void that replaces man's dream of fulfillment is at the heart of his tragedy. The absence of any fixed origin or end opens up the rigid eschatologies of Western thought, however, replacing Christian "free choice" with the free play of the creative mind. Thus the quest for truth gives way to what Adams would call in the *Education* the "new and amusing" (232), an irony that veils a complex view of man and consciousness. Madeleine's myth of the engineer remains a necessary fiction in directing the thought of man in a decentered cosmos. In a letter to Margaret Chanler in 1909, Adams writes: "I am glad you mean to resume your duties in New York society. Except for women, society is now an infinite solution; a mere ocean of separate particles; and you can help it to one little centre. I own that the centre will do nothing; but it may play itself to be real."[27] In the play of the unfixed center itself resides the reality of unity and order. To redefine the center thus as a function rather than as a point or principle, Adams had to turn to the history of ideas for the symbolic expression of his concept.

27. Henry Adams to Margaret Chanler, 9 September 1909; *Letters*, II, 524.

3   The Pluralistic Unity of the
    Virgin in *Mont-Saint-Michel*
    and Chartres

And Kung said "Wan ruled with moderation,
    In his day the State was well kept,
And even I can remember
A day when the historians left blanks in their writings,
I mean for things they didn't know,
But that time seems to be passing."
A day when the historians left blanks in their writings,
But that time seems to be passing."
                    —Ezra Pound, *The Cantos*, XIII, 1930*

In *Mont-Saint-Michel and Chartres* and *The Education of
Henry Adams,* Adams attempts to construct a system of coordinates to define the crisis of modern thought. His own subtitles—
"A Study of Thirteenth-Century Unity" and "A Study of
Twentieth-Century Multiplicity"—appear to reinforce a tendency by critics to simplify the relations between these two
works. *Chartres* is not merely a nostalgic appreciation of medieval art and culture. Adams focuses clearly on the conflict of
intellectual, social, and political forces of the period. His study
of the Virgin's unity is more accurately an investigation into the
origins of modern multiplicity. The failure of the Virgin's centrality in medieval culture is the true subject of the work.
Chartres prepares us for the *Education* by providing an historical point of reference for measuring our modern situation.
With his two "points of relation," Adams "hoped to project

* From *The Cantos.* Copyright 1934 by Ezra Pound. Reprinted by permission of New Directions Publishing Corp. and Faber and Faber, Ltd.

his lines forward and backward indefinitely, subject to correction from any one who should know better" (*EHA,* 435).

The difference between the Virgin of Chartres and the modern Dynamo sufficiently expresses Adams's sense of our modern loss of wonder and imagination. *Chartres* is concerned, of course, with the entropic tendency of history, which Adams later would give a scientific rationale.[1] Adams is, though, fascinated equally with the analogies to be made between medieval and modern problems. The languages may differ, but Adams sees in Thomist theology the same fundamental questions posed by modern physics or classical philosophy. The modern age repeats the struggles of medieval scholasticism: "The schools argued, according to their tastes, from unity to multiplicity, or from multiplicity to unity; but what they wanted was to connect the two. They tried realism and found that it led to pantheism. They tried nominalism and found that it ended in materialism. They attempted a compromise in conceptualism which begged the whole question. Then they lay down exhausted" (*MSM,* 323). *Chartres* ends appropriately with Adams's analysis of Thomist logic, just as the *Education* moves toward Adams's own formulation, "A Dynamic Theory of History." Thomism symbolizes for Adams the origin of modern multiplicity and the limits of the scientific mind. As John Conder has written: "According to Adams, at least, Thomism was the logical beginning of modern science, for what was the Thomistic God but the sum of all energy, and what was medieval religion but a primitive scientific way of controlling it?"[2]

Chartres and the *Education* indicate that man's desire for meaning leads merely to the repetition of fundamental questions about being and consciousness. Although man fails in his attempts to discover unity either in nature or in history, he does find significance in the varied interrogations he makes of his condition. The

1. See "The Rule of Phase Applied to History."
2. John Conder, *A Formula of His Own: Henry Adams's Literary Experiment,* p. 51.

failure of Thomist logic to find unity leaves the artistry of its expression. In *Chartres* and the *Education* Adams redefines the idea of unity as the function of consciousness and man's experience of this function in the relations he composes. Adams may be fascinated with the logic of Aquinas, but most of *Chartres* is devoted to medieval art. What the poetry and architecture finally express is hardly "Thirteenth-Century Unity," but man's longing for just such an impossible order.

We are separated from the "instinct for unity" embodied in Chartres by our fatal self-consciousness. For Adams, man's refusal to accept the limits of his reason and will compel him to reject the reality of the Virgin. The art of the twelfth century celebrates man's ignorance and yearning as the foundations for his being. For Adams, St. Thomas's attempt to resolve the inherent contradictions between God and man, spirit and body, infinite design and individual choice expresses the desire to transcend the conditions that define man and his history. And yet the failure of both Thomist thought and modern science suggests how little man can do but express the "wavering reflection" of his own mind.

The narrative in *Chartres* dramatizes the limitations of the analytic mind. The effort in the thirteenth century to make the universe intelligible necessarily brought about the multiplicity of Western rationalism. In his own way, the modern tourist only violates the Virgin's temple in the attempt to understand it. The uncle's demand that the reader "feel" the passion of Chartres suggests the need for an artistry to express man's alienation and yearning. We discover in *Chartres* that we know even less of ourselves and our world than the architects of the Mount or the poets of the *cours d'amour* knew of theirs. Our ignorance requires that we interpret our world and interrogate our past in order to define our present situation. Thus the uncle's narrative must assume an aesthetic rather than an historical form.

The formal tactics of *Chartres* emphasize Adams's attempt to awaken the imaginative and interpretative powers of his reader. In the preface he turns historical commentary into an intimate discourse in the relation of his fictitious uncle and niece. An immediate analogy is established between the uncle's interpretations and translations of medieval art, architecture, and philosophy and the niece's attempt to understand her nineteenth-century relative.[3] Thus the initial relation in *Chartres* prefigures Adams's avowed aim in the preface to the *Education:* "The training is partly the clearing away of obstacles, partly the direct application of effort. Once acquired, the tools and models may be thrown away" (*EHA,* x). When "the uncle talks," the reader enters imaginatively into his conversation, and this engagement contributes to the art of *Chartres.* John Conder suggests that Adams implicates the reader in his vision of modern multiplicity "by inducing in the reader the same fractured sensibility possessed by the narrator, whose thought has inevitably moved, through the associational method, away from a tenuous faith in the Virgin toward rational analysis," thus making "the reader personally validate the author's theory that thought possesses some kind of inevitable movement."[4] The contrivance of the preface suggests that Adams did not want the "same fractured sensibility" in his reader, but it does argue that *Chartres* is designed to compel the reader to evaluate his modern situation as he engages and interprets the narrator's discourse. The very difference between reader and author, niece and uncle, is funda-

3. See Mabel Hooper La Farge, "A Niece's Memories," in Adams, *Letters to a Niece,* pp. 4–6. A letter by Henry Adams dated January 1, 1909, which was found in George Cabot Lodge's papers as an introduction to "The Rule of Phase Applied to History," reveals much of Adams's distrust of a larger reading audience: "Sugar-coat his idea an inch thick, or disguise it as he will, the teacher cannot force it down unwilling throats; still less induce passive stomachs to digest it; unless the patient has some personal motive, some chance of profit or pleasure to incite his action. This is my apology for appealing directly, personally, to the dozen or two of possible readers who have a personal interest in the subject; —and to no one else." Cater, "A hitherto unknown Henry Adams manuscript," *Adams and Friends,* p. 782.

4. Conder, *Formula of His Own,* pp. 69–70.

mental to Adams's larger historical, philosophical, and aesthetic analyses.

Adams subtitled *Chartres* "Travels / France," and the form of his work seems to bring together the growing medievalism and the vogue for travel books in the latter half of the nineteenth century. *Chartres* is clearly associated with the "cult of the Middle Ages," which in England ran from Browning and Carlyle to Ruskin and the Pre-Raphaelites.[5] Adams's general aims, however, seem more closely related to such modern works as James's *The American Scene,* Pound's *Spirit of Romance,* Williams's *A Voyage to Pagany,* and Lévi-Strauss's *Tristes Tropiques.* By manipulating a dominant literary mode, Adams tries to develop his own individual form in *Chartres.* In the opening chapters of *Tristes Tropiques,* Lévi-Strauss tries to account for the public's fascination with travel books: "I understand how it is that people delight in travel-books and ask only to be misled by them. Such books preserve the illusion of something that no longer exists, but yet must be assumed to exist if we are to escape from the appalling indictment that has been piling up against us through twenty thousand years of history."[6] Adams uses that desperate need for the "illusion of something that no longer exists" to force his readers to confront the crisis in their own civilization. Even the most superficial reader cannot miss the uncle's repeated references to a modern multiplicity which contrasts so sharply with the Virgin's unity.

The Norman's will to power, the Virgin's unity, and the rigor of Thomist metaphysics form the primary structure of *Chartres.* The controlling metaphors for the sections isolate them as three different parts of the medieval crisis, foreshadowing the twentieth-century complexities of the *Education.* The masculine will and energy of the martial Normans culminate in the aspiring *architecture* of Mont-Saint-Michel. In Chartres Adams details the *art* of the Virgin's unity, perhaps best symbolized in the

5. Ernest Samuels, *Henry Adams: The Major Phase,* pp. 259, 208 ff.
6. Claude Lévi-Strauss, *Tristes Tropiques,* p. 39.

stained glass. The rose window becomes a dominant figure for the presence of the Virgin in her temple. The logic of the schools, especially that of St. Thomas in *Summa Theologiae,* is compared to the engineering triumphs of Amiens Cathedral. The concentration in the final chapters is on the birth of such a *scientific* method. The spatial dimensions of Norman order are replaced by medieval scholasticism's architecture of consciousness. Adams interprets medieval thought in terms of the movement, tension, and balance suggested by the relations of those three aspects of the age, which keep the "Unity" of the subtitle precarious. In *Chartres* the Virgin's grand unity is itself a fragile balance of conflicting forces; only for a historical moment did her artistry balance them.[7]

"Saint-Michiel de la Mer del Peril" immediately images the Norman consciousness in the militant energy of Michael. The Archangel stands poised between earth and heaven as the symbol in the eleventh century of man's attempt to make God intelligible. The architecture of the Mount reflects God's uplifting power— its architects building the walls out farther and farther to raise the ceilings and push the spire higher. Michael stands at the heart of the eleventh century, for the Normans dominated western Europe from England to Sicily. Modern man's "two hundred and fifty million arithmetical ancestors living in the middle of the eleventh century" found a political, social, and cultural focus in Norman rule (3). The Normans "stood more fully in the centre of the world's movement than our English descendants ever did," for England's isolation was shattered with Duke William's conquest: "We were a part, and a great part, of the Church, of France, and of Europe" (4). For the American

7. Conder, *Formula of His Own,* p. 79, sees the very structure of the narrative as designed to provide the reader with the sense of movement in the medieval transition: "In fact the book does this very thing, constantly shuttling back and forth between the centuries to emphasize motion and direction in artistic channels, in this way depicting the astonishingly rapid changes within the forces guiding social movement."

tourist Norman culture provides an entrance into an Old World heritage that seems remote in the nineteenth and twentieth centuries. The church door of the Mount is a *pons seclorum*, the bridge "between us and our ancestors." Only the creative attempt to "live again" in the great multitude of arithmetical ancestors makes it possible to cross that bridge "without breaking down in the effort" (5).

The "quiet strength" of the Romanesque is "the absence of display, of effort, of self-consciousness" and offers a peace for the weary nineteenth-century uncle that "no other art does" (7–8).[8] But the repose of the Romanesque is deceptive, perhaps only the fond dream of an old man. The architecture of the Mount expresses an idea that is "the stronger and more restless because the Church of Saint Michael is surrounded and protected by the world and the society over which it rises" (8). There is no Trinity here, only the Archangel pointing toward God. The restless striving of the Normans aspires to that convergence of energy which is divine. Church and State are united in their interpretations of metaphysical and social hierarchies. The unity of the eleventh century is dramatized in Roland's dying, when he proffers his right gauntlet as "an act of homage" to his ultimate feudal Lord (29).

Eleventh-century faith and idealism were, nevertheless, severely limited, as the pressures of history revealed. The unity of God as feudal seigneur depended upon a fundamentally martial society. Action was at the heart of the Norman ferment, and medieval man himself was effaced in the heroism of service to Church and State. Although such a lack of self-consciousness is refreshing to the author of the *Education,* clearly such conditions

8. See Lyon, *Symbol and Idea,* pp. 81–7. Lyon reads the uncle's interpretation of "youth" in contrast to that sense of Wordsworthian "innocence" suggested in the early pages of *Chartres:* "Adams believes that multiplicity is real, and that connecting unity and multiplicity is a destructive process. Yet only the old man sees this truth; the child, living in illusion, believed that unity was alone real and lasting" (86).

could not last. The stabilization of medieval society demanded new ideals, broader symbols for the unity of man and God. In the eleventh century "Roland still prayed his 'mea culpa' to God the Father and gave not a thought to Alda his betrothed." Twelfth-century society required more than the *virtù* of Roland: "In the twelfth century Saint Bernard recited 'Ave Stella Maris' in the ecstasy of miracle before the image of the Virgin, and the armies of France in battle cried, 'Notre-Dame-Saint-Denis-Mont-joie.' What the Roman could not express flowered into the Gothic; what the masculine mind could not idealize in the warrior, it idealized in the woman" (*MSM*, 34).

The restless Norman will-to-live eventually was subsumed by the power and grace of the Virgin at Chartres. Whereas eleventh-century art expresses the aspiration of society, the ideal aesthetic of Mary serves to bring the forces of the twelfth century together. The Mount stands for a highly socialized religious feeling; Chartres represents a metaphysics that defined and ordered the social structure from within. In the uncle's narrative all levels of society serve the Virgin. The Normans worshiped "God the Father—Who never lied!" (48), whereas the architects of Chartres had to cope with the inaccessibility of His Justice. The unity of the Normans is reflected in their sense of completion: the absolute relation of man to God. The Normans finished what they began, whereas most French cathedrals were incomplete in the twelfth century (52). *Chartres* is a study in medieval unity, but it is also the history of the successive breakdown of the old systems of order and the quest for new forms and original symbols. From a modern perspective, the entire volume is a moving picture of decline.[9]

Thus, despite "all the education that Normandy and the Ile de France can give," one approaches Chartres with as much ignorance as at the beginning of the tour (62). The Virgin and her art demand new methods of understanding and feeling. She

9. Michael Colacurcio, "The Dynamo and the Angelic Doctor: The Bias of Henry Adams' Medievalism," p. 705.

is at once a Western Queen, an Eastern Empress, and "the most womanly of women" (73, 74). In the sculpted portals of Chartres, she and her Son displace the Norman ideal of God as feudal seigneur: "She was not a Western, feudal queen, nor was her Son a feudal king; she typified an authority which the people wanted, and the fiefs feared; the Pax Romana; the omnipotence of God in government" (74). In the uncle's recounting of Norman history, the people are conspicuously absent, only the dukes, abbots, and their immediate servants figure in the legends. The Virgin relies on the participation of the common man in a worship that celebrates temporal as well as eternal love. The presence of the Virgin in her temple expresses an idea of unity radically different from the rigorous absolute of a God of Law. The Virgin does not deny the difference and variety of human life with the finality of the Trinity. She is not a fixed and immovable point, the end of definition and the silence of total meaning. The Virgin is constantly in motion and yet as tangible and accessible for her worshipers as the cathedral itself.

No image better illustrates the unity of the Virgin than her rose. Chartres was built out farther and farther to accommodate larger windows to illuminate the interior. The rose windows of Chartres are the very jewels in the Queen's Crown. Within their form the Virgin's unity is the harmony and play of vastly divergent forces. Dante represented God's presence as a blinding burst of pure light. That divine light filtered through the art of the rose window best reflects the Virgin's centrality at Chartres. Her dominion places things in relation, it does not reduce them to a single plane of meaning. She orders events without subjecting them all to the apocalyptic rigor of God's judgment. In the roses of Chartres, medieval men and the saints mingle, Biblical narrative is interspersed with portraits of craftsmen, merchants, and secular princes. All find an appropriate place in relation to their ultimate Mother, the mythic *Venus geneatrix*. As the lines of the rose curve outward from her central presence to the multiplicity of medieval life, the Virgin's creative power is expressed. The mother of Christ, she is the heart of Western Christianity, a primordial source of energy.

As the Virgin's flower, the rose is her virtual incarnation and blossoming for the world of man. Force and its energy may be simple problems of physics for the twentieth-century tourist; they assume the form of majestic art in the Virgin's temple. Ezra Pound sees the loss of a modern aesthetic sense as a separation of the science and art that Adams's Virgin brings into harmony:

> For the modern scientist energy has no borders, it is a shapeless 'mass' of force; even his capacity to differentiate it to a degree never dreamed by the ancients has not led him to think of its shape or even its loci. The rose that his magnet makes in the iron filings, does not lead him to think of the force in botanic terms, or wish to visualize that force as floral and extant (*ex stare*).
>
> A medieval 'natural philosopher' would find this modern world full of enchantments, not only the light in the electric bulb, but the thought of the current hidden in air and in wire would give him a mind full of forms, *'Fuor di color'* or having their hyper-colors.[10]

Similarly, the disparate forces of the Middle Ages come to form in the Virgin's rose. The Trinity judges the world on the basis of an absolute Law. Perfection excludes sin, but the Virgin forgives man. Man's Fall initiates philosophical dualism, the Virgin's love and grace bridge the gap in a way that no rational system ever could. God is absolute in His Word, the *Logos* itself the origin and end of definition. The Virgin's incarnation is seen as the process of the divine defining itself, the activity of grace in the world and the vital relation of man to the universal. The Virgin's cosmos is full of energies unified in her moving center.

At Mont-Saint-Michel the apparent "rest and repose" of Romanesque simplicity reveals a restless striving. The Virgin's

10. Ezra Pound, "Cavalcanti/Medievalism," in *Literary Essays of Ezra Pound,* ed. T. S. Eliot, pp. 154–5. Jordy, *Scientific Historian,* p. 228, points out that Adams was fond of "visualizing science in terms of graphs, and of moving magnets about his desk to watch iron filings fall into Faraday's 'lines of force.'"

unity denies that finality man expects from his absolutes. Her association with a historical period of transition reflects a similar movement on a metaphysical axis. The conflict between the stark Romanesque and the self-conscious grace of the Gothic is harmonized at Chartres, but the stresses and strains of both modes are not brought to rest. Such an architecture is as scientifically valid as it is convenient for modern interpretation. Art historian Henri Focillion describes Chartres in precisely these terms: "In this way the skeleton church was defined—a combination of active forces, in which the cohesion of the parts is ensured by their interaction, by the theorem of functions, by the structure of the specialized members, and even by the type of masonry."[11]

The Virgin does not replace the Trinity as a different center for the medieval cosmos, rather she "absorbs" the Trinity in the very activity of her grace. The equilibrium of the twelfth century is by no means static, but involves the flux of all those opposing forces that would eventually reduce its unity to separate atomies. The balance itself must be precarious if it is to achieve the highest expression, for any final resolution must be the silence of God and the denial of man. Vern Wagner has suggested that Adams refuses in *Chartres* "to accept a fixed position as certain, a truth as absolute," and as a result "remains in a position of teetering inconclusion."[12] Adams's refusal of any final, fixed point reflects the anarchy of the Virgin herself, who disregards law and dogma whenever they conflict with her grace. That grace is precisely an activity and function, immediately meaningful in a human context and emotionally felt.

The ultimate miracle of the Virgin is her repeated metamorphoses. The architecture of Chartres seems to bridge the disparate styles and express an aesthetic unity that no rigid symmetry could

11. Henri Focillon, "The Classic Phase of Gothic Architecture (1938)," from *The Art of the West in the Middle Ages,* as quoted in *Chartres Cathedral,* ed. Robert Branner, p. 117.

12. Vern Wagner, *The Suspension of Henry Adams,* p. 56.

ever accomplish: "In this church the old Romanesque leaps into the Gothic under our eyes; of a sudden, between the portal and the shrine, the infinite rises into a new expression, always a rare and excellent miracle in thought" (*MSM*, 108). Repeatedly, Adams points out the irregularities in the architecture. The west rose is "six or seven inches out of axis with the lancets" (113). According to Viollet-le-Duc, the circular apse defies the contemporary rules of architecture. Such architectural eccentricities were risked to attain ever more lighting, and the desire for windows took precedence over architectural laws (123). Such whims are the Virgin's alone, whose love for the extraordinary and eccentric must have guided the plans. By virtue of its irregularity, "the Chartres apse shows the same genius that is shown in the Chartres rose; the same large mind that overrules,—the same strong will that defies difficulties. The Chartres apse is as entertaining as all the other Gothic apses together, because it overrides the architect" (126–7).

If law implies convention and security, then the Virgin opted for the new and precarious. The freight borne by the expanding twelfth-century trade from the Holy Lands of the Crusades and beyond was "philosophy, poetry, or art." The society that built Chartres was as greedy for mercantile exchange as the nineteenth century, but its "youthful gluttony" assumed more splendid forms (141). Trade brought new ideas, which were adapted to the growing needs of the community. The long Eastern countenances of the sculptures of Chartres reveal a Byzantine grace that combines with Western techniques to surpass even the early Christian mosaics at Ravenna. The Virgin's power resides in this ability to assimilate alien influences and integrate them into an expansive aesthetic. R. P. Blackmur reads *Chartres* in similar terms: "The lesson for modern institutions should be plain; that balance is better than control, that responsibility is better than rule, that risk is better than security, and that stability is death. But the stability and security here spoken of are not the opposites of anarchy and starvation; they are the opposites, rather, of flexibility various enough to receive and react to new impressions."[13]

This twelfth-century unity succeeds where Jefferson's utopian vision and Whitman's confident self-consciousness failed in nineteenth-century America. The Virgin's unity, however, differs also from the transcendent God of the Normans and from the order of other monists. Adams's Virgin seems to resemble William James's "pluralistic God," who is neither infinite nor absolute:

Yet because God is not the absolute, but is himself a part when the system is conceived pluralistically, his functions can be taken as not wholly dissimilar to those of the other smaller parts,—as similar to our functions consequently.

Having an environment, being in time, and working out a history just like ourselves, he escapes from the foreignness from all that is human, of the static timeless perfect absolute.[14]

Unlike James, Adams could not conceive of such a "superhuman consciousness" in the modern age. Twentieth-century man is too self-conscious and rational to escape his own systems and their limits. The Virgin's metaphysics is as anti-systematic as William James hoped his pluralism might be. In both the Virgin's temple and James's pluralistic universe, "your relations with it, intellectual, emotional, and active, remain fluent and congruous with your own nature's chief demands."[15] But for Adams the triumph of Western rationalism signals the decline of this integration of man's intellectual and emotional natures.

The political, social, economic, and religious forces balanced by the Virgin's power were also those forces that would reduce her order to a modern multiplicity of conflicting energies. The Virgin's unity was destroyed by the medieval mentality it had

13. R. P. Blackmur, "The Harmony of True Liberalism: Henry Adams's *Mont-Saint-Michel and Chartres*," p. 17.
14. William James, *A Pluralistic Universe*, p. 318.
15. Ibid., p. 319.

helped to shape and transform. The self-consciousness effaced by the Virgin's faith re-emerged in man's effort to explain his own mysteries. As the figure of historical transition, the Virgin leads to the fragmentation of her own order. Thus, to leave Chartres is to enter a sea of multiplicity, the degeneration of her vast energy into small human conflicts. "The Virgin of Majesty had indirectly achieved her revolutionary purposes," Ernest Samuels writes.[16] And the uncle provides a modern perspective: "We have done with Chartres. For seven hundred years Chartres has seen pilgrims, coming and going more or less like us, and will perhaps see them for another seven hundred years; but we shall see it no more, and can safely leave the Virgin in her majesty, with her three great prophets on either hand, as calm and confident in their own strength and in God's providence as they were when Saint Louis was born, but looking down from a deserted heaven, into an empty church, on a dead faith" (*MSM*, 197).

The triumph of the Gothic led to innovation for its own sake. That which created the reasoned symmetry of Amiens also produced the instability of Beauvais and the extravagance of Sainte-Chapelle's fenestration. Ruskin interprets the decay of the Gothic in terms analogous to Adams's:

So fell the great dynasty of medieval architecture. It was because it had lost its own strength, and disobeyed its own laws—because its order, and consistency, and organization, had been broken through —that it could oppose no resistance to the rush of overwhelming innovation. And this, observe, all because it had sacrificed a single truth. From that one surrender of its integrity, from that one endeavor to assume the semblance of what it was not, arose the multitudinous forms of disease and decrepitude, which rotted away the pillars of its supremacy.[17]

16. Samuels, *The Major Phase*, p. 284.
17. John Ruskin, *The Seven Lamps of Architecture*, p. 61. Adams read both Ruskin and Viollet-le-Duc as early as 1876–1877 as professor of medieval history at Harvard. See Max Baym, *The French Education of Henry Adams*, p. 33. For further influences of Ruskin on *Chartres*, see Samuels, *The Major Phase*, pp. 264–5.

Ruskin's "truth of God" is for Adams the unity of the Virgin, capable of accommodating such innovations in a precarious balance. With the necessary fragmentation of her power, however, architecture became a problem of physics and engineering. In the balance of the high Gothic, man resorted to an idea of unity directly related to the stability of the final structure. As Blackmur points out: "Becoming exclusively conscious, the age made the terrible mistake of trying to balance only congruous forces, seeking to destroy the incongruous forces which weight so much either side of any balance."[18] The restless medieval mind lost the accessible presence of the Virgin. It could only struggle in vain to reach the infinite. The dualism of man and the divine seemed to be reflected in both the architecture and metaphysics of the thirteenth century.[19]

"The proper study of mankind is woman," the uncle says (*MSM*, 198). Eleanor of Guienne, Blanche of Castile, and Mary of Champagne provide a secular trinity for the medieval idealization of woman. In Eleanor and Blanche the history of the Gothic seems to be expressed aesthetically (202). We tend to oversimplify Adams's worship of the feminine as a preference for emotion and instinct over reason and logic. But Eleanor and Blanche were two of the most educated figures of the Middle Ages, emulating the Virgin in their disregard for social conventions and religious orthodoxy. For Adams the intelligent woman of any age combines her natural creativity with a pragmatic reason. Thus, Eleanor and Blanche seem equally skilled in political, social, and aesthetic affairs. Adams's woman symbolizes that "community of feeling and mind" which was the political

18. Blackmur, "Harmony of True Liberalism," p. 3.
19. In *Letters*, II, 80, Henry Adams to Brooks Adams, 8 September 1895, writes: "The Gothic always looks to me a little theatrical and false, like its roofs. The Gothic church, both in doctrine and in expression, is not my idea of a happy illusion. It is always restless, grasping and speculative; it exploits the world and makes profits. . . . Still, it had very great beauties in its best time, and, as an artistic form of illusion, it gives me a sense of reflecting my own ideals and limitations. It is human. . . ."

dream of Jefferson and the philosophical goal of Abélard and Aquinas. The power of Adams's woman is as anarchic as the Virgin's grace, equally relying on human differences for its fluid order.

At the same time that Adams was gathering material for *Chartres,* he was revising the Tahitian memoirs he had collected from his friend, Marau Taaroa, in Polynesia. The "Last Queen of Tahiti" may suggest a primitive ideal, but for Adams she illustrates the marriage of reason and imagination in a fashion analogous to her medieval counterparts. The Tahitian woman has a more important social role than modern women in the West: "Women played an astonishing part in the history of the island. In the absence of sons, daughters inherited chiefteries and property in the lands that went with the chiefs' names or titles, and these chieftesses in their own right were much the same sort of personages as female sovereigns in European history."[20] In a small way, *Tahiti* complements *Chartres* as a study in both the apotheosis and the decline of feminine energy and power. As the Virgin and Eleanor, Blanche, and Mary of Champagne stand on the brink of historical crises, the old chieftess, Arii Taimai, is a last queen. *Tahiti* ends with the precarious peace the Queen has managed to achieve both among her own tribes and with the European powers in Polynesia. Like her medieval counterparts, she copes with political and social crises with a feminine power that is composed as much of cleverness and wile as it is of emotion and instinct. But the end of her reign promises a new disorder, directly related to the "civilizing" influences of the French and English in the South Seas. For Adams at the turn of the century, the exotic Tahiti of Arii Taimai is already as remote as thirteenth-century France. Adams

20. Adams, *Tahiti,* ed. Robert E. Spiller, p. 10. *Tahiti* was first published in Washington late in 1893, in an edition of "not more than ten copies," according to Samuels, *The Major Phase,* p. 100. The Paris edition of 1901 was revised and expanded, the title changed from *Memoirs of Marau Taaroa* to *Memoirs of Arii Taimai E.*

may have referred to the work as "his *Tahiti*," but both he and the old queen's daughter, Marau Taaroa, must have recognized that they were recording the fragments of a lost world.[21]

The power of woman expresses the capacity for an art that reflects a natural variety and creativity. The intelligence of Adams's feminine figures is always used to cope with a confusing world. This is not accomplished solely with the systematic rigor and abstraction of the masculine mind. The Virgin's anarchic grace and accessibility are in radical contrast to both the rigid Law of the Norman God and Thomist logic. The imaginative and creative instincts of woman are *activities* basic to her art. The feminine sense of order dilates in time. It is an immanent and thus active unity, rather than the transcendent and fixed order of God the Father.

In the midst of the medieval poetry that expresses this creativity, conflicting masculine impulses begin to reappear. The thirteenth-century romance *Aucassin et Nicolette* momentarily halts before the medieval peasant whose wary independence foreshadows his enormous power in the fourteenth and fifteenth centuries: "The peasant was a class by himself, and his trait, as a class, was suspicion of everybody and all things, whether material, social, or divine. Naturally he detested his lord, whether temporal or spiritual, because the seigneur and the priest took his earnings, but he was never servile, though a serf; he was far from civil; he was commonly gross. He was cruel, but not more so than his betters; and his morals were no worse" (*MSM*, 235). The stark reality of the peasant's condition suggests the revolution that would shatter the romance of the twelfth and thirteenth centuries. Already he was rising in power, eventually to succeed "in plundering Church, Crown, nobility, and bourgeoisie" (235). The bourgeoisie in-

21. Ibid., pp. 23, 196. Robert Mane in *Henry Adams on the Road to Chartres*, p. 74, relates *Tahiti* and *Chartres* to Adams's own sense of personal alienation from his eighteenth-century heritage: "No doubt Tahiti became all the more sacred because it could offer ground to a secret and personal parable. And so in their turn would the Middle Ages, now that the historian's imagination had received its first liberating impulse."

trudes on the poetry as another potent force that would "cheapen" the art of the age, reducing human endeavors to simple problems in economics.

The impulses of both peasant and bourgeoisie grow increasingly independent of the aesthetic order of the Virgin. In the very progress of the uncle's poetic commentary, new forces emerge to undermine her unity in the twelfth and thirteenth centuries. The study of medieval poetry leads inevitably to William of Lorris's *Romaunt de la Rose* and a nostalgic yearning for the Virgin in the middle of the thirteenth century. Art and life increasingly separate, and Lorris attempts to create an artistic space that would expel "all the unpleasant facts of life." His "court of ideals" is as fanciful as Mary of Champagne's *cours d'amour* were real. The poet no longer sings in the halls of the Mount, but is a wanderer and outcast in an increasingly complex world. For Lorris, poetry is a dream and the awakening is harsh: "He won immortality by telling how he, and the thirteenth century in him, had lost himself in pursuing his Rose, and how he had lost the Rose, too, waking up at last to the dull memory of pain and sorrow and death, that 'tout porrist' " (250). Thirteenth-century art became increasingly self-conscious, as in the reflective mode of Lorris. The intention of society revealed a growing complexity of conflicting forces and desires. Order had been reduced to the level of illusion: "For the first time since Constantine proclaimed the reign of Christ, a thousand years, or so, before Philip the Fair dethroned Him, the deepest expression of social feeling ended with the word: Despair" (250).

In "Les Miracles de Notre Dame" Adams seems to retreat before Lorris's despair. Yet the Virgin's actual miracles were few in comparison with the saints', for her greatest miracle is contained in Chartres itself. Although the activity of Mary's grace is dramatized in the legends of her intercession, actual "miracles" reflect a very human need. What man's poetry could not achieve, the "extraordinary" acts of the Virgin fulfilled. This chapter looks fondly back at the image of unity through

man's hopes and foreshadows "The Mystics." In this context
the Virgin's denial of orthodoxy and dogma reaches its highest
expression: "Mary concentrated in herself the whole rebellion
of man against fate; the whole protest against divine law; the
whole contempt for human law as its outcome; the whole unutterable fury of human nature beating itself against the walls of
its prison-house, and suddenly seized by a hope that in the Virgin man had found a door of escape" (276). Repeatedly, the
Virgin is related to this hope of man in a way that undercuts her
absolute presence at Chartres. If there the Virgin absorbs all
self-consciousness, here she is the "ideal of human perfection,"
the "miracle of miracles *which they felt in their own consciousnesses*" (251, 252; italics mine). The anarchy of the Virgin's
order moves closer to that human multiplicity it had formerly
resolved: "If the Trinity was in its essence Unity, the Mother
alone could represent whatever was not Unity; whatever was
irregular, exceptional, outlawed; and this was the whole human
race" (263). Rather than continue to affirm her vitality and
immanence as the unity that could "explain and include Duality,
Diversity, Infinity—Sex!" (261), medieval man looked for a
logical explanation for her conflict with the Trinity.

In the chapters on Chartres, God the Father is conspicuously
absent. Christ is Mary's Son, who forgives in the image of his
Mother. In "Les Miracles de Notre Dame," medieval thought
begins to struggle with the problem of her relation to the Creator.
With the rise of the middle class and the acceleration of diverse
economic forces, the artistry of Mary was called into question
by both merchants and orthodox theologians: "Mary filled
heaven with a sort of persons little to the taste of any respectable
middle-class society, which has trouble enough in making this
world decent and pay its bills, without having to continue the
effort in another" (277). The loss of her active presence in the
thirteenth century was related intimately to the "self-consciousness" characteristic of theologian and economic man alike. The
attempt to justify the Virgin had to end in a return to an idea

of unity that confirmed the duality of the Christian eschatology: "The Trinity could look on and see her dethroned with almost a breath of relief" (277).

Fifty years before the west porch of Chartres was built, Abélard arrived in Paris to begin an intellectual career that is the "portal of approach to the Gothic thought and philosophy within" (287). His arrival in Paris in 1100 marked the beginning of a period of intellectual ferment that would culminate with St. Thomas's synthetic formulations in *Summa Theologiae*. Abélard used his natural sense of argumentation to attack the realism that had supported orthodox theology. Abélard's nominalism attempted to avoid the implicit contradictions of realism and make possible an interpretation of reality and God more in accord with human experience. William of Champeaux's doctrine of universals affirmed the reality of God's thought and form as the "ultimate substance," whereas Abélard argued that the universal truth "is only the sum of all possible facts that are true, as humanity is the sum of all actual human beings." (294). William began with the assumption of unity, as the Church had always done; Abélard tried to argue from multiplicity to unity. His shift in approach parallels the transformation from the Norman God of Law to the anarchic Virgin, whose unity manifests itself only through man's varied experience of her presence.

Abélard demonstrated the implicit pantheism in the Church's assumption of an omniscient, omnipotent God, while in his own conceptualist arguments he ran the risks of materialism and what Berkeley would define six centuries later as solipsism. As Abélard reflects the vitality and novelty of the Virgin's subsequent order, his very philosophic rigor explains how her power would decline in the thirteenth century. In their attempts to explain their sense of metaphysical unity, the Schoolmen of the twelfth and thirteenth centuries lost their hold on what can be only an "instinct." Nevertheless, there are clear affinities between Abélard's philosophy and the general intention of the Virgin's unity. As Blackmur has written: "Abélard made anarchic hash of official

theology by introducing the human concept into the irreconcilable conflict between Realism and Nominalism: he knew that
that was what men did in practice, or at least it was the practice
of his own mind."[22] Unlike the Virgin, however, Abélard was a
dialectician and theologian, and he preferred to think in terms
of philosophical abstractions.

The pretension of Abélard's scholasticism was that the human
mind could transcend its own inherent limits and explain the
infinite. Despite his affinities with the Virgin's anarchic grace,
Abélard marks the beginning of a scholastic tradition that would
dethrone her. Adams admires Abélard's vitality and rigor, but
he tends to agree with St. Bernard, who distrusted Abélard's
confident syntheses. On the other hand, the mystics' strong
reaction to scholasticism posed equally dangerous problems. The
two extremes suggest the polarities of twelfth-century and thirteenth-century thought, which only the expansive art of the
Virgin resolved: "The Transition is the equilibrium between
the love of God—which is faith—and the logic of God—which
is reason; between the round arch and the pointed" (*MSM*,
321). Abélard's rationalism prefigures modern man's "fatal self-
consciousness." And yet the total effacement of self that characterizes the mystic experience of divinity is equally untenable
for Adams: "The mind that recoils from itself can only commit
a sort of ecstatic suicide; it must absorb itself in God; and in
the bankruptcy of twelfth-century science the Western Christian
seemed actually on the point of attainment; he, like Pascal,
touched God behind the veil of scepticism" (325).

St. Thomas Aquinas attempted to complete Abélard's efforts
to prove unity through multiplicity. His creation of a Church
Intellectual is a necessary complement to the aesthetic triumphs
of Chartres. Adams sympathizes with Thomas's grand project,
for in different terms he too longed for a reconciliation of the
human and divine, of historical and cosmic forces. Thomas tried

22. Blackmur, "Harmony of True Liberalism," p. 4.

to resolve the contradictions of matter and spirit, the individual and the divine, free will and a single creator. For Adams the modern scientist uses different terms to ask the same ageless questions. Man can do little but repeat the fundamental contradiction of his existence with the assumption of a universal order. In the Thomist construction, however, scientific method and aesthetic sense combine in the effort to relate man to God, to locate multiplicity within a structured unity.

Adams marvels at the simplicity and boldness of Thomas's formulation of God as the primal and eternal act of his own creation. Any intervention between God and man seems to be swept away at once. The weighty problems of the Trinity seemed to reinforce Thomist harmony in the thirteenth century: God as He thinks Himself is Himself; as He utters Himself, He is the Son, the Verb Intellectual; as He loves Himself, He is the Holy Ghost (355). And yet the thought that Pope John XXII ultimately would celebrate as a miracle of the Church in 1323 was forced to confront its own very human limits. In his efforts to affirm God as a final "intelligent, fixed motor," Thomas courted pantheism. In his struggle to account for individualization and human multiplicity, he ran the risks of materialism. As Ernest Samuels suggests, St. Thomas became for Adams "the great archetype of intellectual failure."[23] As the uncle puts it: "In his effort to be logical he forced his Deity to be as logical as himself, which hardly suited Omnipotence" (*MSM*, 363). The conflict between form and matter sent Thomas in a variety of different directions, each one threatening the logic of his system. For Adams this is the irreconcilable conflict in Thomist thought. Yet, in his refusal to reject matter for the sake of pure mind or spirit, Thomas suggests man's tragic need to reconcile the polarities of his existence: "He insisted on keeping man wholly apart, as a complex of energies in which matter shared equally with mind. The Church must rest firmly on both" (365).

23. Samuels, *The Major Phase*, p. 303.

Thomas's insistence raised serious questions concerning human freedom. The Thomist notion that man's "free choice" is the reflective power of his judgment prefigures modern determinism for Adams: "The scheme seems to differ little, and unwillingly, from a system of dynamics as modern as the dynamo. Even in the prime motor, from the moment of an action, freedom of will vanished. Creation was not successive; it was one instantaneous thought and act, identical with the will and complete and un-changeable from end to end, including time as one of its func-tions" (374). Although Thomas preserved God's free will by defining it as His choice to act, His constitution of Himself as eternal and primal cause, he could not save both man's freedom and his desire for unity. Adams does not blame Thomist logic, but rather irrational man "who insisted that the universe was a unit, but that he was a universe; that energy was one, but that he was another energy; that God was omnipotent, but that man was free. The contradiction had always existed, exists still, and always must exist, unless man either admits that he is a machine, or agrees that anarchy and chaos are the habits of nature, and law and order its accident" (372). Only the Virgin could tolerate such contradiction and paradox, only her grace could embrace man *because* of his ignorance and irrational desire.

Although Adams labored over the final chapter of *Chartres* for an accurate interpretation of Thomist thought, his St. Thom-as tells us more about Henry Adams than about the author of the *Summa*.[24] Adams lingers over the structural problems of Thomas's church, admiring the effort to reconcile human mul-tiplicity within a divine order. St. Thomas *desired* what the Virgin had achieved for an historical moment—an equilibrium of opposing forces that unified without destroying conflicting

24. See *Letters,* II, 562–3, Henry Adams to Professor Frederick Bliss Luquiens of Harvard, 27 February 1911: "I am even more shy of my theology than of my architecture or linguistics. . . . I care far more for my theology than for my architecture, and should be much mortified if detected in an error about Thomas Aquinas, or the doctrine of Uni-versals."

energies. The limited language of man could reach beyond itself only in symbol and art. The equilibrium Thomas tried to sustain in the *Summa* was as precarious as that of the cathedral of Beauvais, and its "practical use" for the thirteenth-century Church would yield eventually to the changing needs of succeeding cultures. The rigor of his method reveals at last the *art* of his architecture. The failure of man's reason demands new expressions of his ancient questions and new instruments to describe the endless ambiguity of his situation.

Adams's St. Thomas symbolizes the disappearance of the Virgin's vital presence and the increased need for man to rely on his own fallible consciousness: "From that time, the universe has steadily become more complex and less reducible to a central control" (380). In its presentation of the varieties of medieval man's interpretations of his world, *Chartres* dramatizes how "Unity turned itself into complexity, multiplicity, variety, even contradiction" (381). The very energy Aquinas had posited at the center of the cosmos denies any fixed or final definition. Movement remains the enduring paradox in man's attempt to reach some origin or end to his journey. Consciousness must find its meaning only in the activity of defining and expressing itself, for "the universe itself presented different aspects as man moved" (383).

In *Chartres* Adams uses the Virgin to redefine the very idea of unity for twentieth-century man. Her love and grace may be remote and merely symbolic for the manikin of the *Education,* but her very anarchy suggests an alternative to a conception of order as law. St. Thomas struggled to prevent his Church from subjecting man to the ineluctable rule of divine causation. Yet the central power of the Thomist God suggests for Adams a world circumscribed and pervaded by His energetic and active presence. Thomas's God symbolizes for Adams the completion of man's desire, the end of his dream. For Adams man must acknowledge that he knows himself only through the frustration of his desire, the failure of his efforts to know at last. Viewed from such a perspective, history studies the repeated collapse of man's systems for order: "Energy is the inherent effort of every multiplicity to become unity" (332). The breakdown of old orders allows for the free play of the contemporary mind, shuffling elements to create terms to meet new crises. Adams referred to *Chartres* as his "anchor in the past," the point from which he could measure motion. Yet this "granite foothold in the past" reveals at last its own shifting and unstable qualities.[25] *Chartres* exposes the multiplicity of the modern age as it reveals its own complexity.

Chartres and the *Education* assert man's need to bear the continuing burden of his interpretations, but they equally suggest the dangers of his lust for knowledge. Aquinas's grand synthesis heralds modern man's insistence upon a truth accessible to his consciousness alone. Rational man deludes himself that his knowledge might replace the emptiness at the center. In his anxious need for order, he destroys the difference and multiplicity on which his being and world are founded. At the end of *Tristes Tropiques,* Lévi-Strauss suggests that "entropology" should replace "anthropology" as the name for his science:

Man has never—save only when he reproduces himself—done other than cheerfully dismantle million upon million of structures and reduce their elements to a state in which they can no longer be reintegrated. No doubt he has built cities and brought the soil to fruition; but if we examine these activities closely we shall find that they also are inertia-producing machines, whose scale and speed of action are infinitely greater than the amount of organization implied in them. . . . Taken as a whole, therefore, civilization can be described as a prodigiously complicated mechanism: tempting as it would be to regard it as our universe's best hope of survival, its true function is to produce what the physicists call entropy: inertia, that is to say. . . . "Entropology," not anthropology should be the word for the discipline that devotes itself to the study of this process of disintegration in its most highly evolved forms.[26]

25. Samuels, *The Major Phase,* p. 217.
26. Lévi-Strauss, *Tristes Tropiques,* p. 397. These lines were written before I had read Tony Tanner's excellent *City of Words.* In his analysis

It is a similarly entropic tendency that Adams sees in history from the thirteenth century to the twentieth century. For Adams the relentless development of civilized man threatens to separate him from a natural sense of unity. Our modern loss of "the sense of unity in art" is the true subject of the uncle's commentaries on the Normans, the Virgin, and the Schoolmen of the Middle Ages. The self-conscious insistence upon a law to resolve the contradictions of man and natural force is at the heart of modern multiplicity, rather than being the basis for a new human order.

Adams recognizes that man's quest for a monistic order leads, ironically, to the disorder and incoherence it seeks to resolve. Perhaps Adams sees his Virgin of Chartres as a pluralistic alternative to what William James termed theories of a "block universe." Whether viewed in contrast to the Norman God of Law or to a more modern rationalism, Adams's Virgin has clear affinities with that "finite God" William James proposes in *A Pluralistic Universe*: "Everything you can think of, however vast or inclusive has on the pluralistic view a genuinely 'external' environment of some sort or amount. Things are 'with' one another in many ways, but nothing includes everything, or dominates over everything. The word 'and' trails along after every sentence. Something always escapes."[27] In his imagined Virgin, Adams seeks to symbolize an alternative to the fragmentation of modern life that still might allow for the diversity, change, and motion the monists struggled to deny. In his own fashion, Adams attempts to define a "multiverse" less continuous and concatenated than William James's, but equally pluralistic.[28]

---

of Adams as precursive of the contemporary American novelist's obsession with entropy, Tanner cites this same passage from Lévi-Strauss and remarks: "Adopting Lévi-Strauss's word we may say that American novelists of the past two decades have shown themselves to be diligent and concerned entropologists" (152n.).

27. William James, *A Pluralistic Universe*, p. 321.

28. Ibid., p. 325: "Our 'multiverse' still makes a 'universe'; for every part, tho it may not be in actual or immediate connexion, is nevertheless in some possible or mediate connexion, with every other part, however

Both longed for less rigid laws and more flexible philosophies. William James could affirm the individual centers for consciousness as worlds of their own; Adams longed for an antidote to the consuming anthropocentrism that he saw as instrumental in the decline of civilized man.

---

remote, through the fact that each part hangs together with its very next neighbors in inextricable interfusion." Adams was not able to sustain James's confidence in the "continuity" and "interrelation" of the parts of the universe.

4   The Dream of Unity and the
     Experience of Multiplicity
     in *The Education of Henry Adams*

> "You ask Gautama's meaning, for you know
> That since his birth, his thoughts and acts alike
> Have been to me a mirror, clearer far
> Than to himself, for no man sees himself.
> With the solemnity of youth, you ask
> Of me, on whom the charm of childhood still
> Works greater miracles than magicians know,
> To tell, as though it were a juggler's trick
> The secret meaning which himself but now
> Could tell you only by a mystic sign,
> The symbol of a symbol—so far-thought,
> So vague and vast and intricate its scope."
>   —Henry Adams, "Buddha and Brahma," 1895

From behind the mask of Henry Cabot Lodge, Adams remarks in the editor's preface to the *Education:* "He preferred
to leave the 'Education' unpublished, avowedly incomplete,
trusting that it might quietly fade from memory" (*EHA*, viii).
This conception of *The Education of Henry Adams* as unpublishable and incomplete is embedded in such an ironic context
that we tend to question Adams's seriousness. His responses to
publishing inquiries from Ferris Greenslet of Houghton Mifflin
emphasize his intent: "During my life I should not publish the
Education."[1] Many reasons have been suggested for Adams's
reluctance. Reticence before the public eye was a lifelong habit,
perhaps the result of early disappointment when his articles in
the *North American Review* failed to have the political and

1. Henry Adams to Ferris Greenslet, 18 February 1916, *Letters*, II, 637.

economic impact he had expected. His later determination to write for a select audience may well have been confirmed by the failure of the *History* and the largely academic esteem it received. Beyond such practical explanations, however, it appears that Adams wanted to give the impression of personal familiarity between reader and author in both *Chartres* and the *Education*. Adams wrote to Charles Milnes Gaskell shortly after the private edition of the *Education* had been completed: "As my experience leads me to think that no one any longer cares or even knows what is said or printed, and that one's audience in history and literature has shrunk to a mere band of survivors, not exceeding a thousand people in the entire world, I am in hopes a kind of esoteric literary art may survive, the freer and happier for the sense of privacy and *abandon*."[2] Adams was at least free from the demands of publishers who catered to that vast multitude of silent readers with which Henry James had to struggle. If Adams's "esoteric literary art" reflected a definite bitterness and regret, it was at least a mode in which he could manipulate his language for predictable effects.

Publication always involves a certain degree of finality. Once the galleys have been corrected and the type set, the work becomes an artifact to be defended or excused. The incompleteness of the *Education* made it unpublishable for Adams as a total statement. He understood that the diversity of his own life and age could hardly be described in the form of those monumental volumes of "Life and Letters," "Memoirs," or "Autobiography," which had been the tokens of nineteenth-century success. His reluctance to write the biography of his close friend John Hay betrays the ambivalence he felt toward an art that unavoidably distorted men's lives and reputations in its form and style. Much of the confidence underlying his critical portrait of John Randolph vanished in the face of the discovery of radium, the construction of the Cunarder, and the invention of the automobile.

2. Henry Adams to Charles Milnes Gaskell, 10 May 1907, *Letters,* II, 476.

He agreed to write the *Life of George Cabot Lodge,* but it became more accurately literary appreciation rather than historical biography. In connection with the *Education,* Adams wrote to Henry James: "I need hardly tell *you* that my own marginal comment is broader than that of any reader, and precludes publication altogether. The volume is a mere shield of protection in the grave. I advise you to take your own life in the same way, in order to prevent biographers from taking it in theirs."[3]

The hundred blue folio copies that Adams sent out to a select group of readers were printed with those same large margins in which he had invited comments on the earlier drafts of the *History.* As Ernest Samuels suggests: "From first to last he diffidently insisted that the book was 'in the nature of proof sheets,' keeping up the appearance as a kind of *absit omen* years after the book had permanently established itself among an elite public as an unquestioned classic."[4] His request for revisions and corrections was to be largely disregarded—only three annotated volumes were returned. The obsession for revision that Adams shared with James was no pose—by 1907 it was a mental reflex. For years he had relied on an intellectual community of friends as diverse in membership as John La Farge and Clarence King. Famous for his conversation, Adams would draw much material from the talks of the "Five of Hearts" or the famous "breakfast" salons he held in Washington. In 1909 he wrote to Henry Osborn Taylor: "Theoretically all the copies are to be recalled, for corrections, or, as time goes on, I doubt more and more whether the volume is even worth correcting. It served its only purpose by educating *me.*"[5] In both his public and private writings,

3. Henry Adams to Henry James, 6 May 1908, *Letters,* II, 495. Samuels in *The Major Phase,* p. 633, n. 41, points out that there are barely two dozen marginal comments in Adams's own copy of the *Education* in the Massachussets Historical Society.

4. Samuels, *The Major Phase,* pp. 332–3.

5. Henry Adams to Henry Osborn Taylor, 22 November 1909, *Letters,* II, 526.

Adams emphasized his need for writing to be a continuing act of educating himself. He often complained of being a mere spectator to the game of life, and writing provided an active engagement of the world, a vital affirmation of his own sense of being. Like James's concern with the process of consciousness, Adams's obsession was with the need for repeated expression as self-definition.

Any attempt to write the story of a life or an education must confront the puzzle of incompletion suggested by Tristram Shandy, that author so burdened by pressing time. The entire confessional mode from Augustine to Adams is dominated by a desire to order life, to make fragmentary experience meaningful in a larger context. Yet this very need for expression reveals the incompleteness of any education. Adams may fail to project a viable order for his manikin, but he at least liberates him from old dogmas and archaic methods. Such a method leads only to "open air sketches,—just notes of ideas set down for future consideration."[6]

The form and structure of the *Education* rely to a great extent on the example of *The Confessions* of St. Augustine. Both works describe the failures and struggles of youth as the means of demonstrating the emergence of a mature consciousness. Augustine and Adams are concerned with a process of education that will make it possible for them to interpret and understand their worlds. Augustine's narrative up to his conversion in Book VIII and baptism in Book IX traces the awakening of a spiritual consciousness. Only then is Augustine capable of grappling with the problems posed by scriptural exegesis and the meanings of God's Word.[7] Although he has not entirely resolved his spiritual crises in Books X–XIII, Augustine has demonstrated how he is now able to begin to read the meaning of God's plan.

6. Henry Adams to Raphael Pumpelly, 19 May 1910, *Letters,* II, 542.
7. See Gene Koretz, "Augustine's *Confessions* and *The Education of Henry Adams,*" pp. 193–206; Samuels, *The Major Phase,* pp. 340–41; and Levenson, *Mind and Art,* p. 349.

In a similar sense, Adams leads his manikin through the ambiguity of his world until he is compelled to give some systematic explanation of his historical situation. "A Dynamic Theory of History" substitutes the causal patterns of historical change for the finality of God's design. Yet, as Adams leads his subject to the final role of interpreter, the text he reads has hardly the secure foundation of Augustine's "Genesis." The twentieth century's complexities support only the small artist, whose attempts at articulating unity lead inevitably to a reflection of multiplicity. Augustine's interpretation is assured by the confidence God's illumination has inspired. The final books of the *Confessions* begin to resolve the fragments of Augustine's early life in a grand spiritual order. The language of the *Education* ultimately confirms the paradoxes and discontinuities with which the manikin has struggled throughout his life.[8] The failure of "A Dynamic Theory of History" to resolve Adams's questions calls into question all systems of totalizing order. The interpreter at the end of the *Education* shares none of Augustine's confidence in the ends of his knowledge. For Augustine the varieties of scriptural meaning suggest only the diversity of God's truth for fallen man: "From the words of Moses, uttered in all brevity but destined to serve a host of preachers, there gush clear streams of truth from which each of us, though in more prolix and roundabout phrases, may derive a true explanation of the creation as best he is able, some choosing one and some another interpretation."[9] For Adams silence alone is the end of the repeated need for man to interpret and structure his world.

Adams's skeptical method is perhaps more clearly related to the fragments that compose Pascal's *Pensées*. Pascal does not simply deny human reason in favor of a pantheistic God, as St. Francis does in *Chartres*. Implicit in the idea of the "Wager" (*le Pari*) is the paradoxical nature of God, whose existence as

8. See Robert Sayre, *The Examined Self*, p. 111.
9. St. Augustine, *Confessions*, p. 304.

both a presence and an absence demands the activities of faith and reason to continue the game. Although the thought of both Adams and Pascal may be described as dialectical, the form and content of their works are more paradoxical. In Pascal's original classification of the *Pensées,* there is a definite movement from an analysis of the problematic condition of man to the act of the Wager and ending with an historical proof.[10] The general narrative of the *Education* from the "failure" of the manikin to the formulation of "A Dynamic Theory of History" is analogous. Both of these final "historical proofs" refuse to *resolve* the paradoxes of existence. With his law firmly defined, Adams suggests its implications: "Evidently the new American would need to think in contradictions, and instead of Kant's famous four antinomies, the new universe would know no law that could not be proved by its anti-law" (*EHA,* 498). Rather than providing any final intention in the manner of Augustine, Adams suggests an acceleration of man's ambiguity and doubt. Modern science repeats in its own terms ancient philosophical questions. The theory, like Pascal's Wager, sums up the method of any rational education: "The training is partly the clearing away of obstacles, partly the direct application of effort. Once acquired, the tools and models may be thrown away" (x).

The explicitly fragmentary *Pensées* reveals a basic aim often buried in the complex texture of the *Education.* In his study of Pascal and Racine, Lucien Goldmann has argued that both paradox and fragment are fundamental to Pascal's sense of order: "A rationalist thinker can have a logical plan, and a work of apologetics can be written in a way most likely to convince the reader. But there can be, for the tragic work, only one valid form: that of the fragment, which expresses a quest for order that has not succeeded and cannot even begin to succeed. . . . By giving the *Pensées* a paradoxical form, and by leaving them as fragments, he made them into a paradoxical master-

10. Lucien Goldmann, *The Hidden God,* p. 202.

piece, complete by its very lack of completeness."[11] Insofar as tragedy is possible in this modern world, Adams's aesthetics of failure expresses the tragic consequences of a disintegrating historical sense. As an act of the modern mind struggling to define itself, *The Education of Henry Adams* could hardly assume a form as reconcilable as Augustine's or any less paradoxical than Pascal's. For Pascal and Adams, the rational quest for absolute values must acknowledge ultimately the impossibility of determining such values. This very recognition perpetuates the search and necessitates continuing acts of interpretation.

The repeated failures of Henry Adams's education are clarified by the general implications of Pascal's Wager. The necessity of the Wager brings man irrevocably to admit ignorance of the odds of the game itself. Man does not simply cast his bet and peacefully await the outcome of his choice. As Goldman suggests, " 'those who *now* wager' " are the only ones " 'who do not *now* have any doubt' ": "A man who rested and ceased to search, who attained a certainty which ceased to be a wager, would be the complete opposite of the man whom Pascal knew and whom he presented in his work."[12] The manikin of the *Education* is fitted to the motley composed of personal, social, political, economic, scientific, aesthetic, and historical educations. Every "lesson" centers on a choice that can be neither justified nor repudiated on the basis of any enveloping code of values. From his initial decision to accept his family and tradition to the final paradox of his contrived law, Adams repeatedly affirms his own being *now*, making his bets in an ethical and metaphysical void. On this very basis, he is condemned to renew his wager constantly in different forms and by diverse methods, recognizing the impossibility of any final definition.

11. Ibid., p. 196. Goldmann generalizes his argument concerning Pascal's fragments in a similar fashion in "Structure: Human Reality and Methodological Concept," in Macksey and Donato, *Languages of Criticism and the Sciences of Man,* pp. 107 ff.

12. Goldmann, *The Hidden God,* pp. 296, 295; italics mine.

For Pascal "risk, possibility of failure, hope of success" are all synthesized in that "form of faith which is a wager."[13] In Adams's game there are no final stakes. The end is accidental and contingent, by no means suggesting any rules of fair play. Henry Adams's successive wagers in the *Education* are perhaps more closely related to the Nietzschean idea that "to choose is to be," regardless of those external forces that threaten man's freedom on every side. Adams's existential choices certainly include risk and the possibility of failure, but any hope of success involves an absurd contradiction. Man's dream of unity is the instinctive desire for an order that transcends the limits of human reason. In his effort to understand unity, man separates himself from it. In the moment it becomes an idea, unity loses its reality. This alienation from a metaphysical order, however, is what motivates man's renewed projects for being. Like the Virgin at Chartres, Pascal's God is paradoxical. The faith that sustains both involves a leap beyond pure reason. Adams views *man* as paradoxical, driven as he is by an instinctive yearning for unity and a consciousness that cannot transcend itself. This conflict in part explains why Adams himself continues to look for a totalizing historical order despite his insistence that the search is futile.

Goldmann studies Pascal as the origin of modern dialectical thought. In a certain sense, the dialectic is fundamental to Adams's own conception of consciousness. The structure of the *Education*, however, finally suggests the failure of any consistent dialectical method. The first six chapters set up an opposition of forces that poses a tentative order for the work as a whole. Quincy and Boston, Washington and Harvard, Berlin and Rome seem to offer a clear pattern of thesis and antithesis, the Dionysian and Apollonian elements of an education.[14] Such a dialectical argument might also include the synthetic aims of "A

13. Ibid., p. 302.
14. Lyon, *Symbol and Idea,* p. 289n.

Dynamic Theory of History." But the neat opposition within the first six chapters deteriorates into ironic contrasts in such later chapters as "Eccentricity" and "The Perfection of Human Society," or such related chapters as "Foes or Friends" and "Political Morality," "Chaos" and "Failure." Similarly, Adams's own attempts to make clear distinctions between Virgin and Dynamo, unity and multiplicity, instinct and reason constantly break down.

In a dialectical analysis of the *Education,* the concept of unity ought to suggest a synthesis of opposing forces.[15] The failure of all scientific attempts to achieve a totalizing law may in part be traced to this traditional interpretation of order. Adams writes in "The Grammar of Science": "Even Hegel, who taught that every motion included its own negation, used the negation only to reach a 'larger synthesis,' till he reached the universal which thinks itself, contradiction and all" (*EHA,* 451). Yet the vast energy of the Virgin at Chartres provides the modern manikin with a metaphor and image for his own dream of unity. For the twelfth-century worshiper, the Virgin allows contradiction and paradox free play as aspects of her love and grace. As we have suggested, she is lawless and "heretical" on her own terms. Her unity is not the reconciliation of opposites, but an anarchy that encompasses even its own contradiction. Unlike the Trinity, she has no final law on which she bases her activity of grace, unless it be her very unscientific force. In Adams's interpretation, she is approached neither by pure emotion nor by pure reason. She expresses man's instinctive yearning and at the same time surrounds herself with the Masters of the Schools. Her

15. Ernst Scheyer's argument that "Henry Adams was a Hegelian who never knew what it was!" may have some truth in it. The cultural ramifications of Hegel's thought probably had profound effects on Adams and his circle of friends. Adams's views on reason and instinct have clear similarities with Hegel's interpretation of consciousness and its relation to desire. See Scheyer, *The Circle of Henry Adams,* pp. 39–45.

presence at Chartres is a language that makes human meaning and value possible within her own distinctive grammar.

The Virgin's metaphysical sense provides a large contrast to the rational orders of social man. The winter world of Puritan Boston is opposed to the multiplicity of Quincy in the summer. Boston seems to the young Henry to exclude the sensuous riot of the pastoral world at Quincy. Order and law are established at the cost of imagination and variety. The manikin born in the first paragraph of the *Education* is defined and delimited by a taxonomy of names, places, and times: "Under the shadow of Boston State House, turning its back on the house of John Hancock, the little passage called Hancock Avenue runs, or ran, from Beacon Street, skirting the State House grounds, to Mount Vernon Street, on the summit of Beacon Hill; and there, in the third house below Mount Vernon Place, February 16, 1838, a child was born and christened later by his uncle, the minister of the First Church after the tenets of Boston Unitarianism, as Henry Brooks Adams" (3). This paragraph does far more than simply set the stage and define the coordinates for the child's future. It describes a confining heritage designed to exclude alien elements. This Henry Brooks Adams is "branded" and "handicapped" by such restrictions. Throughout the *Education,* Adams is troubled by the paradoxical nature of such attempts at definition. The need for order and unity results in the violation of life's fundamental diversity and change. "Tradition" and "law" always involve artificial arrangements and selections, the establishment of sequences that ignore contradictions and complexities.

Ironically, social power in Boston is wielded by Unitarian clergymen. Their smug complacency in this established world suggests the dangers of all human attempts at order: "For them difficulties might be ignored; doubts were waste of thought; nothing exacted solution. Boston had solved the universe; or had offered and realized the best solution yet tried. The problem was worked out" (34). The application of this inherited system of values immediately leads the young boy into difficulties. Quincy is somehow unaccounted for. The rigorous order of "eighteenth-century, troglodytic Boston" shudders and collapses "in act if not in sentiment, by the opening of the Boston and Albany railroad; the appearance of the first Cunard steamers in the bay; and the telegraphic messages which carried from Baltimore to Washington the news that Henry Clay and James K. Polk were nominated for the Presidency" (5).

In the larger perspective of the *Education,* Boston provides only one pole for the New England consciousness: "The chief charm of New England was harshness of contrasts and extremes of sensibility" (7). As an educational background, New England is an irreconcilable dialectic of forces imaged in Boston and Quincy. Like the seasons of winter and summer associated with the places, the atmosphere of each seems to exclude the other.[16] No synthesis seems possible, but the disparate force of each realm demands explanation. It is in the conflict of these opposing realms that Adams finds the true nature of the New England sensibility to which "resistance" is a fundamental "law": "The double exterior nature gave life its relative values. Winter and summer, cold and heat, town and country, force and freedom, marked two modes of life and thought, balanced like lobes of the brain" (7).

Quincy stands for more than just the multiplicity of nature. The birth of the manikin's senses in the first chapter betrays a romantic naïveté. His instinctive attraction to such natural free-

16. Lyon, *Symbol and Idea,* pp. 133–4, suggests that the initial dichotomy of Boston and Quincy informs the dominant imagery and symbolism of the *Education:* "By associating Boston and school with winter, he also creates the first link between his unity-multiplicity dichotomy and the book's pervasive water symbolism. For winter is a rigid unity, a frozen time of ice and snow. This symbolic use leads directly into the snow, ice, and glacier imagery which appears later in the book" (134). It also suggests the dominant polarities facing the individual in a good deal of American literature: the fear of rigid structures and the narrow spaces that suggest social law, and the metaphysical terror of formlessness and natural anarchy.

dom is later shattered in the apocalyptic vision of "Chaos." Quincy, however, is also related to grandfather John Quincy Adams, just as grandfather Brooks is associated in the boy's mind with Boston. Adams always preferred the Adams side of the family. In all his writings there is implicit respect and tenderness for the man as both president and grandfather. Brooks is associated with the generally restrictive order of nineteenth-century Boston. From a child's view, the president brings gifts of "a little volume of critically edited Nursery Rhymes" and a Bible, "while their grandfather Brooks supplied the silver mugs" (15). Adams shares a curious intimacy with the patriarch of his family. Rustling through the disordered papers and books of the Quincy library, the boy uncovers a spirit to which he feels instinctively drawn. John Quincy Adams has the restless mind and inquiring spirit characteristic of the French *philosophes*. Although neither "The President" nor "The Madam" is able "to impress on a boy's mind, the standards of the coming century," they share the reflective intensity of the mature author (19).

At times the grandfather appears to be a mere dilettante, dabbling in unrelated projects simply for the sake of his own curiosity. This very thirst for new ideas recalls the inventive vitality that had expressed the best in the American character in Adams's *History*: "His was a restless mind, and although he took his hobbies [i.e., hobby-horses] seriously and would have been annoyed had his grandchild asked whether he was bored like an English duke, he probably cared more for the processes than for the results, so that his grandson was saddened by the sight and smell of peaches and pears, the best of their kind, which he brought up from his garden to rot on his shelves for seed" (14). His grandfather seems to offer an alternative to the rigorous values and standards of Boston.

The methods of education offered by Boston and Quincy provide no easy choice for the young man standing on the brink of a new world. The dialectical relation of winter and summer suggests a general figure for the manikin's education: "The bearing of the two seasons on the education of Henry Adams was no fancy; it was the most decisive force he ever knew; it ran through life, and made the division between its perplexing, warring, irreconcilable problems irreducible opposites, with growing emphasis to the last year of study" (9). Only a law that would allow the free play of mind could ever hope to deal with such contraries. Yet throughout the *Education* law involves restraint, confinement, and exclusion. To survive this world demands an active choice, but the alternatives open to the young man offer unity only at the expense of variety and vitality: "If State Street was wrong, Quincy must be right! Turn the dilemma as he pleased, he still came back on the eighteenth century and the law of Resistance; of Truth; of Duty, and of Freedom. He was a ten-year-old priest and politician" (22).

Adams's initial quest for order suggests the alternatives of law, synthesis, and chaos. The history of modern thought could only expose law as fiction, synthesis as compromise. The opposing forces confusing the young boy pose riddles for the old man. The situation at mid-century demonstrates the absolute moral confusion of a mind caught in the web of violent forces. Politics show the fourteen-year-old boy that the attempt to reconcile conflict is frequently effected at the cost of principles. George Washington may be the "pole star" of the Republican heaven, but Adams finds him at the end of the ragged road of Southern slavery and oppression. The question of "how to deduce George Washington from the sum of all wickedness" suggests the inadequacy of those old habits of moral thought he had inherited from his Puritan ancestors. The political lessons of 1850–1851 leave the question unanswered. Any synthesis of alien elements seems impossible. The small boy feels himself a party to that compromise negotiated by the Free Soilers and the Massachusetts Democrats. Trading votes and bargaining for positions reduce statesmanship to an equation in mathematics. Sumner's election to the Senate is accomplished only by placing the Democrat, George S. Boutwell, in the Governor's mansion. The boy's initia-

tion into party politics gives him an inkling of that larger mechanical system that would end in Tammany Hall (50–51). By
supporting Sumner, the boy finds himself condoning compromise
as a method of political and social action: "Thus, before he was
fifteen years old, he had managed to get himself into a state of
moral confusion from which he never escaped. As a politician,
he was already corrupt, and he never could see how any practical
politician could be less corrupt than himself" (50).

As a source for American culture and history, Europe ought
to suggest some answers to the baffling complexities of American
modernity. When he makes the traditional pilgrimage, the manikin confronts simply an intensification of the problems at home.
The "irreducible opposites" of Quincy and Boston, South and
North, freedom and order are repeated in much larger form in
England, Germany, and Italy. His stormy crossing tosses him
into the realms of Dickens and Hogarth, where "aristocracy was
real." The social order of Boston pales before the rigid structures
of nineteenth-century England. The Black Districts of Man-
chester and Birmingham reveal a social oppression that dissolves
the romantic haze of Trollope and Thackeray: "Education went
backward" (73). Europe at mid-century exposed the myth of
scientific and social progress. The mechanization and industrialization of society had created arbitrary classes and irrational
values undreamt of by the most ruthless tyrant. A dictatorship
of abstract force seems to rule everywhere.

Perhaps only the intricacies of the language prevent the young
Henry Adams from studying civil law in Berlin. But for the
weary and aged author, the trouble rests with the idea of law
itself. The lessons of Friedrichs-Wilhelm-Werdersches Gymnasium
teach him more than he ever could have learned at the University of Berlin. The disciplined training of the German Gymnasium dramatizes the methods of a society founded on an
absolute and inflexible interpretation of law. Education is simply
mechanical indoctrination, the leveling of all differences and
variations: "All State education is a sort of dynamo machine

for polarizing the popular mind; for turning and holding its lines of force in the direction supposed to be the most effective for State purposes" (78). The birthplace of Kant, Schopenhauer, and Hegel disposes of reason for the sake of efficiency: "The German government did not encourage reasoning" (78).

It would take the later lessons of Darwin to teach Adams the true significance of treating unity as uniformity, of defining order in terms of fixed laws: "Natural Selection led back to Natural Evolution, and at last to Natural Uniformity. This was a vast stride. Unbroken Evolution under uniform conditions pleased every one—except curates and bishops; it was the very best substitute for religion; a safe, conservative, practical, thoroughly Common-Law deity. Such a working system for the universe suited a young man who had just helped to waste five or ten thousand million dollars and a million lives, more or less, to enforce unity and uniformity on people who objected to it" (225–6). There is more than a mere pun involved in "Common-Law deity." For Adams the entire tendency of Western thought is tied up in the dream of a final and unchangeable order: "Unity and Uniformity were the whole motive of philosophy" (226). The nineteenth-century conception of order could hardly avoid the charge that it was designed to eliminate differences and exclude variety and change. Only the accident of the ganoid fish *Pteraspis* would teach Adams that both lessons in civil law and studies in evolution were doomed to failure in the complexities of the modern age: "The idea of one Form, Law, Order, or Sequence had no more value for him than the idea of none; . . . what he valued most was Motion, and . . . what attracted his mind was Change" (231).

The need for some point of origin becomes more urgent as the manikin stumbles into a world of rapidly accelerating forces. If modern Europe suggests nothing but violence and chaos, then the young man must go directly to the source. When Gibbon trod the ruins of the Forum, history romantically sprang to life for him. The Eternal City was a vast stage on which the drama of ancient history re-enacted itself in his imagination: "After a sleepless night, I trod, with a lofty step, the ruins of the Forum; each memorable spot where Romulus *stood,* or Tully spoke, or Caesar fell, was at once present to my eye; and several days of intoxication were lost or enjoyed before I could descend to a cool and minute investigation."[17] For Adams, too, Rome is "mostly an emotion," but the historical chaos of the city makes "cool and minute investigation" impossible: "In spite of swarming impressions he knew no more when he left Rome than he did when he entered it" (*EHA,* 89, 93). Gibbon was inspired while musing on the steps of the Temple of Jupiter to write the history of the city's decline and fall, but Adams merely stares out at the unfathomable riddle of the ruined Capitol. The only lesson to be learned on the steps of the Church of Santa Maria di Ara Coeli is one of failure. From the Forum to St. Peter's, Adams traces the collapse of the West's two most complicated and extended attempts at historical order, "and nothing proved that the city might not still survive to express the failure of a third" (91).

Like the Virgin, the Dynamo, and *Pteraspis,* the Church of Santa Maria di Ara Coeli is developed into a complex symbol. The Church suggests to Adams the inconsistency of historical change. Reflecting on the violent and catastrophic history of Sicily, Adams sees its anarchy leading directly to Ara Coeli: "For a lesson in anarchy, without a shade of sequence, Sicily stands alone and defies evolution. Syracuse teaches more than Rome. Yet even Rome was not mute, and the church of Ara Coeli seemed more and more to draw all the threads of thought to a centre, for every new journey led back to its steps—Karnak, Ephesus, Delphi, Mycenae, Constantinople, Syracuse—all lying on the road to the Capitol" (367). One might make a chart of forces from Karnak to Rome, from the Temple of Jupiter to the dome of St. Peter's. The design would be a chaos of in-

17. *The Autobiography of Edward Gibbon,* ed. Lord Sheffield, p. 159.

tersecting lines, interrupted connections, abrupt halts. For millennia order and law had implied continuity and sequence. As a temporal system, history ought to deal with successions and relations. Yet lessons as disparate as those learned while viewing the ruins of the Capitol, studying geology, and reading metaphysics all taught Adams that discontinuity and violent crises were basic laws of change. The law of New England was "resistance," and Newton could suggest that any analysis of force involves both action and reaction. But such a vision also implies a consistency of conflict, relegating "crisis" to the realm of "accident." Only when Adams finally came to develop his own theory of history would he fully recognize the value of Ara Coeli's suggestion of discontinuity: "Thus far, since five or ten thousand years, the mind had successfully reacted, and nothing yet proved that it would fail to react—but it would need to jump" (498).

In his appendix to *A Pluralistic Universe* (1909), "On the Notion of Reality As Changing," William James refers to Adams's desire for a totalizing historical law in *Chartres* and the *Education*. James uses Adams to suggest the impossibility of any such scheme for the "synechistic" pluralist who believes in the constantly changing relations of our empirical reality:

A friend of mine has an idea, which illustrates on such a magnified scale the impossibility of tracing the same line through reality, that I will mention it here. He thinks that nothing more is needed to make history "scientific" than to get the content of any two epochs (say the end of the thirteenth and the end of the nineteenth century) accurately defined, then accurately to define the direction of the change that led from the one epoch into the other, and finally to prolong the line of that direction into the future. So prolonging the line, he thinks, we ought to be able to define the actual state of things at any future date we please. We all feel the essential unreality of such a conception of "History" as this.[18]

18. William James, "On the Notion of Reality As Changing," appendix to *A Pluralistic Universe*, pp. 351–2. The reference seems to be clearly to James's friend and correspondent, Henry Adams. William requested a copy of the *Education* from Adams in a letter dated 7 December 1907;

James's remarks are apt responses to the historical formulations of the *Education*. Yet the failure of "A Dynamic Theory" is the result of the manikin's repeated confrontations with the discontinuity of historical events and their effects. At the end of the *Education* Adams still may long for the rigorous historical scheme James views as unreal, but his own experiences seem to have shown him the need to think in contraries and discontinuities. William James struggled to admit "novelty" into his philosophy without repudiating experiential continuity.[19] Adams could not resolve the question, and he found himself compelled to grant that discontinuity was fundamental to change and motion. The general outlook of the *Education* repudiates Adams's own desire for historical coherence and suggests a tentative pluralism. Despite Adams's disagreements with William James, he confronts in the *Education* problems equally fundamental to such "synechistic" pluralists as Peirce, Bergson, and William James.[20]

The violence and chaos of the Civil War years provide contemporary justification for the manikin's reflections on historical discontinuity. As an arbitrary point for measuring Henry Adams as a force, the period 1860–1867 virtually severs him from his own past. As his father's secretary he observes society at large become the "helpless victim" of the uncontrolled forces of the War (*EHA,* 109). His first-hand experience of Anglo-American diplomacy teaches him only that politics and history are often the results of individual psychology. The attempt to determine finally the honesty or dishonesty of a figure like Lord Russell ends in confusion and moral doubt. The author himself attempts to reconstruct the facts forty years later, and he assembles an

and sent his impressions of the *Education* to Adams in a letter of 9 February 1908. See also Henry Adams to William James, 9 December 1907, *Letters,* II, 485.

19. See William James's discussion of the problem of novelty and continuity in *Some Problems of Philosophy,* pp. 152–3, 215–19; and in *A Pluralistic Universe,* pp. 350–51.

20. *A Pluralistic Universe,* p. 352.

impressive array of evidence from the letters and diaries of Palmerston, Russell, Gladstone, and Charles Francis Adams. His conclusions, however, simply confirm his youthful bewilderment. The confusion of historical causation is often the result of man's own ambivalence and inadequacy. No historical law could explain or order the inconsistencies of men in power. Ernest Samuels has summarized Adams's predicament during this period: "The years in England from 1860 to 1868 seemed in retrospect the most significant, for though they opened wide all the main avenues of experience and knowledge that the philosopher statesman needed to traverse, international diplomacy, war, politics and statecraft, science, art, social psychology, national character, yet from the highest standpoint he had made no advance toward a career or a final philosophy of life. Each experience, appraised in terms of the philosophic calculus of 1905, is manipulated to demonstrate failure, mistake, misconception, ignorance and futility."[21] Forced to rely on men acting out of confused motives of self-interest, patriotism, or cunning, Adams sees only the disorder of a history founded on human "reason." The attempt to view historical movement in terms of man's will and power breaks down in the inconsistencies of individual psychology: "Here, then, appeared in its fullest force, the practical difficulty in education which a mere student could never overcome; a difficulty not in theory, or knowledge, or even want of experience, but in the sheer chaos of human nature" (*EHA*, 153). Beneath all the reasoned and deliberated judgments of the agents of power, Adams sees a confusion of instinctive impulses, unconscious prejudices, and cultural differences.

The manikin's quest increasingly becomes an interrupted sequence. His personal response to the assassination of Lincoln provides a metaphor for his own sense of self: "His identity, if one could call a bundle of disconnected memories an identity, seemed to remain; but his life was once more broken into sepa-

21. Samuels, *The Major Phase,* p. 368.

rate pieces; he was a spider and had to spin a new web in some new place with a new attachment" (209). The evidence of history argues that the fault is with man alone. All Adams's various educations attempt to affirm the power of man to order his world. The only alternative appears to be an analysis of that force which impels man helplessly through a universe of random motion and change. The language of science seems the least subject to the inconsistencies of human judgment. There must be some facts that do not lie.

New developments in the natural and physical sciences appear to promise an order for the manikin's education. Without the training or background to question the scientific mind, the young Adams willingly trusts the soothing answers of Darwin and Lyell: "Neither he nor any one else knew enough to verify them; in his ignorance of mathematics, he was particularly helpless; but this never stood in his way. The ideas were new and seemed to lead somewhere—to some great generalization which would finish one's clamor to be educated" (224). The very idea of uniform evolution simply repeats in new terms the entire thrust of his eighteenth-century heritage. Substituting natural selection for historical sequence, natural uniformity for divine design, Darwinian theory seemed "the very best substitute for religion." Regardless of the method, the intent remains the same, "that the best way of reaching unity was to unite. Any road was good that arrived" (226). Yet in the attempt to affirm his new faith Adams discovers its inherent contradictions. Writing a review of Sir Charles Lyell's *Principles of Geology* in order "to clear the minds of American geologists about the principles of their profession," Adams becomes a critic of the very idea of evolution. The act of interpretation again seems to imply the destruction of its subject, just as Volume IX of Adams's own *History* in part repudiates the aims of Volume I.

From Lyell himself Adams learns that his original ancestor "was a very respectable fish, among the earliest of all fossils" (228). The riddle of *Pteraspis* shows the failure of evolutionary theory to account for accident and mutation. Like the Church of the Ara Coeli, *Pteraspis* suggests that discontinuous change is fundamental to geological and natural processes. Like Adams's later "Dynamic Theory of History," all evolutionary theory seems to begin by begging the question: "Ponder over it as he might, Adams could see nothing in the theory of Sir Charles but pure inference, precisely like the inference of Paley, that, if one found a watch, one inferred a maker. He could detect no more evolution in life since *Pteraspis* than he could detect in architecture since the Abbey. All he could prove was change" (230). Based on an inference analogous to Thomist theology, evolution simply repeats the inescapable conclusion that unity is the illusion of man's hope. The overwhelming evidence seems to support a theory of catastrophism in nature similar to the violence expressed in human history. Adams accepted the argument of his friend Clarence King, proposed in *Catastrophism and the Evolution of Environment* (1877), that upward evolution was a fiction. The complexity of natural forces results in catastrophic upheavals of the environment and sudden leaps in the mutation of species.[22] The collapse of the idea of evolution involves the failure of an age-old habit of thought. The implicit faith placed by man in order and sequence breaks down in the face of *Pteraspis:*

Out of his millions of millions of ancestors, back to the Cambrian mollusks, every one had probably lived and died in the illusion of Truths which did not amuse him, and which had never changed. Henry Adams was the first in an infinite series to discover and admit to himself that he really did not care whether truth was, or was not, true. He did not even care that it should be proved true, unless the process were new and amusing. He was a Darwinian for fun. [231-2]

In the *Education* the very term "evolution" comes to stand for man's general dream of an ordered sequence and a unified

22. See Jordy, *Scientific Historian*, pp. 174 ff., on King's theories of catastrophism; and Samuels, *The Major Phase*, pp. 480-84, for their general impact on Adams's thought and writings.

history. As Adams translates the word out of its purely scientific context, evolution provides an ironic scale whereby he measures the failure of his age. President Grant, Garibaldi, Syracuse, the Virgin, modern Russia, and Adams himself are all described for a variety of reasons as "denials of evolution." *Pteraspis* also assumes a symbolic importance transcending its highly technical name. Adams finds an ironic paternity in it, because *Pteraspis* confirms his own instinct for lawlessness: "He had reckoned from childhood on outlawry as his peculiar birthright" (243). The nineteenth-century idea of sequence excluded discontinuity and complexity as "accidental," but Adams gradually comes to see his entire education in contradictory terms. The failure of Darwin or Lyell to account for *Pteraspis* leads him inevitably back to Rome and the steps of Ara Coeli: "The long ten years of education had changed nothing for him there. He knew no more in 1868 than in 1858. He had learned nothing whatever that made Rome more intelligible to him, or made life easier to handle" (236).

Nevertheless, the play of science seems to keep the game interesting. The interpretative activity promises at least some education, even if only in the repeated attempt to uncover order in the confusion of man's languages. The abstractions of scientific theory, however, break down in the image and fact of his sister's death. Just as human fallibility reveals itself in the inconsistencies of the Civil War, so the chaos of nature breaks through his romantic memories of Quincy in the harsh reality of Bagni di Lucca. Although Adams may have longed for the simplicity of St. Francis's mysticism, he could never reconcile such blind faith to the disorder of existence. In *Chartres*, St. Francis greets " 'our sister death' " as "the long-sought, never-found sister of the schoolmen, who solved all philosophy and merged multiplicity in unity" (*MSM*, 346). To Adams death is the final expression of that multiplicity in nature that denies her romantic associations with the feminine. In the setting of Shelley's and Byron's

Italy, the accidental death of Louisa repudiates any transcendental relation of man to nature. Hardly " 'our sister,' " death destroys Adams's sister both factually and symbolically. Perhaps the only firm basis for Adams's moral sense in the first half of the *Education* is the vitality of his sister's intellect. Her lesson alone seems to have any constant ethical value for his education: "Women have, commonly, a very positive moral sense; that which they will is right; that which they reject, is wrong; and their will, in most cases, ends by settling the moral" (*EHA*, 85).

Like the paralysis that ends the restless curiosity of John Quincy Adams, the convulsive rigidity of tetanus quickly breaks the will of Henry's sister:

He had never seen Nature—only her surface—the sugar-coating she always shows to youth. Flung suddenly in his face, with the harsh brutality of chance, the terror of the blow stayed with him thenceforth for life, until repetition made it more than he could call on himself to bear. He found his sister, a woman of forty, as gay and brilliant in the terrors of lock-jaw as she had been in the careless fun of 1859, lying in bed in consequence of a miserable cab-accident that had bruised her foot. Hour by hour the muscles grew rigid while the mind remained bright, until after ten days of fiendish torture she died in convulsions. [287]

Adams's immediate response to Louisa's death suggests that a maleficent force revels in man's suffering. Even more terrifying for Adams than a hangman God, however, is the idea of an absolutely unconscious cosmos of colliding forces. Such a vision is an apocalyptic nightmare, the total denial of man's will and freedom:

The first serious consciousness of Nature's gesture—her attitude towards life—took form then as a phantasm, a nightmare, an insanity of force. For the first time, the stage-scenery of the senses collapsed; the human mind felt itself stripped naked, vibrating in a void of shapeless energies, with resistless mass, colliding, crushing, wasting, and destroying what these same energies had created and labored from eternity to perfect. Society became fantastic, a vision of pantomime with a mechanical motion; and its so-called thought merged in the mere sense of life, and the pleasure in the sense. The usual anodynes of social medicine became evident artifice. [288–9]

The language of the passage dramatizes Adams's inability to describe that "void of shapeless energies" surrounding him. The multiplication of adjectives, nouns, and verbs suggesting mere physical motion denies the tendency of language to build a complex of meaning. The style affirms "a mechanical motion" subject to no supplementary order or sequence. Adams's language in this context is destructive of its own inherent aims. The punctuated cadence seems to expose the inadequacy of man's signs.

Symbolically, the death of Louisa accounts for the ominous silence separating "Failure" (1871) from "Twenty Years After" (1892). The "repetition" of "accident" in his wife's suicide is "more than the will could struggle with; more than he could call on himself to bear." "Chaos" is the virtual end of education, just as the death of Marian suggests the end of all meaning. The act of the *Education* itself would necessarily end on Horatio's note: " 'The rest is silence!' " (504). The apocalyptic vision of "Chaos" reflects the entire tone of the work. The loss of the feminine principle, imaged in his sister's death and implied in the absence of his wife from the *Education*, reveals man's quest for order as a futile dream. As Melvin Lyon has written: "The ultimate dream of man is that reality is unity; the ultimate drama is man's attempt to make the multiplicity of reality conform to that dream. But since the dream is an illusion, the drama must be always a tragedy."[23] The end of education is the recognition of its impossibility in the modern world. Even "accidental education" can do little but "warp the mind." The forms of the mind merely reflect the illusions of the senses.

Stopping at Ouchy "to recover his balance in a new world," Adams finds a concrete image for his nightmare in Mont Blanc.

23. Lyon, *Symbol and Idea*, p. 155.

His response to the mountain is an ironic answer to Shelley's question in the fifth stanza of "Mont Blanc":

> The secret strength of things
> Which governs thought, and to the infinite dome
> Of Heaven is as law, inhabits thee!
> And what were thou, and earth, and stars, and sea,
> If to the human mind's imaginings
> Silence and solitude were vacancy?

That power seen by Shelley in his poetic dream of Mont Blanc looks to Adams "what it was—a chaos of anarchic and purpose-less forces" (289). Shelley affirms the imaginative ability of the mind to expand and fill the "silence and solitude" with its projected meaning: the "inaccessible" power assumes diverse forms in the minds of men. For Adams the peak returns to its primal anarchy. The mind can only "sugar-coat" the terrifying reality of its own helplessness; the process of consciousness involves a negative struggle. It is an anxious trial and a desperate gamble to protect man from the terror or ennui of his imprisoned condition.

"Chaos" leads to the anticlimax of "Failure." The first half of the *Education* is confirmed in Adams's experiences as Professor of History at Harvard: "In essence incoherent and immoral, history had either to be taught as such—or falsified" (301). In the midst of despair, however, Adams instinctively clings to the restless spirit of inquiry that characterized John Quincy Adams. He attempts to teach his students to deal with chaos and multiplicity on their own terms, suggesting that motion and change might be studied by developing appropriate methods rather than final laws. Even lessons in Anglo-Saxon law could dramatize his own dynamics of failure as a tentative mode of cognition. His students "learned, after a fashion, to chase an idea, like a hare, through as dense a thicket of obscure facts as they were likely to meet at the bar; but their teacher knew from his own experience that his wonderful method led nowhere, and they would have to exert themselves to get rid of it in the Law

School even more than they exerted themselves to acquire it in the college" (303). The pursuit itself provides the significance, instead of the dogma and law of old Unitarian Boston. By teaching his students how to develop viable methods for appropriate subjects, Adams teaches them the lessons of his own education. Knowledge becomes a means of survival rather than a desire for final definition or identity. The process of inquiry itself reveals how meaning and understanding depend upon the activity of making problematic choices between conflicting evidence. Such choice and selection make the game possible and "amusing," turning education into a vital experience. Adams's own sense of incompleteness and failure become the bases for a modern educational theory.

Adams could hardly feel secure as Professor of History in the conventional sense of both words. The long years of systematic and accidental education had taught him that "complexity precedes evolution." All quests for origins and ends must fail: "The *Pteraspis* grins horribly from the closed entrance. One may not begin at the beginning, and one has but the loosest relative truths to follow up" (303). "Chaos" and "Failure" mark the end of the desire that "education might lead somewhere." Darwin had taught Adams at least one lesson—survival is an instinctive need. The last movement of the *Education* is an ironic attempt to survive in a rapidly crumbling world. The method must be open where the foundations of knowledge are dangerously unstable.

From "Twenty Years After" to "Nunc Age" Adams acts as the interpreter of his age. The manikin assumes a professorial tone and role that frequently verge on the didactic. Unable to define a History, Adams struggles to develop a method of education based on his own incomplete knowledge: "Education should try to lessen the obstacles, diminish the friction, invigorate the energy, and should train minds to react, not at haphazard, but by choice, on the lines of force that attract their world" (314). The critical narrative of the last fifteen chapters attempts to develop an epistemology whereby the mind might be able "to react . . . by choice." If "Chaos" seems to suggest the futility of the attempt, the effort itself expresses both the limits and possibilities of human consciousness in an alien universe. In a sense, such a division of the *Education* is the artifice of criticism. The entire narrative is a sequence of interruptions, the halting journey of a prodigal who cannot return. But in these final chapters, Adams becomes aware of his own limits and the futility of any desire for a totalizing historical order. At the same time he prophesies the acceleration of man's confusion and ignorance, he views his own fin-de-siècle pronouncements with ironic detachment.

David Minter has suggested two intellectual methods that characterize the American consciousness. In nineteenth- and twentieth-century literature, he distinguishes between the "man of design" and the "man of interpretation": "The man of design participates in modern man's continuing faith in design, in careful planning and concerted devotion as means of assuring success; the man of interpretation participates, on the other hand, in modern man's tendency, especially in art, to make interpretation—both as historical recounting (historical narrative) and as imaginative translation (artistic narrative)—a means of taming unexpected and unacceptable failure."[24] Adams's systematic failure in the first part of the *Education* to discover any trace of historical design forces him into such an interpretative role. As Minter suggests, interpretation depends upon the failure and discontinuity reflected in the consistent collapse of a design.[25] This critical activity ultimately affirms only motion and change as absolute in the study of historical relations. The intention of such interpretation is pragmatic rather than eschatological. Instead of struggling to articulate a final order or meaning, Adams's speculative philosophy of history attempts to develop viable

24. David L. Minter, *The Interpreted Design as a Structural Principle in American Prose*, p. 6.
25. Ibid., pp. 30–31.

points of reference that will enable one to survive the confusion of the modern world. "A Dynamic Theory" uses science and philosophy to confirm the inadequacy of any attempt to resolve the contradictions of a chaotic universe. The restless mind of Henry Adams attempts to *use* those forces that would otherwise deny the validity of any conscious action or choice. Knowledge is redefined in the *Education* as the function of man's interpretations. If order is the dream of man, then it is shaped by the discordant attempts of man to realize it. Thus Minter argues that the manikin of the *Education* is compelled to choose interpretation over design: "Faced with deep and wide resistance— confronted with a world in which every experience and fact, including his own aesthetic and intellectual bent, has 'conspired to ruin his sound scheme of life, and to make him vagrant as well as pauper'—Adams moves toward the interpretive role."[26]

This conflict of design and interpretation in the *Education* makes the work a central text in the study of American modernity. These two different intellectual methods may be clarified in the more generalized language of Lévi-Strauss. Both Madeleine Lee and the young Henry Adams seek that engineer of power who is the agent of historical change (*D,* 9). The scientific interpretation of history demands a unified origin for a continuous sequence of cause and effect relations. Confusion and disorder are the results of human limitations, the failure of man to pierce the veil of time and change. Lévi-Strauss uses the figure of the *engineer* to express an epistemology that is fundamentally intentional. The engineer possesses a scientific mind that attempts to *create* events and thereby *change* his world.[27] His tools and materials are carefully designed to complete the work of his prior plan. Without his blueprints his task is impossible, his vocation denied. The structures he builds are justified by their use. In a linguistic sense, he is the artificer who would construct

26. Ibid., p. 117.
27. Lévi-Strauss, *The Savage Mind,* pp. 22 ff.

ex nihilo a "general grammar" of universal applicability. As Derrida interprets Lévi-Strauss's engineer, he "should be the one to construct the totality of his language, syntax, and lexicon." The engineer himself ought to be "the absolute origin of his own discouse."[28]

Differentiated from the engineer, Lévi-Strauss's *bricoleur* copes with the immediate needs of his condition. He is a translator who turns the finite resources of his world into temporary materials for an unanticipated project. His language must remain tentative and incomplete, an exploration of the possibilities of what meaning a given sign might bear:

The "bricoleur" is adept at performing a large number of diverse tasks; but, unlike the engineer, he does not subordinate each of them to the availability of raw materials conceived and procured for the purpose of the project. His universe of instruments is closed and the rules of his game are always to make do with "whatever is at hand," that is to say with a set of tools and materials which is always finite and is also heterogeneous because what it contains bears no relation to the current project, but is the contingent result of all the occasions there have been to renew or enrich the stock or to maintain it with the remains of previous constructions or destructions.[29]

A Jack-of-all-trades, the *bricoleur* utilizes elements defined by projects other than his own. His aim is to create a viable structure to deal with a current need, using "whatever is at hand." His activity is destructive of *any* intentional goal, any eschatological ordering of a world. The significance of his activity is described by the various choices he makes. The engineer makes one primal choice in his commitment to a plan. Meaning, value, and use are restricted to the conditions of his design. But the *bricoleur* must interpret what effects his rearrangement of elements will have on each component. Each redistribution involves

28. Derrida, "Structure, Sign, and Play," pp. 256–7.
29. Lévi-Strauss, *Savage Mind,* p. 17.

the displacement of conventional meanings. Without a clear idea of his final structure, the *bricoleur* relies on a knowledge of the most precarious sort.[30]

Bricolage is a practical illustration of the implications of interpretation as a function. As a metaphor for the interpretative role of the manikin in the *Education,* it suggests an alternative to that totalizing history Adams desires. What really distinguishes the language of the engineer from the discourse of the *bricoleur* is the status of their signs. The success of the engineer depends upon the reliability of his tools and materials. He must have faith in the scientific tradition, which has defined a certain object as an I-beam, for example. The *bricoleur*'s activity, however, is made possible only by the substitutions of meaning he can make for a given collection of objects. He relies on the absence of any outside authority for his activity. His discourse depends upon and makes possible what Derrida terms "freeplay": "a field of infinite substitutions in the closure of a finite ensemble."[31] The play of signification is, in a sense, an attempt to *supplement* that *lack* of a center or fixed principle with the interpretative *activity* itself.

Adams's manikin is more than a literary device, it dramatizes the implications of decentering the structures of thought and language. In the context of Adams's thought, the conventional notions of "author" and "subject" cannot be sustained. If Adams's man is pushed, pulled, and trapped by forces beyond his control, he may hardly be termed the author or originator of his own life. Offered as merely a tool or model to be discarded once it has served its purpose for the reader, the *Education* denies any final definition. Like *Chartres,* it is a pre-text for further interpretations, a structure to be dismantled in hopes of other translations. Autobiography as the discovery of one's self is denied in favor of education as the opening up of possibilities and the disclosure of supplementary meanings. As Adams repeats through-

30. Ibid., p. 19.
31. Derrida, "Structure, Sign, and Play," p. 260.

out the work, "This is a story of education—not a mere lesson in life" (*EHA,* 243). By no means an Everyman, the manikin of the narrative substitutes his own blankness for the traditional subject.[32] Adams's manikin is an ironic archetype for the protagonist of modern literature. Like that of so many later existential figures, the identity of Henry Adams in the *Education* is defined by his *desire* for a coherent self. It is just this absence the manikin expresses, forcing Adams and his readers to recognize what has become a dominant theme in modern literature and philosophy: "Man's essence is a function of his desire, that is to say, it is dependent upon non-realization."[33]

Adams's symbolism repeatedly demonstrates the collapse of its own design. In the absence of any scientifically verifiable law for historical movement, Adams resorts to images and symbols such as Quincy, Ara Coeli, and *Pteraspis.* As mythic origins, both Ara Coeli and *Pteraspis* serve destructive functions. Revealing the impossibility of fixing any solid point of departure for a modern education, they suggest only mystery and paradox as the ends of knowledge. Within the aesthetic structure of the *Education* they are negative forces that direct the reader toward the apocalyptic vision of "Chaos."

The symbolism of the Virgin, the Dynamo, the Saint-Gaudens sculpture at Rock Creek, and "A Dynamic Theory of History"

32. Lyon, *Symbol and Idea,* p. 116, remarks: "The likeness of the names 'Adam' and 'Adams' is used to suggest that Adams and his forebearers share in the human nature all men have inherited from Adam. 'Henry Adams' is Everyman." The archetypal value of the manikin resides in his flexibility, not in those associations that would fix him in a mythic pattern. He is like Adam, Cain, and the Prodigal in his restless need to name, destroy, wander, and build. Yet his role in the narrative is designed to expose the inadequacy of any system—whether mythic or scientific—for explaining man's "fallen" condition.

33. Anthony Wilden, "Death, Desire and Repetition in Svevo's *Zeno,*" 112. Wilden, however, is simply paraphrasing what is a central concept in Heidegger, Sartre, and other existential philosophers. Sartrean existentialism depends upon just this notion. One might compare Adams's dynamics of failure to the implicit failure of Sartrean man. See Chapter 8.

function in a different fashion. Adams's education up to 1871 teaches him the ephemeral value of man's signs. It is just such a relativity of meaning that Adams begins to manipulate in the later chapters of the *Education*. As the interpreter of his age, he ironically affirms the power of consciousness to assign meanings to the accidental forces of a physically impelled universe. It is the function of those meanings, however, that makes survival possible. Adams's later symbolism operates within a system of relationships that attempts to structure movement and change. The Dynamo and the Virgin, for example, are not used to construct an historical dialectic. Adams plays them off each other to reveal the *absence* of the Virgin's unity in the very image of the hollow Dynamo. Inextricably connected, they are imaginative means of measuring man's historical motion without using a static and exclusive frame of reference. Taken individually, neither Virgin nor Dynamo can approximate the violent changes involved in Adams's general vision of history. It is their very difference that allows their relation to bear meaning for the student of chaos.

The Saint-Gaudens monument at Rock Creek Church is a paradigm for Adams's symbolic process. The figure is a composite of diverse theological and philosophical ideas from Eastern religions, mythic archetypes, and the modern arts. It expresses an ironic unity that denies the languages of man. Nevertheless, meaning and value are made possible in the very ambiguity of the figure. Interpretation is not external to the sculpture but fundamental to its art: "From the Egyptian Sphinx to the Kamakura Daibuts; from Prometheus to Christ; from Michael Angelo to Shelley, art had wrought on this eternal figure almost as though it had nothing else to say. The interest of the figure was not in its meaning, but in the response of the observer" (*EHA,* 329). Unlike that of the vision of Mont Blanc in "Chaos," the silence of the figure is not a denial of man and consciousness. Rather, it embodies the dream of man for unity as it reveals the fundamental silence of any such total order. Adams's own plan for the figure describes the universality he wanted Saint-Gaudens to express: "The whole meaning and feeling of the figure is in its universality and anonymity. My own name for it is 'the Peace of God.' LaFarge would call it 'Kwannon,' Petrarch would say '*Siccome eterna vita e veder Dio*' and a real artist would be very careful to give it no name that the public would turn to a limitation of its nature."[34] The struggle to name the inexpressible results in the symbolism of man's interpretations. "Isis of the ten thousand names," Ortega y Gasset calls reality, and the Egyptian goddess is a fitting model for the mystery at Rock Creek.[35] The enveloping shroud hiding the figure expresses the tendency of all human forms to veil the reality they seek to disclose.

Adams's restless mind could not sustain for long the conception of a totally deterministic universe. Natural force itself may deny the validity of man's meanings and values, but its very indeterminate quality makes definition possible. For Adams unity is redefined as the interchange of man and the cosmos. The play of conscious choice and uncontrollable forces describes the discordant processes of historical definition. The modern "seeker of truth—or illusion—would be none the less restless . . ." (*EHA*, 402). In any final synthesis anarchy and unity would lose their meanings. The idea of chaos depends upon consciousness, just as unity is the dream of man. Adams accepts an important Thomist notion: "Without thought in the unit there could be no unity; without unity no orderly sequence or ordered society. Thought alone was Form. Mind and Unity flourished or perished together" (429).

Such recognition is hardly a joyous affirmation for Adams. Consciousness remains peripheral to a force that denies order or sequence (421). Relation replaces truth, and man becomes responsible for the meanings he constitutes from the available

34. Henry Adams to Richard Watson Gilder, 14 October 1895, in *The Letters of Mrs. Henry Adams 1865–1883*, p. 458.
35. José Ortega y Gasset, "The Dehumanization of Art," p. 53.

possibilities. If the Dynamo replaces the Virgin as an image for modern energy, it suggests more than simply the chaos of "anarchic and purposeless" force that had threatened modern man's dream of order. The Dynamo symbolizes the failure of man's art and science to give vital form to abstract force. The Virgin's absence in the modern age suggests how man's desire for knowledge has lessened his capacity for graceful illusion. Scientific man seems to have become an obstacle to himself and to have restricted his imagination. The art of the Middle Ages relied on the mystery of the human condition; modern man insists on resolving an ambiguity basic to his artistic and spiritual needs. Thus man becomes increasingly determined by forces that are more and more alien to him. The triumph of the architects of Chartres was their ability to name and express natural forces. In this way they accommodated themselves to such powers, giving them human significances and relations. Unable to name or symbolize force, modern man only intensifies the destructive aspects of his knowledge.[36]

With education at a final impasse, only speculation can fill the void of despair. "A Dynamic Theory of History" emphasizes the confusion and paradox that make up *The Education of Henry Adams*. Playing upon one of his favorite images, Adams expresses his theory in the figure of the spider and its web: "For convenience as an image, the theory may liken man to a spider in its web, watching for chance prey. Forces of nature dance like flies before the net, and the spider pounces on them when it can; but it makes many fatal mistakes, though its theory of force is sound. The spider-mind acquires a faculty of memory, and, with it, a singular skill of analysis and synthesis, taking

36. Lynn White, Jr., in "Dynamo and Virgin Reconsidered," pp. 183–194, argues that the dialectic of the Virgin and Dynamo depends upon the Virgin's "Spirituality" and the Dynamo's "materiality." It does not seem to me that the relation of the Dynamo to the Virgin is really dialectical. Both attempt the same symbolism, with varying degrees of success in expressing their respective cultures.

apart and putting together in different relations the meshes of its trap" (474). Like the *bricoleur*, the spider-mind survives not as a result of its theory, no matter how sound it may be, but in the activity of "taking apart and putting together in different relations the meshes of its trap." Failure and incompletion become laws of adaptation, suggesting the constant effort needed to make any sense out of a constantly changing universe. The image of the spider and its prey is inverted curiously. In a conventional deterministic scheme, *man* would be the prey of forces beyond his control. Yet here the forces are the victims of the trap, the mind acting as the weaver of the pattern. The center of man's meaning is his own design, as elusive as the shifting interpretations he makes of his world.

"A Dynamic Theory of History" is largely important for the method it suggests, rather than for the history it offers.[37] Adams makes a rough survey of history from the Fall of Rome to the modern age. The argument suggests that man's loss of any principle of order or faith is dependent upon his failure to "assimilate forces as he assimilated food" (475). History may be considered the long trace of man's alienation from nature, his severance from those primal forces which accelerate and multiply like gases swirled in space. Yet the theory itself attempts to account for the discontinuous nature of the manikin's various educations. Translating the image of the spider and web into the language of science, Adams formulates his law: "A dynamic law requires that two masses—nature and man—must go on, reacting upon each other, without stop, as the sun and a comet react on each other, and that any appearance of stoppage is illusive" (478). Such action and reaction involve incompletion as the basis of the law. Man is condemned to the critical activity of making tentative meanings to deal with natural forces. Human his-

37. Conder, *Formula of His Own,* p. 186: "It was, after all, in the form of art, not of science or history, that he presented a dynamic theory of history to a reading public."

tory is described in the patchwork woven by man, which, like Penelope's shroud, requires the infinite activity of weaving and unraveling.

The value of any segment of man's attempts to make meaning depends largely on historical perspective. In this regard Adams remains a confirmed relativist. Whether we choose to look nostalgically at the Middle Ages as a period of unity or consider the modern age an enormous advance over the brutishness of thirteenth-century social life reflects only how we measure force. For Adams only a degradationist theory seems to account for the modern leveling of differences, the loss of the discrimination and aesthetic sense that characterized medieval art and culture. The technology of the modern age reflected in the Dynamo seems to confirm the historical evidence that "man depended more and more absolutely on forces other than his own, and on instruments which superseded his senses" (485). Man's alienation paradoxically results from his longing for a habitable world. The quest for unity always seems to end in multiplicity.

"A Dynamic Theory" is concerned basically with the relation between consciousness and external nature. For the philosophical tradition the answer seems obvious: "The Baconian law held good; thought did not evolve nature, but nature evolved thought" (485). But an entire system of value depends upon man's ability to affirm his own power to define his world, however illusory such a world might be. If thought is simply another manifestation of natural force, choice becomes an absurd gamble, a mad throw of dice. The question remains at the heart of the *Education*. Adams recognizes that the mind "defies law" and cannot be encompassed by any rational construct (489). In all his writings, Adams affirms the inconsistent and paradoxical qualities of mind. Any attempt to define the activity of consciousness must beg the question: "The doubt persisted whether the force that educated was really man or nature–mind or motion" (501).

The question is partially answered by the *Education* itself.

The enormous effort of composition and recollection seems to deny that the mind is a mere particle in a sea of supersensual chaos. Cutting and piecing together the history of his education, Adams constitutes meaning in the very struggle to find a place in a bewildering modern world. The constant imperative that one must choose in order to be remains amidst the fragmentary narrative of a life. Although the scientific rigor of "A Dynamic Theory" collapses, the artistry of the *Education* remains, and Adams dramatizes his own notion that "unable to define Force as a unity, man symbolized it and pursued it, both in himself, and in the infinite, as philosophy and theology; the mind is itself the subtlest of all known forces" (476). Adams's *felix culpa* defines multiplicity as the law of the cosmos, unity as the dream of man. Only the function of consciousness itself enables man to react successively to a constantly changing universe of force.

The manikin of the *Education* is the archetype for the modern man of interpretation, a figure condemned to the unreliability of his language. Free play and the activity of the *bricoleur* replace the unified intention of the engineer. As Derrida has suggested, man must experience such a condition with either a joyous release or an anxious dread.[38] Clearly, the impossibility of total History and the absence of any metaphysical origin or end account for Adams's apocalyptic tone in the *Education*. There is hardly that Nietzschean affirmation in Adams that one detects in Henry James, or even the cautious meliorism one finds in William James. In his darkest moments, Henry James still affirms his own consciousness without demanding anything but the amusement its relations offer. Henry Adams plays the game begrudgingly, nostalgically yearning for a simpler world where at least the illusions of order and unity remained unquestioned. The artistry of the *Education* results from the failure of history. Crisis and discontinuity suggest to Henry James the possibility of new vitality. Adams's need to begin again and again becomes

38. Derrida, "Structure, Sign, and Play," p. 264.

an increasingly burdensome task, ending in silence. Even Adams's "optimism" is sudden, unexpected, and inconsistent. The entire strain of the *Education* moves toward Shakespeare's "silence" as a final chord, yet Adams adds a dangling comment: "Perhaps some day—say 1938, their centenary—they might be allowed to return for a holiday, to see the mistakes of their own lives made clear in the light of the mistakes of their successors; and perhaps then, for the first time since man began his education among the carnivores, they would find a world that sensitive and timid creatures could regard without a shudder" (505). The modern reader must grimace at the failure of the prophecy. The dream of such a return is the bitter irony of the confirmed skeptic. Like the false hope posed by Melville at the end of *Clarel*, it exposes only the true darkness of Adams's final vision.[39]

Adams despairs at last of that very process James finds so novel and enlivening. The endless necessity of interpretation confirms Adams's degradationist views of man and culture. James would come to see the failure of the modern age as its inability to sustain the free play of human signification. The unity Adams vainly longs for is the true "beast in the jungle" for James. Adams would respond to James's *Notes of a Son and Brother* with characteristic gloominess: "Why did we live? Was that all? Why was I not born in Central Africa and died young. Poor Henry thinks it all real, I believe, and actually lives in that dreamy, stuffy Newport and Cambridge, with papa James and Charles Norton—and me! Yet, why! It is a terrible dream, but not so weird as this here which is quite loony."[40] James would answer Adams's objections by affirming the problematic knowl-

39. Melville, *Clarel*, p. 523:
    But through such strange illusions have they passed
    Who in life's pilgrimage have baffled striven—
    Even death may prove unreal at the last,
    And stoics be astounded into heaven.
40. Henry Adams to Elizabeth Cameron, 8 March 1914, *Letters,* II, 622. This letter more than likely captures the mood of Adams's lost letter to James concerning *Notes of a Son and Brother.*

edge offered by man's interpretations with a confidence Adams could never sustain. James, of course, sees the destructive possibilities of modern man's freedom, but he recognizes also the vitality and significance of consciousness as man's only possible justification:

I still find my consciousness interesting—under *cultivation* of the interest. Cultivate it *with* me, dear Henry—that's what I hoped to make you do—to cultivate yours for all it has in common with mine. *Why* mine yields an interest I don't know that I can tell you, but I don't challenge or quarrel with it—I encourage it with a ghastly grin. . . . It's, I suppose, because I am that queer monster, the artist, an obstinate finality, an inexhaustible sensibility. Hence the reactions—appearances, memories, many things go on playing upon it with consequences that I note and "enjoy" (grim word!) noting. It all takes doing—and I *do*. I believe I shall do yet again—it is still an act of life.[41]

Henry James seems to moderate some of the pessimism of Adams's final vision with this tentative affirmation. His attitude has similarities to his brother's pluralism: "Pluralism . . . is neither optimistic nor pessimistic, but melioristic, rather. The world, it thinks, may be saved, on condition that its parts shall do their best. But shipwreck in detail, or even on the whole, is among the open possibilities."[42] And yet one senses in the false hopes held out in the final pages of the *Education* that Adams too allows for such possibilities of redemption in his own pluralistic universe. In his dynamics of failure, Adams develops a method for expressing the functional interchange between man's dream of unity and experience of multiplicity that is as effective in its own way as William James's radical empiricism or Henry James's social consciousness.

41. Henry James to Henry Adams, 21 March 1914, *The Letters of Henry James,* ed. Percy Lubbock, II, 373–4.
42. William James, *Some Problems of Philosophy,* p. 142.

5 The Imaginative Construction
   of Historical Order in
   The American Scene

> 1907. *The American Scene,* triumph of the author's long prac-
> tice. A creation of America. A book no "serious American" will
> neglect.
>
> —Ezra Pound, "Henry James," 1918*

In his early travels James was a pilgrim to the shrines of
European culture and art, as awed as the naif Hyacinth Robin-
son. His travel sketches concentrate primarily on architecture,
painting, literature, and language. These writings are eminently,
almost decadently, "civilized" in tone and subject. The tea-rose
world seems all too prevalent for heartier appetites. And yet for
all this the museum remains in James's writings a dominant
image for dead history, the separation of the aesthetic process
from its final product. In Adam Verver's "House of Civilization," James not only parodies the American's sense of culture,
but also attacks the idea of history as an arrangement of sequences. Prince Amerigo is a *morceau de musée* in the Ververs'
collection, as dehumanized as the volumes of his family history
in the British Museum. In both *The American* and *The Wings
of the Dove,* James uses the figure of the museum copyist to
expose the flatness of all purely mimetic art. In general, the
museum becomes a symbol for all that has been allowed to die
in European history and culture. The American collector who

imports the wealth of Western history in crates and bundles betrays a similarly hollow interpretation of history as things.

For James art relies on the vitality of the imagination. The kind of history with which he is concerned is intimately related to his sense of the aesthetic process. All the travel sketches that James wrote have at least one thing in common: the center of interest from *Transatlantic Sketches* to *The American Scene* and *Italian Hours* is the restless analyst himself. James pays as much attention to the traveler's methods of observation, selection, and expression as he does to his subject or scene. The titles themselves emphasize the perspective demanded. "Sketches," "Portraits," "Scene," and "Hours" express the need for the painter's frame, the historian's order, and the writer's form. Repeatedly in *The American Scene* the narrator reminds us that he is reading as much *into* a given scene as he is reading *out of* it. Like James's "dusky, crowded, heterogeneous back-shop of the mind," the museum stands for simply the artifacts of history and the aesthetic process (*AN*, 47). As Ortega y Gasset has suggested:

In the museum we find the lacquered corpse of an evolution. Here is the flux of that pictorial anxiety which has budded forth from man century after century. To conserve this evolution it has had to be undone, broken up, converted into fragments again and congealed as in a refrigerator. Each picture is a crystal with unmistakable and rigid edges, separated from the others, a hermetic island.

And, nonetheless, it is a corpse we could easily revive. We would need only to arrange the pictures in a certain order and then move the eye—or the mind's eye—quickly from one to the other.[1]

Clearly this is the sort of revival that James attempts in *The American Scene* or the collected essays of *Italian Hours*. When the reader enters the museum world through the Jamesian lens, it is brought to life in the very movement of that inner eye, weaving and dancing a pattern of its own.

1. Ortega y Gasset, "On Point of View in the Arts," in *The Dehumanization of Art*, p. 107.

In this general sense, the modern museum is a vast warehouse of the artifacts of reason and imagination. Ordered and arranged by periods to show historical developments, it predicates linear time as fundamental to the historical consciousness. Such systems of order repeatedly blur discrimination, spreading the thickness of history in a long, thin swath of tradition or continuity. We are simply given the forms of history, the hollow vessels of lost art. André Malraux describes the violence the modern museum does to art:

In the past a Gothic statue was a component part of the Cathedral; similarly a classical picture was tied up with the setting of its period, and not expected to consort with works of different mood and out-look. Rather, it was kept apart from them, so as to be the more appreciated by the spectator. True, there were picture collections and *cabinets d'antiques* in the seventeenth century, but they did not modify that attitude towards art of which Versailles is the symbol. Whereas the modern art-gallery not only isolates the work of art from its context but makes it forgather with rival or even hostile works. It is a confrontation of metamorphoses.[2]

What those long galleries so fatally lack is tone and style, that depth of history that is made through our appropriation of the past.

James is concerned primarily with the process of historical consciousness. History is not validated by an order external to man for James, but in the successive attempts of humanity to define itself. Clearly, such an historical sense is always moving toward art, providing a *method* for a larger aesthetic context.[3] Thus James's history has no real independent intelligibility, but

2. André Malraux, *The Voices of Silence,* p. 14. Compare with Henry Adams's remark in *Chartres,* p. 149: "One's first visit to a great cathedral is like one's first visit to the British Museum; the only intelligent idea is to follow the order of time, but the museum is a chaos of time, and the cathedral is generally all of one and the same time."

3. See Christof Wegelin, *The Image of Europe in Henry James,* p. 77: "His view of the process of art, moreover, was closely paralleled by his view of the process of history, both being integral to his view of life."

is inextricably related to what we internalize, live, and apply. In this sense it is as illusory and ephemeral as any imaginative form, subject to the same questions of validity. Just as James's novels repeatedly expose their own artistry, any historical consciousness must ultimately betray its mythic quality.

The failure of the "Dynamic Theory of History" dramatizes Henry Adams's own struggle to develop a totalizing order beyond consciousness and will. Adams's system leaves only the artistry of his method amid the ruins of his scientific formulations. The very priority that James accords consciousness Adams struggles against, doomed to acknowledge it at last in an aesthetic born of failure. He wavers between the equally unacceptable alternatives of St. Francis and St. Thomas, Pascal and Descartes. History as a means of relating the individual to some external continuity evades Adams. Such order seems to be an illusion implicit in man's social instinct, sustained by the idea of community. In the simplest sense, what James considers history Adams defines as education—the movement of the mind toward some idea of history. Adams must recognize that for the historian any total history could be conceived of only as chaotic.[4] Beyond the "illusions of his senses," Adams always confronts a "chaos of anarchic and purposeless forces" (*EHA,* 289). This cosmic disorder is implicit in James's later writings, compelling the aesthetic consciousness to carve forms and shapes out of nameless worlds of change.

4. Viz. "Chaos," in the *Education*. In the final chapter of *The Savage Mind* ("History and Dialectic"), Lévi-Strauss explores the differences between that "historical consciousness" we have associated with James and the desire for an historical order external to man as investigated by Adams. Lévi-Strauss accurately sums up the problems of any historical vocation, p. 257: "Consequently, historical facts are no more *given* than any other. It is the historian, or the agent of history, who constitutes them by abstraction and as though under the threat of an infinite regress. What is true of the constitution of historical facts is no less so of their selection. From this point of view, the historian and the agent of history choose, sever and carve them up, for a truly total history would confront them with chaos."

Thus for James the very terms of cognition rely on man's vitalization of history out of the dead past suggested by the museum. To track and pursue the ghost of consciousness describes this aesthetic reading of the past. The *donnée* of history is the presence of those artifacts and texts on which we base our interpretations. Such history is a calling forth of consciousness. Our "reading of," "writing about," or "talking around" a given verbal or plastic arrangement defines our historical sense. Thus history and art are intimately related through language. James would have understood that Paul de Man's "literary interpretation" is just as applicable to historical documents as it is to *The Sacred Fount*: "To become good literary historians, we must remember that what we usually call literary history has little or nothing to do with literature and that what we call literary interpretation—provided only it is good interpretation—is in fact literary history. If we extend this notion beyond literature, it merely confirms that the bases for historical knowledge are not empirical facts but written texts, even if these texts masquerade in the guise of wars or evolutions."[5]

In this more limited sense, history expresses the phenomenology of the critical mind. The process of consciousness that replaces any essential self suggests equally radical changes in our conception of historical sequence. The order of James's historical consciousness moves away from any temporal system that would seek its validation in a definitive origin or end. James's history depends upon its forms, the means whereby one comes to see his relation to the past in the present. History becomes the very incarnation of the origin in the interpretation of the past. It is the artistic act of making the past intelligible, regardless of how transitory such knowledge ultimately may appear.

In *A Small Boy and Others* James relates his early historical sense to the birth of an aesthetic consciousness. Looking back

5. Paul de Man, "Literary History and Literary Modernity," in ed. Morton W. Bloomfield, *In Search of Literary Theory*, p. 267.

over the growth of his imagination, the mature author sees his own early impressions of the Louvre in the "confounding air" of the modern museum. The things of history constitute an overwhelming vastness for a small boy and his brother, both as yet lacking any sense of style or tone:

> We were not yet aware of style, though on the way to become so, but were aware of mystery, which indeed was one of its forms— while we saw all the others, without exception, exhibited at the Louvre, where at first they simply overwhelmed and bewildered me.

> It was as if they had gathered there into a vast deafening chorus; I shall never forget how . . . they filled those vast halls with the influence rather of some complicated sound, diffused and reverberant, than of such visibilities as one could directly deal with. To distinguish among these, in the charged and coloured and confounding air was difficult—it discouraged and defied; which was doubtless why my impression originally best entertained was that of those magnificent parts of the great gallery simply not inviting us to distinguish. They arched over us in the wonder of their endless golden riot and relief, figured and flourished in perpetual revolution, breaking into great high-hung circles and symmetries as squandered picture, opening into deep outward embrasures that threw off the rest of Paris somehow as a told story, a sort of wrought effect or bold ambiguity for a vista, and yet held it there, at every point, as a vast bright gage, even at moments of felt adventure, of experience.[6]

This passage is the starting point for young Henry's initiation into the mysteries of style and form. The *objets d'art* of the gallery are not described, but instead the form of the Galerie d'Apollon itself is his initial subject. James's attempt to recapture his early impressions of bewilderment and wonder depends upon the form and architecture of the gallery. The "golden riot and relief" of the high-arched ceiling and "the embrasures that threw off the rest of Paris somehow as a told story" emphasize the young visitor's need to develop his own form for the tumult

6. James, *A Small Boy and Others*, pp. 345–6. Hereafter cited in the text as *SBO*.

of history presented there. The fascinating confusion of the hall contrasts with his lack of the sense of style as a means of discrimination. The description of the swirling intricacies of the ceiling decoration offers an objective correlative for the boy's own emotions. He longs for some means of relating himself to this wealth of art and history.

It is appropriate that James should have selected the Galerie d'Apollon in the Louvre in which to re-enact this birth of the imagination. The gallery contains the Louvre's collections of "Orfèvrerie et Émaillerie" (gold work, jewelry and enamels, medals).[7] It is thus a collection of forms—those bowls, vases, and reliquaries that so often provide the novelist with metaphors for the form or vessel of consciousness itself. In addition, the gallery houses a number of enameled copper reliefs, medals, small medieval altar screens, and triptychs. The enameled, stamped, and painted surfaces relate to the other dominant image James uses to describe consciousness assuming a form: the "prepared plate," which is either "etched," "painted," or "enamelled."[8]

In the actual and metaphoric forms of the Galerie d'Apollon, James's historical and aesthetic outlooks coincide. History is enshrined in the shapes that express the artists' interpretations of their relation to the world. For James the historical consciousness is precisely such an aesthetic activity: a reading of texts that in themselves are interpretations of their worlds. History and consciousness converge in the aesthetic act. Like those precious objects, the form of consciousness is refined, hammered to a fine thinness, and embellished with one's impressions and reflections. Filling the vessel is equally a process of developing its surface, of elaborating the form as an appropriate container for its vital fluid or "jelly."

7. See André Michel and Gaston Migeon, *Le Musée du Louvre,* pp. 108 ff.

8. See James, *The American Scene,* p. 454. Hereafter cited in the text as *AS*.

James's reconstruction of that experience moves the young Henry from a sense of the mystery of style to a burgeoning historical sense that is style itself. The process of recollection matches the movements of the youth *into* the aesthetic history of the Galerie:

This comes to saying that in those beginnings I felt myself most happily cross that bridge over to Style constituted by the wondrous Galerie d'Apollon, drawn out for me as a long but assured initiation and seeming to form with its supreme coved ceiling and inordinately shining parquet a prodigious tube or tunnel through which I inhaled little by little, that is again and again, a general sense of *glory*. The glory meant ever so many things at once, not only beauty and art and supreme design, but history and fame and power, the world in fine raised to the richest and noblest expression. [*SBO*, 346–7]

The vision of the young man and the language of the artist work together to transform that bewilderment and sensuous riot into a veritable "bridge over to Style." The passage itself moves, like the fictional "I," from an unawareness of to an initiation into style. That "glory," salvaged from "some complicated sound" echoing in the ornate hall, becomes the suggestive germ of a burgeoning aesthetic.

The artist of *A Small Boy and Others* completes the young man's rite of passage in the subsequent text. James appropriately presents the birth of his imagination in the young man's nightmare "many years later." Just as the author's recollection assumes the form of the work itself, so the young man's dream provides a form for his impressions. The natural order of the dream emphasizes how fundamental James considers aesthetic form to the activity of consciousness. In order to attain a meaningful shape, the young man's dream must be "read" upon "awaking" "in a summer dawn," just as the author must provide a reading of the entire experience in relation to the autobiographical intentions of his own work. Such complexity is after all descriptive of the aesthetic process itself, constantly turning history over to shape the present. James's description of his nightmare provides us with a clear expression of such a process of consciousness, in its wild pursuit of the ghost of the past. The length of the passage suggests the tortuous density of James's reflective mode:

The climax of this extraordinary experience—which stands alone for me as a dream-adventure founded in the deepest, quickest, clearest act of cogitation and comparison, act indeed of life-saving energy, as well as unutterable fear—was the sudden pursuit, through an open door, along a huge high saloon, of a just dimly-descried figure that retreated in terror before my rush and dash (a glare of inspired reaction from irresistible but shameful dread,) out of the room I had a moment before been desperately, and all the more abjectly, defending by the push of my shoulder against hard pressure on the lock and bar from the other side. . . . Routed, dismayed, the tables turned on him by my so surpassing him for straight aggressions and dire intention, my visitant was already but a diminished spot in the long perspective, the tremendous glorious hall, as I say, over the far-gleaming floor of which, cleared for the occasion of its great line of priceless vitrines down the middle, he sped for *his* life, while a great storm of thunder and lightning played through the deep embrasures of high windows at the right. The lightning that revealed the retreat revealed also the wondrous place and, by the same amazing play, my young imaginative life in it of long before, the sense of which, deep within me, had kept it whole, preserved it to this thrilling use; for what in the world were the deep embrasures and the so polished floor but those of the Galerie d'Apollon of my childhood? [*SBO*, 347–9]

With a vital difference, the nightmare echoes the famous vision of "fear and trembling" that was the crisis in the intellectual life of Henry James, Sr.[9] The elder James's crisis leads him from a paralyzing dread to the consolations of Swedenborg.

9. The experience referred to is reprinted from *Society the Redeemed Form of Man* in F. O. Matthiessen, *The James Family,* pp. 161 ff. William James records several similar moments of supernatural terror in *Varieties of Religious Experience* and in his diary (especially in entries dated February 1, 1870 and April 30, 1870).

His sublime terror represents the destructive forces of self-consciousness and isolation. Society in a philosophic sense becomes
the source of the ego's redemption from its own fears. Despite
its obvious parallels with his father's crisis, Henry's hallucination
marks the difference in outlook between the nineteenth-century
father and the twenieth-century son. Whereas the elder James
resists the urge to rush wildly from his room, sitting rooted in
his chair, Henry makes his dream-ego pursue that presence
through the vast, cleared space of the Galerie d'Apollon. More
important, the "awful agent, creature or presence" is equally
"terrified" by Henry, who ultimately pursues the ghost through
the historical space of the gallery. The contrast between the
father's *paralysis* and the son's *movement* aptly describes their
divergent attitudes toward consciousness. The elder James's
advice to his sons to "be" something rather than "do" something
reflected his confidence in the transcendental *telos* he had
appropriated from Swedenborg.[10] For Henry James, Jr., "being"
is defined in the activity of *coming-to-be,* in the expanding movement of the aesthetic and historical imaginations.

When James includes his father's objections to Hegel (in a
letter to Eliot Cabot) in *Notes of a Son and Brother,* he reveals
much of the romanticism, transcendentalism, and mysticism of
his father's philosophy. One can hardly read his reconstitution
of the Galerie d'Apollon nightmare without placing him on the
side of Hegel:

Personal or phenomenal existence is constituted by referring itself to
a foreign source, or, what is the same thing, confessing itself created:
so that the fundamental word of Philosophy, by Hegel's own for-

10. James, *Notes of a Son and Brother,* p. 47: "What was marked in
our father's prime uneasiness in presence of any particular form of success
we might, according to our lights as then glimmering, propose to invoke
was that it bravely, or with such inward assurance, dispensed with any
suggestion of an alternative. What we were to do instead was just to *be*
something, something unconnected with specific doing, something free
and uncommitted, something finer in short than being *that,* whatever it
was, might consist of." Hereafter cited in the text as *NSB.*

mula, is creation; which, however, as I understand him, he denies in any objective sense of the word. This then is what I complain of in him . . . that he makes existence *essential* to being, so that take existence away and being becomes nothing. It would not be a whit less preposterous in me to say that thought is essential to thing, subject to object, marble to statue, canvas to picture, woman to wife, mother to child. . . . Being implies existence of course just as picture implies canvas, or as personality implies reality, or as chick implies egg; but it implies it only to a lower intelligence than itself, an unspiritual intelligence to wit, which has no direct or inward intuition of being, and requires to be agitated to discerning it.   [*NSB*, 268]

In the nightmare it is precisely the pursuit that is essential to the recognition. We may apply any number of conventional philosophical terms to describe the presence that interrupts the digestion of Henry, Sr.: "fear and trembling," "sickness unto death," *Angst.* The "ghost" of Henry, Jr., defies such categorization. It is the sense of the past, the aesthetic process, the process of consciousness, the recollective act. Crucial for his recognition is not the name of that presence, but the name of that which it brings him to see: the Galerie d'Apollon of his youth. The push through the door and his rush down the long cleared hall after the retreating visitant evokes in the dream-Henry the " 'scene of something.' " The whole press and push of the language leads to the recognition, at the end of his nightmare, of the Galerie d'Apollon of his childhood. In that naming, the germ of his imagination's growth is reconstituted. The dream assumes a form in the midst of the history and art enshrined in the ornate gallery. Like Ralph Pendrel, the historian of *The Sense of the Past,* the author of *A Small Boy and Others* vitalizes history in the act of reading and composing the scene. The ghost in the dream is frightening in its vagueness and formlessness, but alluring in its energy and promise. The dreamer's pursuit is partially fulfilled as he gives form to his sense of that presence in the very recognition of the Galerie d'Apollon.

The presence pursued by Henry evokes paradoxical responses

from the dream figure. The nightmare itself is "founded in the deepest, quickest, clearest act of cogitation and comparison, act indeed of life-saving energy, as well as unutterable fear." The process of his pursuit is vital, full of the powers of the youthful imagination attempting to come to terms with the ambiguity of the actual. The bursting of the double-locked door, defended from both sides, is an act of will on the part of the dream-Henry. As such, the chase is the birth of the aesthetic process itself, pursuing history in the form of one's own expression.

The intricacy with which the hallucination is composed once again emphasizes that "thickness" and "layering" of impressions that provide the individual's relation to his more public history. Within the dream itself, enclosed by the author's recollective act, the dream-Henry is startled "in the suddenest wild start from sleep, *the sleep within my sleep.*" Thus the young imagination remains submerged until that sudden wild start resurrects a suggestive image. The germ is neither an object nor a thing, but a vital process. Just as the initial visit to the Louvre is a movement from the mystery of style to the recognition of style itself, so that "awful agent" retreats down the long gallery, sweeping the dream figure into the bristling scene. In the magic of the dream and the author's language, the Galerie d'Apollon becomes the space in which the past is incarnated in the present. In *Notes of a Son and Brother* James would write of his own autobiographical method: "So at least do I read back into blurred visions the richest meanings they could have" (305–6). James gives this idea a more general application in *The American Scene:* "I draw courage from the remembrance that history is never, in any sense, the immediate crudity of what 'happens,' but the much finer complexity of what we read into it and think of in connection with it" (182).

For James the acts of recollection and recognition violate conventional notions of the past. The attempt to make the past present calls into question a history of continuity or uniform sequences. The present is built up through the impressionistic layering of the subject's reading of the past. Such a process provides the critical analyst with an historical relation in the midst of the infinitely receding past. James's artistic technique often reveals such a shift in attitude toward temporality. In the novels, time is either a predicated frame to structure events and actions or it is another method of developing the scenic context. In itself time is simply ineluctable change, which compels man repeatedly to define forms and develop contexts in order to make his life intelligible. It is James's "destructive element" in much the same sense that Conrad's Stein uses the phrase. Subject to time, man recognizes his mortality and the ambiguity of his situation. Yet this awareness also involves the need to create meaning and value out of and in relation to the incessant displacement of time.

In the opening paragraph of *The Portrait of a Lady* James initiates the time of the novel in the very act of composing the scene. The characters themselves have tried to give an order to the waning day in the ritual of afternoon tea: "Under certain circumstances there are few hours in life more agreeable than the hour dedicated to the ceremony known as afternoon tea" (*PL*, I, 1). Yet, as James paints this special little hour in his "peculiarly English picture," we recognize that the very atmosphere that gives the tone to this ritual will soon end it. Time becomes an integral part of the scene in its spatial representation: "Part of the afternoon had waned, but much of it was left, and what was left was of the finest and rarest quality. Real dusk would not arrive for many hours; but the flood of summer light had begun to ebb, the air had grown mellow, the shadows were long upon the smooth, dense turf. They lengthened slowly, however, and the scene expressed that sense of leisure still to come which is perhaps the chief source of one's enjoyment of such a scene at such an hour" (1). Out of the design cast on the broad lawns, Mr. Touchett, Ralph, and Lord Warburton emerge at the center of the composition.

The success of James's painting is carefully balanced against the failure of Mr. Touchett to arrange his own scene. James creates a setting with characters; the Touchetts simply mimic the English ritual of tea. Mr. Touchett has purchased a dead little world. The waning afternoon reflects not only the old banker's impending death, but Ralph's fatal illness and the end of the Touchett line as well. Lord Warburton himself is struggling with the disappearance of the old values of the landed aristocracy and the rise to power of a modern bourgeoisie. The scene and the ritual that Mr. Touchett consecrates by lifting his large, brightly painted teacup to his lips suggest the timeless paradise he had hoped to buy from England's history and civilization. This *"innocent* pastime" takes place in "the *perfect* middle of a splendid summer afternoon," a time that can only be described as "a little *eternity . . .* an *eternity of pleasure"* (I, 1; italics mine)'. But this unfallen Eden, perfect even in the absence of an Eve, reveals only its own deadness. In the lengthening shadows and with the entrance of Isabel, James brings us back to the time and change these three men all fear.

In a single scene, James initiates time and place and their thematic functions in the novel. By contrasting his own narrative composition to the emptiness of the afternoon tea ritual, he dramatizes the need for Isabel to be educated into a world of time and change. The dynamics of the scene suggests James's basic notion that time achieves meaning through man's composition of reality, in the constructive vision that places people and things in relation. Whereas the social ritual of tea fails to constitute values, James's description of the scene gives shape and dimension to the formless flow of time as change. Time informs and is informed by the scene, thus achieving presence through the activity of the artist's consciousness.

It is this kind of scenic and aesthetic time that has led Georges Poulet to speak of the divestment of the past in the Jamesian novel: "Its characters undergo an infinity of experiences and incessantly discover themselves in new relationships with each other, but these experiences and relationships are oftenest the

direct effect of present junctures; they are a new disposition of
beings that corresponds to their displacement. An affair of the
surface, and not one of depth; a movement in space and not
one in time."[11] This is an accurate assessment of the originality
of the present demanded of James's conscious characters. Yet
it is hardly "an affair of the surface, and not one of depth." As
the above passage from *Portrait* should indicate, James's time
is constituted frequently in spatial terms; but it is precisely such
a treatment that results in what James would call the "depth" of
history. This depth expresses the vitality and variety of the
critical imagination, expanding and revising its interpretations
of a constantly changing world. Thus consciousness manifests
itself in the effort of the individual to deal with the "new dis-
positions" and "displacements," which are the very signs of
temporal change. It would be more accurate to say that many
of James's characters divest themselves of a dead past through
the vital act of making their own history. The fading world of
the Touchetts and Lord Warburton confronted by Isabel in the
opening pages of *Portrait* clearly indicates that she must develop
an aesthetic vision in order to avoid such hollow forms and
rituals.

Thus time and history become functions of the individual's
particular phenomenology of perception. James's spatialization
of time suggests a primary interest in psychological duration.
Poulet is quite right to see James's "aesthetic time" in terms of
point of view, rather than chronological sequence:

He invents a new kind of time, what one might call aesthetic time.
It consists in establishing about a center a moving circle of points
of view, from one to the other of which the novelist proceeds. There
is no change except in point of view. Thus time is constituted by
passage, not from one moment to another, but from one point of
perspective to another. This process is demonstrated to perfection
when there is found situated at the center an entity, an object or an
ensemble of objects, as in *The Spoils of Poynton*. For these objects
have no past, they are not situated in time but in space. The only

11. Georges Poulet, *Studies in Human Time*, p. 351.

time one finds here is that which would be employed in contemplating a statue from all angles, in the course of discussing it with other connoisseurs. This is "the law of successive aspects," by which James carefully reduces time to a local duration, and by which he saves himself from being lost in the "admirable immensity."[12]

To speak of a "local duration" should not indicate a simplification of James's aesthetic time, but rather clarify the subjective and impressionistic foundations for his historical sense. It is quite true that objects in the present are frequently germinal for James's sense of the past. All his travel sketches depend upon the "relics of the past" in his historical and aesthetic readings. But the *objet d'art* itself is merely suggestive of that interpretative act which shaped it originally.

James and his characters are faced with the infinite muddle of actuality and the need to define forms out of it. The breakdown of any viable *telos* or center for the structures of thought and language demands a revision of traditional conceptions of time and history. The collections in the modern museum lose their evolutionary order when the origin and goal of such a development have been withdrawn. The translation of the classical center from an eternal universal to a temporal function necessitates an *interpretative* imagination as the modern medium of expression. The beginning and end of history for James are contained in his *recognition* of the Galerie d'Apollon. The differential relationships of the young man's first visit to the gallery, his unconscious shaping of the experience in the nightmare, his reflective construction of it on awaking, and his aesthetic development of the entire experience in terms of his autobiography describe the function of consciousness itself. The play of mind expressed in these variant movements is an historical process. Thus history blooms in the Galerie d'Apollon from the dead collections of the past into the vitality of the present. This kind of museum visitor finds each small artifact bristling with relations and possibilities in the willful activity of the roving eye.

12. Ibid., p. 352.

History becomes a perpetual incarnation, a variation on Nietzsche's eternal return. As Jacques Derrida has written: "The *Telos* becomes totally open, becomes the [act of] opening itself. To say that it is the most powerful structural *apriori* of historicism is not to designate it as a static and determined value that informs and encloses the genesis of being and meaning. It is the concrete possibility, at once the birth of the history and the meaning of becoming in general. It is then structurally genesis itself, both origin and growth."[13] The play of consciousness itself defines the historical space. When translated onto the stage of the imagination, Malraux's "confrontation of metamorphoses" may well develop the necessary contexts.

No work of James's more explicitly deals with the problems of an historical consciousness than *The American Scene*. In the expatriate's return to his homeland, the impressions rendered describe clearly the nature of both James's own historical sense and the effacement of historical value in modern America. Both the style and the narrative method of *The American Scene* reflect the structural complexities of the novels of the Major Phase. Thus, it provides a valuable introduction to the highly wrought aesthetic forms of *The Ambassadors, The Wings of the Dove,* and *The Golden Bowl.* Written after these three novels, *The American Scene* provides special insights into the operation of that critical consciousness that is the focus of the novels. By investigating aesthetic form in terms of the historical analogy, James clarifies the process of consciousness coming-to-be—the basic subject of these novels. Most important, however, *The American Scene* is a critique of modern America, explicitly dealing with James's idea of the crisis in Western thought. It is, as Ezra Pound has described it, a "large volume," "but one should in time drift through it. I mean any American with pretences

13. Derrida, " 'Genèse et structure' et la Phénoménologie," in *L'écriture et la différence,* p. 250; translation mine.

to an intellectual life should drift through it. It is not enough to have perused 'The Constitution' and to have 'heerd tell' of the national founders."[14] James describes himself as a "restless analyst," whose own imaginative diversity contrasts sharply with the sterile uniformity of modern American society.

James attempts throughout the entire work to discover meaning and purpose in recent American history. In the absence of this order, he finds value in the historical relations made possible through his own interpretative activity. In the imaginative rendering of his impressions of America, James puts himself in touch with the creative vitality he feels this society has lost or destroyed. The American scene appears to be "figured by a great gray wash of some charged moist brush causing colour and outline . . . effectually to run together" (455). In his response to Charleston, James analyzes the effects of a characteristic American blankness: "It was only another case of the painting with a big brush, a brush steeped in crude universal white, and of the colossal size this implement was capable of assuming. Gradations, transitions, differences of any sort, temporal, material, social, whether in man or in his environment, shrank somehow, under its sweep, to negligible items; and one had perhaps never yet seemed so to move through a vast simplified scheme" (305). The brush wielded by this modern democracy eliminates all discriminations in the name of equality. This historical thinness is the result of the American tendency to generate collections without contexts—a manifestation of the undefined energies of the American leviathan. Meaning and purpose are improvised without any relation to the past or the future. In *The American Scene* James describes the enormity and vastness of America's production: the proliferation of events, things, actions incarnated in the shuffling herd of the people. The collected array presents a monolithic blur, reflecting

14. Pound, "Henry James" (1918), in *Literary Essays of Ezra Pound*, p. 327.

the absence of the forms of the creative mind. Ironically, the impression of thinness depends upon quantity and mass, the vast conglomerate of the "stuff" of American business and economics. That vast pile lacks the variety and tone that transform the chaos of actuality into readable history, social manners, or general culture. James receives "the sense that . . . as Nature abhors a vacuum, so it is the genius of the American land and the American people to abhor, whenever may be, a discrimination" (305).

In his visit to Carpenters' Hall in Philadelphia, James finds a rare source for the deep impression, which almost universally fails him in the American cities. The exception of that little historic structure tends to emphasize the more extensive blankness of the American experiment:

> It makes for the sense of complexity, relieves the eternal impression of things all in a row and of a single thickness, an impression which the usual unprecedented length of the American alignment (always its source of pride) does by itself little to mitigate. *Nothing in the array is "behind" anything else—an odd result, I admit, of the fact that so many things affirm themselves as preponderantly before.* Little Carpenters' Hall *was*, delightfully, somewhere behind; so much behind, as I perhaps thus fantastically see it, that I dare say I should not be able to find my way to it again if I were to try. . . . *It might have been, for this beautiful posteriority, somewhere in the City of London.*   [294; italics mine]

The ironic intention of the passage builds to the final sentence. The rare discovery of historic tone in old Philadelphia—its evocations of Franklin and Independence—emphasizes the modern void in American history. With a perfect sense of contrast, James associates Carpenters' Hall with London, as if its charm were a rejection of the modern American glare.

Repeatedly, James associates the felicity of early American history with Europe. The lack of chronological history that Cooper sought to fill with the density of American events does not pose a problem for James's retrospective glance.[15] For James, American history before the Civil War finds depth and tone in its relation to the European heritage. Thus, old Phildelphia recalls the London of Christopher Wren, and Duplessis's portrait of Franklin glows with the light and dark of one of Rembrandt's Elders. Yet James's entire pilgrimage through modern America emphasizes the effacement of any such relation, the failure of the possibility of a truly American history. For James the economic, social, and political forces of the post-Civil War era seem to rely on the quantity of production and the collectivization of man. The modern American tendency seems to repudiate the interpretative and creative methods that defined the wealth of European history.

The restless analyst who struggles to understand the confusion of modern America is a curious blend of detached observer and yearning expatriate. His dislocation in the places he knew in his youth gives personal authenticity to the contrasts between early and modern America. The narrative voice repeatedly shifts from "I" to "he" to "we." The "I" most often speaks from the reflective distance of Lamb House, where James shaped his sketches and impressions into the final work. That "I" provides us with the wealth of historical sense bred into the author from long association with England and the Continent. James's "he" provides the reader with an immediate image of the analyst at work, absorbing impressions and searching for relations. The less frequent "we" develops the collective sense of analysis that clearly marks the work as a sharp stab at the discriminating American. The processes of perception, reflection, recollection, and creation make the narrator a protean figure. He is not an omniscient nar-

15. For example, see James Fenimore Cooper, *The Deerslayer*, I, 13: "On the human imagination events produce the effects of time. Thus, he who has traveled far and seen much is apt to fancy that he has lived long, and the history that most abounds in important incidents soonest assumes the aspect of antiquity. In no other way can we account for the venerable air that is already gathering around American annals."

rator, for he is constantly surprised and bewildered by this new world. The complexity of the narrative voice, however, defines a journey that is much more than, for example, Tocqueville's sociological study. James's voyage is developed through his diverse impressions of the failure of the American imagination. The phenomenology of the analyst's vision acts to vitalize his sense of the possibility of an American history—if only for the lonely author at Rye.

When the narrator disembarks in America, the "monstrous form of Democracy" reveals not only the general loss of historical tone, but the effacement of his own personal origins: "*The will to grow* was everywhere written large, and to grow at no matter what or whose expense" (54). Change of that nature is the denial of form, order, and meaning. James sees only the accelerating entropy of the cultural machine, a view that complements Adams's historical pessimism: "The illustration might be, enormously, of something deficient, absent—in which case it was the aching void to be (as an aching void) striking and interesting"(56). In New York James sees the indiscriminate will to grow best expressed in the skyscraper, as appropriate an image of the modern tendency as Adams's Dynamo. Its massiveness and height represent the accumulation of business wealth and power. Its architectural monotony and sharpness dramatize the effacement of discrimination and taste. The crowning of the skyline with lofty spires is hardly reminiscent of Renaissance London or Florence. Skyscrapers represent the extemporaneous and ephemeral quality of modern America, the repudiation of an historical sense: "Crowned not only with no history, but with no credible possibility of time for history, and consecrated by no uses save the commercial at any cost, they are simply the most piercing notes in that concert of the expensively provisional" (77).

The loss of cultural discriminations is given dramatic expression in the view of Trinity Church, whose "simplified Gothic" is lost in the riot of Wall Street (78). The expatriate is forcibly impressed with New York's disregard for history by the razing of his birthplace in Washington Square. He views it as a symbolic amputation of his ties to both his own youth and an earlier America. Modern American history is not the vitalization of the present from a sense of the past, but the eradication of the past in the rush of the present. As James remarks at several points in *The American Scene,* beauty depends upon form, and the forms of the present must be generated from a critical interpretation of the past.

Much criticism has been directed against James's apparent condemnation of the alien in his analyses of the mass immigration laws. In connection with New York, James's views of the immigrants and his trip to Ellis Island provide metaphoric expression for the formlessness of American Dollar Democracy. He recognizes clearly enough that mass immigration was one more operation of the dehumanizing machine of the profit motive. The increasing demands for cheap labor by American business radically undercut the traditional idealism of the Statue of Liberty's motto. The dehumanization of the immigrant, his loss of cultural and individual identity in the American web, is for James one more manifestation of that "monotonous male commonness, of the pushing male crowd." His views on the immigrant's place in America are hardly elitist. In his descriptions of the alien, he criticizes the skyscraper civilization that transforms equality into commonness: "He resembles for the time the dog who sniffs around the freshly-acquired bone, giving it a push and a lick, betraying a sense of its possibilities, but not—and quite as from a positive deep tremor of consciousness—directly attacking it. There are categories of foreigners, truly, meanwhile, of whom we are moved to say that only a mechanism working with scientific force could have performed this feat of making them colourless" (128). The American "identity" becomes a vast destructive force, which has "profited by their sacrifice" (129). Ultimately, America itself must suffer from the loss of distinctions in the dissolution of its own form. Peter Buitenhuis has called James's impressions of the Bowery and the ghettoes of

New York some of the best writing in *The American Scene*.[16]
In those sections James seeks to uncover the remaining cultural
flavor of the immigrants. James sees that the American melting
pot unfortunately tends to end in the garbled language of the
alien. In Europe various cultures interact without loss of cultural
pride or integrity (128). Languages and customs change on
their own terms, vitalizing different societies. In America the
evidence of the alien's corruption of language and customs reflects
a breakdown of both cultures. Our attention should be directed
less to James's proverbial condescension than to his recognition
of the future plight of the immigrant. In such conditions men
are transformed into simply the "properties" of the American
Trust. America's assimilation of the alien subjects him to the
predetermined coordinates of the democratic machine and its
economics. The integration of alien cultures into the American
scene ought to enrich its heritage rather than contribute to a
growing vagueness and loss of tone. From our modern perspective, James's vision of the failure of American methods of cultural
assimilation ought to be considered prophetic.

The disappearance of an American historical sense is manifest
everywhere in *The American Scene* in the massive production
and conspicuous consumption of the post-Civil War era. At the
heart of the new American forces James finds an absence of any
social, metaphysical, or intellectual principle of order. The work
itself is structured around a quest for the center of American
life. With the exception of the first chapter, "New England," the
book is divided according to cities as focal points for regional
culture. Yet those cities expose the blankness and confusion at
the heart of American life. As the economic center of America,
New York reveals only the ceaseless change that is the thrust of
devouring capitalist motives. In New England, the "vast and
vacant" space of the old meeting house represents the absence of
the social and religious order of the early Americans (24).

16. Peter Buitenhuis, *The Grasping Imagination,* p. 190.

James's climactic description of Washington, D.C., captures that essential vacancy he finds characteristic of the modern American scene. In a discussion of the disappearance of organized religion James defines the "negative" as the center of American life. For James the absence of "religious faith" must be read in terms of the loss of cultural or historical consciousness and intention:

Washington already bristles, for the considering eye, with national affirmations—builded forms of confidence and energy; . . . but something is absent more even than these masses are present—till it at last occurs to you that the existence of a religious faith on the part of the people is not even remotely suggested. Not a federal dome, not a spire or a cornice pretends to any such symbolism, and though your attention is thus concerned with a mere negative, *the negative presently becomes its sharp obsession.* You reach perhaps in vain for something to which you may familiarly compare your unsatisfied sense. You liken it perhaps not so much to a meal made savourless by the failure of some usual, some central dish, as to a picture, nominally finished, say, *where the canvas shows, in the very middle, with all originality, a fine blank space.* [380–81; italics mine]

Clearly the religious faith is not intended to evoke European Catholicism or the Church of England. Absent in America is that spirituality that is the expression of consciousness in its collective and social forms. This is surely the only "religion" James may be said to have subscribed to. This central blankness in the American landscape provides the single most important metaphor for James's analysis of the society, culture, manners, and people he encounters.

His earlier description of Washington as a city of conversation develops the idea of the capital in process of formation, struggling to define itself. Such a tendency is constantly undercut by indiscriminate growth. The attempt of American women to create a "Europe of their own" in Washington is seen as impossible in the very differences between sexual relations in America and in Europe (352). The polarization of the sexes in America, a constant theme for Henry Adams, reflects a fundamental abyss in

American life, descriptive of the central absence. The effacement of the American male, nominally ascribed to his preoccupation with business, is analogous to the death of a more essential
father for the American scene. In the modern air, the social *logos*
has been reduced to mumbo-jumbo. As James remarks much
earlier in the work: "The *il*legible word, accordingly, the great
inscrutable answer to questions, hangs in the vast American sky,
to his imagination, as something fantastic and *abracadabrant*,
belonging to no known language" (121–2). The "alien language" of the American text is more often than not "*il*legible"
to even the most accomplished cultural linguists.

It is with such a sense of emptiness that the narrator must
struggle. His impressions of Washington end in an almost
melodramatic scene, painfully expressive of the failure of democratic ideals. Pacing the marble pathways of the Capitol, James
comes upon a "trio of Indian braves, braves dispossessed of
forest and prairie" decked out "in neat pot-hats, shoddy suits
and light overcoats, with their pockets, I am sure, full of photo-
graphs and cigarettes" (363). The incongruity of their presence
amid these marble colonnades suggests to the narrator "an image
in itself immense, but foreshortened and simplified—reducing
to a single smooth stride the bloody footsteps of time." In the
whirr of the democratic machine every trace of its mad production vanishes: "One rubbed one's eyes, but there, at its highest
polish, shining in the beautiful day, was the brazen face of history, and there, all about one, immaculate, *the printless pave-
ments of the State*" (364; italics mine).

If James seems to mourn the loss of a viable *telos* for American
history, he is not, however, advocating the fixed and static centers characteristic of European church or aristocracy. His novels
illustrate clearly enough that both are as hollow in the modern
age as the social and economic values of modern America. The
Catholicism of Prince Casamassima or of Prince Amerigo is a
mere reflex, a dead social form providing only catch phrases and
epithets. The Jamesian center is a creative activity, which pro-

vides contexts in the forms it makes from the "admirable immensity" of the actual. The American need for such an historical sense is sought in extemporized symbols. In "Philadelphia," James explicitly analyzes the implications of such ephemeral centers for the structures of the American consciousness:

> The collective consciousness, in however empty an air, gasps for a relation, as intimate as possible, to something superior, something as central as possible, from which it may more or less have proceeded and round which its life may revolve. . . . But the difficulty is that in these later times, among such aggregations, the heroic and romantic elements, even under the earliest rude stress, have been all too tragically obscure, belonged to smothered, unwritten, almost unconscious private history: so that the central something, the social *point de repère*, has had to be extemporized rather pitifully after the fact, and made to consist of the biggest hotel or the biggest common school, the biggest factory, the biggest newspaper office, or, for climax of desperation, the house of the biggest billionaire. [290–91]

The need to "dress" the social "doll" with color and tone is the fundamental need of social man to provide himself with a context. The tone of the passage leads us away from any conception of the center as a fixed transcendental principle. For James heroic or romantic implies the validation of the actual in the transcendental. It is the dualism implied in his description of the "romance" as a balloon untethered from the earth (*AN*, 33–4). Modern America structures its social consciousness about a center that is "extemporized rather pitifully after the fact." Rather than becoming a principle for order, it merely reflects cultural indirection. The "biggest factory" can do little but suggest the failure of quantity or size as a true measure of value.

In the subsequent paragraph James describes his own perceptual process in a manner clearly intended to relate to his critique of the American imagination. The perceptive consciousness must recognize that history and societies are *made* in the forms they assume. Such forms must reflect a vital interrelation of man and his world, not simply of the forces and energies that dominate and repress him: "Such an observer has early to perceive, and to conclude on it once for all, that there will be little for him in the American scene unless he be ready, anywhere, everywhere, to read 'into' it as much as he reads out. It is at best for him when most open to that friendly penetration, and not at its best, I judge, when practically most closed" (*AS*, 291). This inter-penetration of man and his world transforms the social *product* into a cultural *expression*, the living record of a civilization.

Earlier, James had in a similar mood pondered the enclosure of Harvard Yard. The fence itself provides an apt metaphor for the relation of form to meaning. He complains of the incomplete-ness of the wall, gates, and iron palings; but recognizes an at-tempt at privacy and value conspicuously absent in the rest of the American scene:

This special drawing of the belt at Harvard is an admirably inter-esting example of the way in which the formal enclosure of objects at all interesting immediately refines upon their interest, immediately establishing values. . . . Nothing is more curious than to trace in the aspects so controlled the effect of their established relation to it. This resembles, in the human or social order, the improved situa-tion of the foundling who has discovered his family or of the actor who has mastered his part. [62]

The final line is particularly appropriate for the expatriate nar-rator, who finds Harvard's Alumni Hall "closed to him" and who "had to enter, to the loss of all his identity . . ." (61). Throughout *The American Scene* James finds that the places of his past provide only pale or sentimental associations. He finds his homeland in the images and metaphors he carves out of the current landscape.[17] Thus the formal enclosing of Harvard Yard is comparable to his own activity of giving shape and dimension to the formless and often chaotic world he encounters. It is, after all, the artist who runs the risks of the return trip, and his identity is as inextricably as ever related to the form of his expression:

17. See Wright Morris, "Henry James's *The American Scene*," in *The Territory Ahead*, p. 191.

"Really, universally, relations stop nowhere, and the exquisite problem of the artist is eternally but to draw, by a geometry of his own, the circle within which they shall happily appear to do so" (*AN*, 5).

In his *Notebooks* James makes the connection between the enclosure of Harvard Yard and the aesthetic process even clearer. As such an enclosure allows the values of formal composition and definition, so "*dis*closure" is the characteristic tendency of the modern machine as it strips away formal boundaries:

> I was fumbling, I was groping through the little Cambridge haze that I was, by the same stroke, trying to make "golden," and I noted for my recall "The Gates—questions of the Gates and of the fact of enclosure and of disclosure in general—the so importunate American question (of *Dis*closure—call it so!) above all." This, with some possible peep . . . of my vision of the old high Cambridge and Oxford *grilles* and their admirable office of making things look interesting . . . as for instance how, *within* the College Yard, its elements and items gain presence by what has been done (little as it is, of enclosure—with a glance at the *old* misery!) and how I may put it that the less "good" thing enclosed, approached, *defined,* often looks better than the less good thing *not* enclosed, not defined, not approached.[18]

As it "makes a sense," the Yard bears aesthetic value for the roving eye. In the fragments of James's notes on the journey we catch the sense of the artist struggling to constitute meaning where the past grows thin and the rushing present blurs the outlines of things. The "foundling" and the "actor" of the earlier passage are intimately related, for the family and country James rediscovers belong to his own creative imagination.[19]

18. *The Notebooks of Henry James,* ed. F. O. Matthiessen and Kenneth Murdock, 11 December–30 March 1905, p. 316.

19. The complexity of James's response to Harvard Yard makes Leon Edel's account of the episode in *Henry James: The Master* seem inadequate. Although Edel suggests the "novelist's need for shape and form" as part of James's response, he concentrates on James's reflection that the Yard "was still not sufficiently enclosed" (p. 245). The tone of both *The American Scene* and the *Notebooks* entries suggests that James sees the

In "Philadelphia" and the chapters on the South James investigates two examples of the separation of early America from
the post-Civil War era. In these sections James contrasts America's early history with the blankness of the modern age. Quaker
Philadelphia and the "romantic" Old South are different attempts to shape a society around a central principle of order.
Both social experiments provide insights into the vitality or
deadness of a collective historical consciousness. Most important
to note is James's sense of the modern loss of distinction, which
has swept the differences between Philadelphia and Charleston
into the unrelieved monotony of the current scene.

Quaker Philadelphia was established on an essential *consanguinity,* which transformed the city from a place into "an
absolute final" social condition (278). It is in part the conscious
contrivance of such a social interrelation, the naming of brother
and sister, that contributes to James's sense of the drabness of the
Quaker. Yet the Friends' social vision was founded on the vitality of *organic* relations. The idea of basing a society on organic
consanguinity necessarily ought to imply "not only a family"
but "a 'happy' one" at that. The society ought to be able to
accommodate growth, development, and new influences. The
historic tone James finds in his rambles through the old streets
of Philadelphia depends upon that social intimacy of the Quakers which is so absent in the rest of America. James receives a
genial impression of William Penn's original social ideals in the
few remaining traces of the old Quaker world (280–1). This
rare social sense, however, quickly fades in the modern glare.
Modern Philadelphia represents the horror of the "American
case," "the way in which sane Society and pestilent City, in the
United States, successfully cohabit" (283). What "genius for
life" James found in the Quaker experiment is lost in this modern
cohabitation. It is a social *danse macabre,* the breakdown of any

---

value of the Yard's enclosure in contrast to the general "*dis*closure" he
sees written everywhere in modern America.

order that might offer historical or cultural relation. The immersion of the old America in this new world suggests to James the image of "a society dancing, all consciously, on the thin crust of a volcano" (285).

The organization of the chapter "Philadelphia" reflects this modern tendency. James begins with his impressions of the old Quaker world, full of its "serenity," "consanguinity," "homogeneity," and "morality." Independence Hall and Carpenters' Hall seem to reflect this balance and harmony, but the chapter ends with James's impressions of the Pennsylvania Penitentiary: "This huge house of sorrow affected me as, uncannily, of the City itself, the City of all the cynicisms and impunities against which my friends had, from far back, kept plating, as with the old silver of their side-boards, the armour of their social consciousness" (300). This is an enclosure quite different from that of Harvard Yard. The prison becomes a metaphor for the modern American city's denial of social relation and its failure as a truly organic community. The "individual sequestration" that James finds at the prison seems to suggest more significantly the fear and alienation of the American citizen.[20]

James's impressions of the Old South provide another contrast to his vision of the society of Penn and the Quakers. The closed world of the South was founded not on an organic principle of growth and vitality but on the rigid system of slavery. Instead of establishing a social relation to the rest of the world, the a priori values of the slave states led to a radical isolationism. The "romance" of the South is analyzed by James in terms of its disjunction from the historical and cultural reality surrounding it:

Since nothing in the Slave-scheme could be said to conform—conform, that is, to the reality of things—it was the plan of Christendom and the wisdom of the ages that would have to be altered. History,

20. See Michel Foucault, *Madness and Civilization*, p. 61, for a related analysis of the fundamental "confinement" of modern bourgeois societies.

the history of everything, would be rewritten. . . . This meant a general and a permanent quarantine; meant the eternal bowdlerization of books and journals; meant in fine all literature and all art on an expurgatory index. It meant, still further, an active and ardent propaganda; the reorganization of the school, the college, the university, in the interest of the new criticism.   [374]

This kind of social closure leads to a collective solipsism that results in violence when forced to confront a reality other than its own. With penetrating analysis, James's impressions of the Old South gauge the essential quality of Southern monomania. The "romantic view" becomes a subversive force that enslaves, represses, and exploits. At this point, James comes very close to Twain's attacks on Southern romanticism.[21] He sees the Old South as its own best victim, trapped by forces and superstititions fundamental to its social identity.

Everywhere along his rumbling train ride through the modern South, James finds the fragments of the great slave scheme. The waste of the Civil War is symbolized in the decaying halls of the Southern plantation house. The obliteration of the slave system has not prepared the ground for a more vital social order. The text of the Old South is unreadable, the scattered *ostraka* of some vanished race. Any sense of regional character has been replaced by the monotony and commonness of modern America. The crisis of the war—the break with past history—has made the new South a garbled array of "senseless appearances." In Richmond and Charleston James finds that his impressions simply won't compose. In the wasteland of the modern South, James experiences the general ephemerality of the American scene.

The possibility of a viable form for modern American society vanishes in the sweeping forces, spoken in the Pullman's rumbling voice: " 'See what I'm making of all this—see what I'm making, what I'm making!' " The weary James, struggling with

21. Twain's attacks on Southern romanticism in *Life on the Mississippi, Huckleberry Finn,* and *Pudd'nhead Wilson* are basic to his criticism of nineteenth-century American society's illusions.

the immensities of his journey and the ambiguities of America, gives his final answer:

"If I were one of the painted savages you have dispossessed, or even some tough reactionary trying to emulate him, what you are making would doubtless impress me more than what you are leaving unmade. . . . Beauty and charm would be for me in the solitude you have ravaged, and I should owe you my grudge for every disfigurement and every violence, for every wound with which you have caused the face of the land to bleed. No, since I accept your ravage, what strikes me is the long list of arrears of your undone; and so constantly, right and left, that your pretended message of civilization is but a colossal recipe for the *creation* of arrears, and of such as can but remain forever out of hand." [463]

If James finds anything in America worth preservation, it is the land and nature itself. The ravage of the American Dream is reflected in the landscape, whose scarred face resists the portraiture of the artist. The wilderness remaining is already threatened by the great leveling machine, which removes even natural differences and discriminations. The lush tropical climate of Florida has become the setting for the false-front hotels dotting its beaches. The "hotel-spirit" and "hotel-civilization" provide the final symbols of the American synthesis: the digestion of the past.

The American Scene ends on a note of foreboding as it prophesies the triumph of the superficial and ephemeral in America. The last pages foreshadow the possible nature of another volume of impressions that was planned, to be entitled *The Sense of the West*.[22] As an alternative to Florida, James looks forward to California as a source of potential vitality, "a sort of prepared but unconscious and unexperienced Italy, the primitive *plate,* in perfect condition, but with the impression of History all yet to be made" (462). The example of Florida and its hotel

22. Buitenhuis, *Grasping Imagination,* p. 204. The distinction between the two projected volumes is important. As James wrote to W. E. Norris from Rye: "(I have indeed practically done one volume of 'Impressions' —there are to be two, separate and differently titled;) . . ." *The Letters of Henry James,* II, 46.

civilization nevertheless seems to foredoom the expansion of the American Common to the very edge of its borders. As Peter Buitenhuis has summarized James's response to California and the West: "He had an unhappy vision of how that history *might* be made."[23] One need hardly speculate about James's response to the California of the nineteen-seventies.

The narrator of *The American Scene* shapes his images as points of reference for understanding the circuit of his journey. As such, they bear value in their creation, interrelation, and change. James suggests how dependent meaning and value are on the active engagement of what is there. In "Baltimore" he contrasts his role with that of the journalist who tries to tally his impressions into some "careful sum." James borrows the journalist's slate—itself a reminder of the ephemeral quality of the modern American text—and draws upon it the shape of his own perceptual process:

If it was a question of a slate the slate was used, at school, I remembered, for more than one purpose; so that mine, by my walk's end, instead of a show of neat ciphering, exhibited simply a bold drawn image—which had the merit moreover of not being in the least a caricature. The moral of this was precious—that of the fine impunity with which, if one but had sensibility, the ciphering could be neglected and in fact almost contemned: always, that is (and only) *with* one's finer wits about one. Without them one was at best, really, nowhere—even with "items" by the thousand. [308–9]

It is the "finer wits" James relies on at last. The pilgrimage of the artist is made in his creative activity, dramatized in the enormous depth and flow of what has often been viewed as merely a collection of impressions. The real story is that of the analyst, who maintains himself just in proportion as he is sentient and restless: "That was the real way to work things out, and to feel it so brought home would by itself sufficiently crown this particular small pilgrimage" (309).

Tony Tanner recalls James's *The American Scene* toward the

23. Buitenhuis, *Grasping Imagination*, p. 205.

end of his recent study of contemporary American fiction.[24] James's vision is certainly prophetic of the risks the modern American artist has had to confront. The work leaves us with the sense that there is "really too much to say," and thus reminds us of what remains: the indomitable presence of the critical analyst himself. Like so much modern American literature, *The American Scene* reflects the failure of the Dream—and perhaps the more generalized failure of Western history. America's failings suggest the need for the creative imagination to use its "finer wits" to vitalize a history in its own artistry. In his own impressions the narrator finds a basis for an historical outlook. The tension between the interpreter and his vast object of study must be resolved in his favor. His American pilgrimage becomes an act of existential affirmation, the survival of that peculiar Jamesian ego in the storm of its transatlantic crossing.

24. See Tanner, *City of Words,* pp. 416 ff.

perne structurefor body burning
gyre SPIN ocean currents

6   The Realism of the Symbolic Process in *The Wings of the Dove*

> O Sages standing in God's holy fire
> As in the gold mosaic of a wall,
> Come from the holy fire, perne in a gyre,
> And be the singing-masters of my soul.
> Consume my heart away; sick with desire
> And fastened to a dying animal
> It knows not what it is; and gather me
> Into the artifice of eternity.
>
> Once out of nature I shall never take
> My bodily form from any natural thing,
> But such a form as Grecian goldsmiths make
> Of hammered gold and gold enamelling
> To keep a drowsy Emperor awake;
> Or set upon a golden bough to sing
> To lords and ladies of Byzantium
> Of what is past, or passing, or to come.
>
>   —Yeats, "Sailing to Byzantium," 1927*

The American Scene centers on the tension between the narrator's perceptual activity and the modern historical tendency toward social conventionality and conformity. A similar conflict is fundamental to James's epistemology in the later novels from *The Sacred Fount* (1901) to the unfinished *The Ivory Tower*. In James's writings there is a clear homology between historical consciousness and aesthetic consciousness. The "blankness" of modern American society compels the restless analyst to make his own sense out of the jumble of appearances, relying more on

homology=shared ancestry between pair of genes or

his vital imagination than on the dreary facts. Similarly, in the later novels he consistently deconstructs the characters' hopes for a secure reality or historical order, forcing them either to embrace their own unstable "truths" or to submit themselves to the "lies" of others. The majority of James's characters end possessed by conventional values, which they are unwilling to reinterpret and thus revitalize. Prince Amerigo and Charlotte Stant in *The Golden Bowl* refuse to embrace the fundamental ambiguity of human relations, and thus retreat from potential freedom into the security of social forms; Maggie Verver uses her imaginative awakening only to preserve social appearances and thus avoid the true instability of the human situation. Even Milly Theale, who alone seems successful in making something authentic of her brief life, does so only sacrificially. Forced to confront her mortality, Milly has little choice but to assert herself. Unlike Kate Croy and Maggie Verver, she cannot be lured by hopes of future beauty and truth.

James's later novels are fundamentally concerned with the problematics of human knowledge and being in time. Their "realism" depends basically on the homology between the structures of literary language and ordinary human consciousness. In its highly self-conscious form, the novel is always concerned with the methods whereby man creates new signs and discards or revitalizes old ones. Imaginative writing seems to be defined by its tendency to make explicit the tension between linguistic normalization and the need for innovation. Ferdinand de Saussure recognized that such a dialectic is essential to the continuity and vitality of language as an institution.[1] The Prague linguist Jan Mukařovský considers the development of every literary

1. See Ferdinand de Saussure, *Course in General Linguistics*, p. 74: "In the last analysis, the two facts are interdependent: the sign is exposed to alteration because it perpetuates itself. What predominates in all change is the persistence of the old substance; disregard for the past is only relative. That is why the principle of change is based on the principle of continuity."

phenomenon to embody such an opposition. In Felix Vodička's summary of Mukařovský's view, "Development, as a necessary process through which things are changed in time, is conceived of as the result of two opposite tendencies: on the one hand a series maintains its character during its evolution because without a permanent identity it could not be understood as a continuity in time. On the other hand it violates its identity since no changes would be possible without this violation. Violation of identity stimulates the motion of development; through permanency of identity a regular pattern is imposed upon evolution."[2] Mukařovský himself would argue the homology between this literary function and the social and historical functions of man. As Vodička suggests, "Patterning and depatterning of art and literature necessarily depend on the patterning and depatterning of the systems of functions that occur in the life of an individual in a concrete historical situation."[3]

James's later novels announce not only the ambiguous world in which his characters are forced to live but the unstable nature of the linguistic sign as well. Trapped by conventional truths or acceptable realities, James's characters not only surrender their own individuality but also threaten the arbitrariness of the sign that assures the vitality of language.[4] Thus, in the same sense that Milly Theale uses her life and death to disillusion Kate and Densher about London society, James's later novels are concerned with the deconstruction of habitual modes of signification. Yet James does not offer his own discourse as an alternative for the reader, because his language is too intimately tied to

2. Felix Vodička, "The Integrity of the Literary Process," p. 11.
3. Ibid., p. 14.
4. See De Saussure, *General Linguistics*, p. 73: "The arbitrary nature of the sign is really what protects language from any attempt to modify it. Even if people were more conscious of language than they are, they would still not know how to discuss it. . . . The symbol has a rational relationship with the thing signified; but language is a system of arbitrary signs and lacks the necessary ground for discussion. There is no reason for preferring *soeur* to *sister*, *Ochs* to *boeuf*, etc."

the subject of his critique. By opening up the dead categories of social language, James offers the possibility of interpretative thought and renewed meaning. Thus he deftly skirts the dogmatism and didacticism he condemns so vigorously in many of his characters.

The symbolism in the later works suggests a similar tension. The impulse toward symbolization itself involves an attempt to assign meaning to the ambiguous. There is a conscious duplicity in the Jamesian symbol: it suggests both man's longing for truth and the unfulfillable nature of such a desire. A character such as the narrator of *The Sacred Fount* offers a distorted image of this conflict in the later novels. His "scientific" quest for a "law" that might explain the devouring master-servant relations among the guests at a weekend party is a parable for the aims of most of James's characters. Like Lambert Strether, Kate Croy, or Maggie Verver, the narrator longs for a secure sense of self. And yet his quest reveals the elusiveness of identity in a world where any "fount" for knowledge must reveal itself inevitably as "extemporized," "specious," or "spurious" (as James referred to his own structural centers in the Prefaces). His weekend investigation is a process of disillusionment, during which he learns to abandon scientific rigor for an imaginative play which gives life successive colors and forms. *The Sacred Fount* and the novels that follow it are written expressly against hopes for certainty, truth, or revealed meaning. They demonstrate the tension between the desire for formal definition and the need for innovation, which is central to James's conception of aesthetic process.

Like the wings of the dove, the sacred fount the narrator struggles to define is ultimately evasive. In itself it comes to symbolize the *absence* that man must confront with his varied interpretations. In a central scene in the novel, the characters view a painting of " 'the man with the mask in his hand,' " as May Server first calls it.[5] The painting demonstrates this par-

5. James, *The Sacred Fount*, p. 54. Hereafter cited in the text as *SF*.

adoxical relationship between definition and free play, suggesting the problems the imaginative characters in these novels must face:

The figure represented is a young man in black—a quaint, tight black dress fashioned in years long past; with a pale, lean, livid face and a stare, from eyes without eyebrows, like that of some whitened old-world clown. In his hand he holds an object that strikes the spectator at first simply as some obscure, some ambiguous work of art, but that on a second view becomes a representation of the human face, modelled and coloured, in wax, in enamelled metal, in some substance not human. The object thus appears a complete mask, such as might have been fantastically fitted and worn. [SF, 55]

On one hand, the painting reveals the essential blankness and deathliness beneath the masks we design for our appearances in the world. Thus, May Server changes her title to " 'the Mask of Death' " (56). Such a reading implies that the painting is intended to reveal a basic human truth, as if exposing our social lies. On the other hand, the narrator affirms the vitality of the "modelled and coloured" mask, despite the fact that its material is distinctly artificial. To the narrator the mask represents the possibility of creating meaning where there may have been none to begin with. The young man's face is meaningless and dead without a role to play, a mask to wear. Yet his deathliness is in part like the white foundation a clown uses to prepare his face for the makeup. For the mask to be "blooming and beautiful," imagination and artistry are required to draw order and harmony from the confusion of life at large. The mask is "living" insofar as it implies a vital act of interpretation and composition. It evokes not only the artistry of its maker but also that of the actor who uses it in the play. From this standpoint, the painting does not reveal the "pale, lean, livid face" of life in the figure of the young man alone. By associating life with the art of the mask, the narrator suggests that reality can never be separated from appearance. Truth is reduced to the function of the critical intelligence itself and all meaning must be understood in terms of the particular form of its expression.

The painting seems to dramatize the crisis of art itself. The design of art cannot hope to reveal any fundamental truth, but simply to evoke possibilities for meaning by suggesting new modes of vision. Like the subtle composition of Jamesian society, the painting depends upon the relations constituted within its frame. Those relations—the man and his mask—demand the critical interpretation of the viewers. Art violates the stream of life by framing relations and constituting values. Any form attempting to give cognitive clarity to pure experience must reveal itself as an artifice, a mere instrument for purposes of tentative understanding. In the same sense that William James recognized that his pluralistic universe must be "unfinished," Henry sees that the structures of consciousness and their defining language rely on incompletion.[6] It is this openness of form in the mind and its art that makes interpreted meaning possible as a functional response to a changing world.[7] The narrator of *The Sacred Fount* learns that our conceptions of the world are mere sketches, incapable of containing the shifting reality they seek to possess.

Thus the symbolism in the later novels constantly frustrates the characters' demands for meaningful definition. The mystery of the painting, like the secret of relations at the weekend party, lingers in the paradoxical confrontation of the man's death-in-life countenance and the mask's colorful artificiality. Like Kafka's parables, James's symbols are ambiguous texts and remain "symbolic" only insofar as they resist conventional understanding and require an imaginative act of interpretation. Milly Theale is perhaps the best example of this process of interpretation in the later novels. In *The Wings of the Dove* there is a constant pressure to give Milly an immediate, iconographic significance. Not only do Kate Croy, Susie Stringham, Maud Lowder, Merton Densher, and Lord Mark make Milly over in their own images; but the writer himself pushes her repeatedly

6. See William James, *A Pluralistic Universe,* p. 329.
7. See Holland, *Expense of Vision,* pp. 198–9.

toward the level of allegory. She is the "fairy princess" (Susie), the "dove" (Kate), "the little American Girl" (Densher), or the Bronzino portrait (Lord Mark). The entire Christian context in which James so explicitly places Milly, from her first appearance in the Alps to her final covering "flight," threatens to transform her into a fixed and determinate value. Yet it is only as Milly manages to avoid an allegorical identity that she truly achieves a symbolic force in the novel. In her effort to maintain herself as a "symbol of differences," Milly gives herself a creative authenticity rarely achieved by James's other characters.

The central myth of the novel—the Incarnation, Passion, Crucifixion, and Ascension of Christ—is manipulated to destroy any possibility of fulfilled meaning. Milly's association with the dove and with the ultimate immanence of the Holy Spirit evokes the ambiguity of the Word diffused in the world by Christ's sacrifice. The novel remains a world unto itself, any meaning beyond it being reduced to silence and void. The final symbolism of Milly's absence must be read in the relics of her memory in the world of Lancaster Gate—the letter, fortune, and lost love she bequeaths to Merton Densher. In a Christian context, interpretation is born of the discourse of the Scriptures. The dissemination of the *Logos* demands the continuing interpretations of scriptural exegesis as the means of uncovering the infinite mystery of the divine in a fallen temporal world.

Unlike Scriptures' reliance on a transcendental *logos,* a novel is a delimited linguistic world. The signs constituting the text are the only reality of the work. To transcend the world of the novel is simply to escape its confines and substitute another system of related signs for its meaning. Such a departure may take the form of another discourse, such as this one, which serves to see the literary work in a new, different form. Although the relation of this criticism to the text of the novel may contribute to a third understanding, it necessarily discloses meaning in its own unique play of language. If a novel dramatizes its essential fictionality, as *The Wings of the Dove* repeatedly does, then the attempt to determine final meaning is a violation of the work's aesthetic integrity. It is in the very nature of the novel as a literary form that any governing principle for its structure must be evasive. Insofar as James sees the creative process as homologous with the function of human consciousness itself, such a conception may be extended to the domain of actual experience. More immediately important, however, is the fact that the language of a literary text does not carry the reader on a magical journey toward its final revelation. Rather, the reader's voyage is a quest, an active engagement of the language of the work and a creative transposition of that language into the forms for his own understanding.

James's difficulty with the central consciousness, the misplaced middle, and the structural centers for his works betrays an ultimate recognition that the governing principle for the creative process is always diffused in the flow of language itself. If the Prefaces express a faith in the artist's imagination, it is only in the shapes and forms it projects that the imagination ever assumes apprehensible significance. The potential energy of the creative imagination is a vast fluidity, a chain of associations that must be shaped and delimited in the form of the work of art. In any teleological system to transcend the ambiguity of human discourse is a loss of individual being for the sake of a larger unity. Yet in James's aesthetic cosmos to transcend language is to end only in silence, the absolute void of meaning, the loss of value. As Jacques Derrida has suggested, the impossibility of any transcendental reality transforms our own discourse into the essential mystery of our condition: "This moment was that in which language invaded the universal problematic; that in which, in the absence of a center or origin, everything became discourse . . . that is to say, when everything became a system where the central signified, the original or transcendental signified, is never absolutely present outside a system of differences. The absence of the transcen-

dental signified extends the domain and interplay of signification *ad infinitum*."[8]

Although Christ's Incarnation and Crucifixion announce the
unity of God's kingdom, it is His presence in our memory that
constantly reminds us of our fallen, fragmented condition. As
the resolver of differences, Christ is also the great symbol of
differences, manifesting the essential disrelation between self and
other, as well as that between our temporal realm and the timeless domain of the kingdom of heaven. In analogous fashion,
Milly Theale ultimately brings the characters of the novel to a
consciousness of one another, forcing them to recognize the
distance that separates their respective desires. The effect of
Milly's sacrifice on Lancaster Gate is by no means redemptive,
but is rather a revelation of the hollowness at the heart of such
social games. At the end of *The Wings of the Dove*, we are left
with a shattered, fallen world become conscious of itself. Aunt
Maud's tears at the end are more for her own loss than selfless
expressions of love for Milly. Milly's death does not promise an
ultimate reconciliation of differences, but simply makes those
differences manifest, revealing the impossibility of Kate's and
Merton's "temple of love," the emptiness of Maud Lowder's
historical "collection," and the deathliness of Lord Mark's
Bronzino portrait.

At Milly's climactic dinner party in the Palazzo Leporelli Merton Densher enters Kate's own consciousness through the white
light of the "dove's" presence and recognizes Milly's ultimate
role as a "symbol of differences":

As she [Kate] saw herself, suddenly, he saw her—she would have
been splendid; and with it he felt more what she was thinking of.
Milly's royal ornament had—under pressure now not wholly occult
—taken on the character of a symbol of differences, differences of
which the vision was actually in Kate's face. It might have been
in her face too that, well as she certainly would look in pearls, pearls
were exactly what Merton Densher would never be able to give her.

8. Derrida, "Structure, Sign, and Play," p. 249.

Wasn't *that* the great difference Milly tonight symbolised? She unconsciously represented to Kate, and Kate took it in at every pore, that there was nobody with whom she had less in common than a remarkably handsome girl married to a man unable to make her on any such lines as that the least little present.[9]

The very icons of Milly's symbolism (here her pearls) become meaningful only as interpreted by others. Densher's reflection on Kate's thoughts takes place through the medium of Milly's presence. It is the wordless vision of Milly that reveals to him the distance separating him from Kate and the fulfillment of his love. In the specificity of Densher's interpretation, Milly's full symbolic power is revealed. When Densher speculates "Wasn't *that* the great difference Milly tonight symbolised?" he refers to the fact that "pearls were exactly what Merton Densher would never be able to give her [Kate]." Although it is ironic that Milly's total symbolic power should be reduced to the simple material want of Merton Densher, there is another significance in the figure of the pearls. In contrast to the "temple of love" wherein Kate and Densher hope to consecrate their perfect love, the pearls as icons of perfect spiritual love suggest the impossibility of the consummation of such a vision. The union of the material and spiritual figured in the pearls also reveals a fundamental paradox in the relation between Kate and Densher. Although their love is born in the timeless space surrounding the "temple" and on the lofty, imaginative summit of the garden wall, their love is always brought back to the material and physical. In fact, it is Milly's "smile, the lustre of her pearls, the value of her life, the essence of her wealth" that brings them together again and puts "the reality . . . into their plan" (*WD*, II, 229). It is on the basis of this "reality" that Kate agrees, in the closing line of the chapter, to come to Densher and, by consummating their love physically, to shatter the illusion of any more spiritual communion.

9. James, *The Wings of the Dove*, II, 218–19. Hereafter cited in the text as *WD*.

The specificity of Densher's reading of Milly as "a symbol of differences" should not lead us away from its far wider application to the world of the novel. The conscious distance separating the characters at the end, from Susie's geographical distance in America to the more poignant separation of Kate and Merton and the estrangement of Kate from Maud and family, is succinctly summed up in Kate's last word: " 'We shall never be again as we were!' " The very illusion of social order and personal relations is that they bring about a harmony that would shield man from his fundamental isolation. Yet, built upon the "lies" of "another man's truth," neither society in general nor inter-subjective relations can ever hope to bridge the abyss of human differences.[10]

Milly's ultimate symbolic function is to disclose differences and manifest the ambiguity of human relations. The collapse of the various roles which the characters give Milly reveals that human "wisdom" will never "taper, however tremulously, to a point," as Susie Stringham thinks it must (II, 107). The themes, images, and metaphors that repeatedly relate Milly to the Incarnation ultimately leave us with the immanence of her memory in the world of Lancaster Gate, without the possibility of transcendental revelation. *The Wings of the Dove* reinterprets the Christian myth in a significant manner. Rather than calling forth the image of Christ's Passion to give Milly an authority in this world, the theological echoes call into question all systems of meta-physical order as absolute sources for meaning. Milly's symbolization through the various points of view encircling her in the novel

10. See Joseph Conrad's letter to E. L. Noble, 2 November 1895, as quoted in G. Jean-Aubry, *Joseph Conrad: Life and Letters*, 2 vols. (Garden City, N.Y.: Doubleday, Page and Co., 1927), I, 184: "No man's light is good to any of his fellows. That's my creed from beginning to end. That's my view of life—a view that rejects all formulas, dogmas and principles of other people's making. These are only a web of il-lusions. We are too varied. Another man's truth is only a dismal lie to me."

does not lead to a sacred fount of origins, but into the ambiguity and mystery of consciousness itself.

The appearance of Milly Theale in Book Three emphasizes the rejection of any external or transcendental source for order. From a precarious perch on an Alpine ledge Milly contemplates the alternatives of being in time and annihilation. When Susie Stringham finds Milly hovering over the abyss, she is at first frightened that Milly has "a horrible hidden obsession" to leap. She soon recognizes, however, that Milly's sublimity expresses her self-conscious possession and strength: "She was looking down on the kingdoms of the earth, and though indeed that of itself might well go to the brain, it wouldn't be with a view of renouncing them. Was she choosing among them, or did she want them all?" (I, 124). As she quietly withdraws, Susie jots a note on the Tauchnitz volume Milly has left behind: "She had stopped at the point of the path where the Tauchnitz lay, had taken it up and, with the pencil attached to her watchguard, had scrawled a word—*à bientôt!*—across the cover; after which, even under the girl's continued delay, she had measured time without a return of alarm" (125). In one swift, compact gesture Susie brings time and language back, in the same way as the pencil hangs from her watchguard. Milly's choice to live will involve a descent into a realm of time and language, both of which will demand her active interpretation. Written as it is on the cover of the Tauchnitz edition, "*à bientôt!*" speaks for the text as well as for Mrs. Stringham. "Uncut and antiquated," the book suggests Milly's indecision before she descends from the lonely height of the Brünig. Although she has carried with her the ambiguity of language, she has thus far avoided any reading of it, afraid to engage a world that would only reveal to her the tragic condition of her life.

As the "heiress of all the ages," dispossessed of her own private past, Milly becomes a symbol of differences. Just prior to the contemplation on the Brünig, the narrator clarifies Milly's symbolic function in the novel: "She worked—and seemingly quite without design—upon the sympathy, the curiosity, the fancy of her associates, and we shall really ourselves scarce otherwise come closer to her than by feeling their impression and sharing, if need be, their confusion" (I, 116). The passage foreshadows James's own remarks in the Preface to the novel and as such constitutes the novel's own critique of its internal movement. It is precisely in "the sympathy, the curiosity, the fancy" she evokes in her associates that Milly is great: "She reduced them, Mrs. Stringham would have said, reduced them to a consenting bewilderment; which was precisely, for that good lady, on a last analysis, what was most in harmony with her greatness. She exceeded, escaped measure, was surprising only because *they* were so far from great" (116–17). By attributing these lines to the style of Mrs. Stringham, the narrator demonstrates his own critical dictum. Any approach to Milly, as we circle closer, throws us by a kind of centrifugal force out toward all that which surrounds her.

Milly begins with everything, as Mrs. Stringham, Kate, and Aunt Maud remind her throughout the novel. Yet it is her "possession" of "all the kingdoms of the earth" that makes her own personal sense of being so difficult. Her final disappearance is the apotheosis of a triumph that begins with her social success *in absentia* at Maud Manningham's dinner party at Lancaster Gate. From the beginning Susie characterizes Milly as "the girl with the background, the girl with the crown of old gold and the mourning that was not as the mourning of Boston" (109). Yet Milly's background is the "general shipwreck" of her family and the reduction of her legacy to a material fortune. The crown she wears is one that Susie has laboriously hammered and beaten in her own romantic imagination. Milly has no past to which she can appeal; all her friends are "of recent making" (105). When she descends from the alpine heights she truly has "all the world before her."

Milly is the innocent heiress of her New York heritage. In *The*

American Scene New York stands for the vast complexity of a swarming, haggling population that leveled the differences creating discrimination, taste, and value. Milly's freedom is in part related to this modernity, and her youthful potentiality needs the forms and values of European history and tradition. Yet the "boundless freedom" that drives her "restlessly" through Europe inevitably leads to her awareness of the "abyss" and the silence that her own particular fate promises. Like all the illusions of freedom in James's fiction, from Roderick Hudson's and Isabel Archer's to Maggie Verver's, Milly's possibilities for life are as ephemeral as "the wind in the desert" (110). Although Densher repeatedly characterizes Milly as "the little American Girl," the problem of her existence goes far beyond the simple cultural implications of the American in quest of a history.

The social world of London into which Milly descends is in the throes of radical upheaval. Europe and America no longer express the clear separation of worlds so fundamental to James's earlier international themes. The tendency of America has become the growing force in Europe as well. The "monstrous" leveling of history and tradition James found in turn-of-the-century America rears its head in the midst of a London that had formerly called forth romantic images. Social institutions, mores, and relations are no longer vital springs for human behavior in industrial and financial London. The economics of relationships have been reduced to the pure quantity of their yield. Maud Lowder, the "Britannia of the Market Place," sees social order and historical value as items to be entered in a ledger, sums to be subtracted, added, and balanced. The new England, ruled over by "the false gods of her taste and false notes of her talk," demonstrates the effects of modern capitalism. Maud's immensity is that of London itself, increasingly ahistorical and unimaginative: "Mrs. Lowder *was* London, *was* life—the roar of the siege and the thick of the fray" (32). In the society of Lancaster Gate, manners are simply appropriated to mask a primitive rapacity, they are not the graceful expression of an internally ordered system of relations. The space of Maud's "tall, rich, heavy house" serves to ensnare visitors rather than invite them. This Britannia is "unscrupulous and immoral," and she is not "afraid to lie" (31).

Money takes the place of traditions or the accumulated heritages and values of families as the organizing principle for social relations. Kate Croy's relation to her Aunt Maud depends upon her acceptance of a "great" and therefore "rich" suitor. Indeed, Maud cuts all social ties with Kate's sister Marian, because she has married "poorly." The cheques Maud sends to Marian on her marriage and on the funeral of her husband, Mr. Condrip, demonstrate how money carries an absolute power of acceptance or rejection. Yet, if *The Wings of the Dove* seems "all about money," it is more vitally concerned with "what money can make of life" in terms of social relations.[11] In a vital social order money simply stands for the possibilities of its use and application, but in the world of Lancaster Gate money is a value in itself. Milly's fortune represents a freedom she ultimately will use to create and preserve life and love, but Aunt Maud's gold never transcends the artistry of its own stamped image.

Aunt Maud is attempting to buy a history, much as the American collector goes to Europe to borrow a tradition. Maud's concept of history is as limited as her moral vision. Lord Mark is simply a name—literally a "mark"—a title to be worked into her peculiar design. In her initiation into this alien world, Milly learns from Lord Mark the nature of the modernity that levels differences and denies vital social relations:

He explained, for that matter—or at least he hinted—that there was no such thing to-day in London as saying where any one was. Everyone was everywhere—nobody was anywhere. He should be put to it—yes, frankly—to give a name of any sort or kind to their hostess's "set." *Was* it a set at all, or wasn't it, and were there not really no such things as sets in the place any more? —Was there

11. Millicent Bell, "The Dream of Being Possessed and Possessing: Henry James's *The Wings of the Dove*," p. 97.

any thing but the groping and pawing, that of the vague billows of some great greasy sea in mid-Channel, of masses of bewildered people trying to "get" they didn't know what or where?   [I, 150]

Like the vast collection of furniture in the rooms of Lancaster Gate, massive and artless in their arrangement, the tradition Maud devours is reduced to a tedious sameness, a linear array or show of the things in themselves. Like the subject of Pound's "Portrait d'une femme," Aunt Maud is a kind of Sargasso Sea of what Mrs. Stringham terms her "accumulated contents—a packed mass . . . of curious detail" (169). She aptly represents the modern tendency in the size of her surface as a substitution for an inner depth and quality. For Milly she is "English and distinct and positive, with almost no inward but with the finest outward resonance" (168).

It is in Aunt Maud's social cage that Kate Croy finds herself at the beginning of the novel. In a world where "everyone," as Milly remarks, seems "to think tremendously of money", relations reveal positions, not viable personalities (195). Kate's immobility in the opening chapter suggests a vast energy held in check by the tensions of her social and familial conditions. Possessed by everyone, she has nothing of her own, and the future promises neither escape nor relief: "She waited, Kate Croy, for her father to come in, but he kept her unconscionably, and there were moments at which she showed herself, in the glass over the mantel, a face positively pale with the irritation that had brought her to the point of going away without sight of him" (3). The very syntax of the sentence imprisons her, parenthetically naming and defining her: "Kate Croy" and "a face positively pale." The father for whom she waits is a cheap confidence man, whose "vulgar little room" evokes the taste of "the faint flat emanation of things, the failure of fortune and of honour" (3–4). Her visit is a futile attempt to find some vital source of identity and meaning as an escape from her imprisonment at Lancaster Gate. Chirk Street, however, reflects only the failure of her family feeling. Milly's lost past gives her at least freedom, but Kate must constantly confront the living fragments of her heritage, heaped in the back streets of Lexham Gardens or wearily tending a bawling brood in Chelsea. At the heart of this general wreck, Lionel Croy dramatizes the lies on which her family name rests: "This was the weariness of every fresh meeting; he dealt out lies as he might the cards from the greasy old pack for the game of diplomacy to which you were to sit down with him" (7). It is the absence of truth (rather than the presence of falsehood), the loss of meaning and relation, that Kate feels so poignantly in the novel's opening chapter.[12]

Willing to sacrifice everything for her family, Kate realizes that for her father and sister she is simply "chalk-marked for auction" and valuable only insofar as she "pays." Family feelings have grown "stale" and empty, and she finds that her only inheritance is her name: "It was the name, above all, she would take in hand—the precious name she so liked and that, in spite of the harm her wretched father had done it, wasn't yet past praying for. She loved it in fact the more tenderly for that bleeding wound" (6). She is determined to transform that name from a mere emblem into a meaningful quantity. She is in quest of a fount for order and value that will revive her own history and provide her with an independent relation to the world:

Her father's life, her sister's, her own, that of her two lost brothers —the whole history of the house had the effect of some fine florid voluminous phrase, say even a musical, that dropped first into words and notes without sense and then, hanging unfinished, into no words nor any notes at all. Why should a set of people have been put in motion, on such a scale and with such an air of being equipped for a profitable journey, only to break down with-

12. Lionel Croy's name suggests that at the heart of Kate's family are a devouring force and potential violence. As Laurence Holland has pointed out in *The Expense of Vision*, p. 315: "Croy, in a dialect of the penny-pinching Scots, means the legal penalty paid, whether in goods or cash, for murder."

out an accident, to stretch themselves in the wayside dust without reason? [4]

Her constant demand for reasons, explanations, and meanings informs the driving will of Kate Croy: "She hadn't given up yet, and the broken sentence, if she was the last word, *would* end with a sort of meaning" (6). Kate Croy longs to act in a salvatory manner. She desires to save the intention of that family phrase from the silence and meaninglessness that threaten it. By making for herself a history and a future she hopes to complete that meaning in the peculiar art of her final plan.

Significantly, Milly repeatedly expresses her desire simply "to live" and "to keep everything" in her love for the very taste of life. Kate Croy lives only to complete her meaning, in quest of an impossible utopia. Her envisioned marriage to Merton Densher expresses exactly such an intention, and it is their mutual pledge of love that makes any united action possible. From their very first meeting, their love is an escape from the world around them. Their detachment from that "party given at a 'gallery' hired by a hostess who fished with big nets" is described in the romantic imagery of Kate's aspiring imagination:

She had observed a ladder against a garden wall and had trusted herself so to climb it as to be able to see over into the probable garden on the other side. On reaching the top she had found herself face to face with a gentleman engaged in a like calculation at the same moment, and the two enquirers had remained confronted on their ladders. The great point was that for the rest of that evening they had been perched—they had not climbed down; and indeed during the time that followed Kate at least had had the perched feeling—*it was as if she were there aloft without a retreat.* [53; italics mine]

Unable to escape from her family, Kate is left only with the vertical thrust of her own fantasy. Romance and youth make the first meeting of the couple appear to be a complete, immediate communion. Their love and passion keep them "perched" in their own remote world for a much longer time than the remainder of the evening. Their private engagement constitutes a sacred space, an unfallen garden of innocence: "They had accepted their acquaintance as too short for an engagement, but they had treated it as long enough for almost anything else, and *marriage was somehow before them like a temple without an avenue. They belonged to the temple and they met in the grounds:* they were in the stage at which the grounds in general offered much scattered refreshment" (59; italics mine). In place of Kate's family history and Densher's own scattered past, the temple becomes a principle of unity and order. It defines in its own language their intention and action, their love and honor.

Their system for order and meaning, however, in its effects resembles Aunt Maud's. Their temple is built at the expense of others. In Conrad's view, to live you must " 'to the destructive element submit yourself, and with the exertions of your hands and feet in the water make the deep, deep sea keep you up.' "[13] A similar recognition informs Milly's descent into the swirling sea of Maud Lowder's London. Yet Densher and Kate, like the young Stephen Dedalus, are "hydrophobes" and their fear of drowning drives them back to an insistent faith in their own illusions. In the text of the novel, the temple of love magically appears as if in response to their passionate decree, like Kubla Khan's sacred pleasure dome. To transcend the confines and limitations of the world is always a kind of death. The created space of their garden remains unrelated to life and human discourse. Kate and Merton appear to suffer from the same conflict of determinism and free will that plagued Adam and Eve. Unlike Eden, however, their closed world offers only an illusory freedom from time's constraints. As Milly's final bequest reveals, Kate's and Merton's greatest act of deceit is toward themselves. Living in hopes of fulfilling their dream for the future, they twist and distort their own lives in pursuit of an impossible desire.

13. Joseph Conrad, *Lord Jim,* p. 214.

In the world of the novel, everyone is to a greater or lesser degree an artist, transforming individual impressions into systems of value. One of the richest sources of reference for the characters in *The Wings of the Dove* is the world of the arts. Art is viewed by most of them as something to be possessed—a glittering, jeweled object—rather than as an activity and process. Maud and Kate strive to replace the ambiguity of the present with the truth and fulfilled meaning their designs and plans imply. It is the art of a sleight-of-hand *artiste*, who wants to substitute her own quantity for what is given. Both Maud and Kate appear to transform the social scene, when in fact they are only replacing its confusion with the more desirable orders of their own fictions. Their artistry is not a means for them to engage more directly the reality of their social situations, but merely a reflection of their selfishness.

Milly's social acceptance and success in London depend upon her role as an element in the various schemes and plots of these *artistes*. As Milly gradually learns the special language of this closed world from the Lord Mark and Kate, she discovers that everyone is either the "worker" or the "worked" (I, 179). To live in such a world, one must eventually " 'pay through the nose,' " in Kate's explicit phrase. When Milly visits Matcham, she finds her presence crucial to the social drama, and she begins to realize how much she is controlled and handled by others. "The great historic house" suggests an "almost extravagantly grand Watteau-composition," and she sees herself a figure in another's picture (208). Even the name "Matcham" emphasizes the artificial arrangement of relations involved in this social drama. The day is ironically "a high-water mark of the imagination" for Milly. Her consciousness blossoms with the shock of recognizing the high cost involved in submitting herself to social games.

Milly sees her true function in this world when she views the Bronzino portrait. During their circuitous approach to the painting, Lord Mark implores, " 'Do let a fellow who isn't a fool take care of you a little' " (220). Milly suddenly recognizes that Lord Mark, Kate Croy, and Maud Lowder all want to take care of her in an extraordinary manner, as if she were a garden to be tended or a work of art to be preserved. For Lord Mark *Milly* is the "image of the wonderful Bronzino," once again demonstrating how the art of this world provides the primary frame of reference (217). In such a reversal, art is not an expressive form shaped from the impressions of life, but a determining system imposed on the ambiguity of experience.

Although the painting provides Lord Mark with a simple image to describe Milly, for Milly herself it is "the mysterious portrait" viewed through the mist of her tears:

Perhaps it was her tears that made it just then so strange and fair—as wonderful as he had said: the face of a young woman, all splendidly drawn, down to the hands, and splendidly dressed; a face almost livid in hue, yet handsome in sadness and crowned with a mass of hair, rolled back and high, that must, before fading with time, have had a family resemblance to her own. The lady in question, at all events, with her slightly Michael-angelesque squareness, her eyes of other days, her full lips, her long neck, her recorded jewels, her brocaded and wasted reds, was a very great personage—only unaccompanied by a joy. And she was dead, dead, dead. Milly recognised her exactly in words that had nothing to do with her. "I shall never be better than this." [220–21]

Lord Mark's identification of Milly with a Renaissance noblewoman may be taken as an attempt to wed his private desire to the needs of his aristocratic position. When he refers to the painting he really means its subject, the historical woman. Milly recognizes the absence of joy inherent in the work, literally reflected in the late Renaissance mannerist style ("Michael-angelesque squareness").

Like all Milly's pronouncements, " 'I shall never be better than this' " is subject to various interpretations. Lord Mark thinks she is referring to the historical woman, but "he hadn't understood." On one hand, Milly compares her own condition within the frame of Matcham and Maud Lowder's London to the deathly art of the portrait. On the other hand, she refers to the beauty and wonder of her success—"the pink dawn of an apotheosis"—which surround her at the moment (220). Both possibilities are enclosed by the intensity of her consciousness in the act of recognizing and feeling her private predicament. Never will her life be more intense or highly charged than in that moment when she realizes the expense of its loss.

Like the Veronese painting that Mrs. Stringham composes in Venice, the Bronzino is an important image for Milly's translation into a symbolic presence. Miriam Allott has identified the painting with convincing accuracy as Bronzino's "Lucrezia Panciatichi," painted between 1532 and 1540.[14] In that painting the subject sits rigidly facing the spectator, dressed in stiff red brocade. She wears a rope of pearls around her neck with a jeweled pendant and a longer chain, on the links of which is carved the motto AMOUR DURE SANS FIN. Her long, stiff hands contribute to the deathly quality of the painting. The right hand rests on an illuminated book, the text framed by a decorative border. Around her waist is another gold chain, similar to the band framing her head. The painting fades into a background of neutral brown, barely revealing a niche that frames her torso.[15] Her blonde hair is braided and parted to form a kind of stiff corona around her elongated head.

The motto she wears is an ironic coda for the theme of the novel itself, but many more details are revealing in relation to Milly. The chains, necklaces, and jewels—manifest symbols of the Renaissance nobility's wealth—dramatize how Milly both "wears" her fortune for this society and is at the same time tied and chained by such riches. Both in the open illuminated text and the carved motto, language is associated with art and the necessary interpretation mirrored in the resting hand. The expression of the subject and her glowing paleness reflect a spiritual

14. Miriam Allott, "The Bronzino Portrait in Henry James's *The Wings of the Dove*," pp. 23–5.
15. Arthur McComb, *Agnolo Bronzino*, p. 60.

denial of her material accoutrements. As Viola Hopkins Winner
has noted, the painting expresses "a general characteristic of the
mannerists, who, in reaction to the High Renaissance celebration
of the beauty and vigor of the human body, expressed in their
works the spiritual unease, a lack of faith in mankind and matter."[16] The elongated distortion of the figure reveals a movement
toward an ecstatic peace beyond the confining limits of the
world. The red dress, purple sleeves, and jewelry conflict with
the spirituality of her intensely conscious and intellectual expression.

An interesting comparison may be made between this portrait
and Bronzino's "Panciatichi Madonna," painted for the same
family between 1532 and 1535. It hangs in the Uffizi where
James probably saw the "Lucrezia Panciatichi." It is a painting
of the Holy Family, with John kissing the Christ child in the
foreground, as the Virgin and Joseph adoringly look on. The
Madonna is turned three-quarters profile, looking down from
her height on the Child, but there is still a striking similarity in
her features and figure to Lucrezia Panciatichi. The angular
features and hands, the elongated head and body parallel those
of the portrait. The Virgin is also dressed in red with a white
breast cloth, but her dress is a filmy tunic in muted red. Her
body is in motion, leaning to her left, her head turned, and her
eyes clearly in the act of looking, in contrast to Lucrezia's distant
stare. The Madonna's hair is also blonde and parted in the
middle, but it ripples around the sides of her head, a stray wisp
trailing over her right shoulder, in contrast to Lucrezia's braided
and set hair. The jewels and chains are gone, with the exception
of a single jeweled pin where her tunic comes to a point. The
chain at the waist has been replaced by a loose tie sash. In her
left hand the Madonna holds a *closed* book and there are scattered scrolls below the Christ child in the center bottom foreground.

16. Viola Winner, *Henry James and the Visual Arts*, p. 83.

The entire composition of the "Panciatichi Madonna" dramatically expresses in form and color the spiritual love to which Lucrezia Panciatichi aspires. The motto on Lucrezia's necklace and the text in her hand have been replaced by the presence of the Word itself in the incarnation of Christ. The painting is the closest Bronzino ever comes to expressing a vital spiritual love. The relation of these two paintings, whether or not James himself made the comparison, illustrates the problem of Milly's life and death. To live in the perpetual "pink dawn of an apotheosis" is to die to the world of time and change—either physically or in the manner of Matcham's social art. To live with the consciousness of one's own mortality, as Lucrezia Panciatichi does, is to yearn for a transcendent beauty. In a world where transcendence is simply the abyss that Milly confronts in the Alps, the vision of love and grace in the "Panciatichi Madonna" requires a self-conscious act of the creative imagination. It is from this point on that Milly studies "the dove-like," assuming roles and masks, and living in the "as if" of an other's vision and image of her.[17] Only in this manner may she assume her own vital role as artist of the beautiful. Milly's "incarnation" is not divine; it is the sacrificial diffusion of herself as a disembodied presence in the art of her symbolism.

As the narrator of *The Sacred Fount* complains, art cannot save, it can only preserve; Milly's sacrifice preserves what he terms the "precious sense of their loss, their disintegration, and their doom" (*SF*, 273). Kate and Densher do not betray the private principles on which Milly has founded both her life and her death. What they plan to take from her is precisely what she is prepared to give as her final sacrifice. The passionate desire for love expresses Milly's need to live in an other as an escape from the perpetual consciousness of her mortality and decay. It is the memory of her that possesses Merton, Kate, Susie, Maud,

17. See Holland, *Expense of Vision*, p. 302: "In Milly's *acting as if* and in the patterns of her action are the manner which yields the appearance, at least, if not the very image of Milly herself."

and Sir Luke Strett at the end. When she remarks to Kate: " 'I think I could die without its being noticed,' " she is expressing more than simply her stoic resignation in Venice (*WD*, I, 228). Her physical absence is noticed only insofar as she persists in the minds of others, in the consciousness of time and death that she has brought forth. Like the Bronzino portrait, Milly as symbol is brought to life only in the recognition Kate's memory of her evokes: " 'We shall never be again as we were!' "

It is in order to live, both physically and psychologically, that Milly leaves the artificial world of London and assumes her role as the princess of the Palazzo Leporelli. For the little American girl in quest of a past, Venice is a "vast museum" and "a modern curiosity shop." In contrast to the ascendant mercantilism of modern London, the great Renaissance republic of trade and commerce is now in decline. Whereas the language of Lancaster Gate is contrived and deceptive, the squares of Venice resound with the easy dialogue of the natives. As James wrote in *Italian Hours:* "Their delightful garrulous language helps to make Venetian life a long *conversazione*. This language, with its soft elisions, its odd transpositions, its kindly contempt for consonants and other disagreeables, has in it something peculiarly human and accommodating."[18] Their language and the variety of their dialect have the grace of centuries, the depth of linguistic change and adaptation. This is in direct contrast to the guttural and toneless conversation James found so characteristic of the modern glare in America. Venice as a city in decay offers a kind of openess and freedom impossible in New York or London. The Piazza San Marco is "a great social saloon, a smooth-floored, blue-roofed chamber of amenity, favourable to talk" and "the drawing-room of Europe" (*WD*, II, 189, 261). Its milieu allows Milly a certain free play, an imaginative range beyond the rigid systems of Lancaster Gate.

Despite the pleasant summer atmosphere, Venice in the novel

18. James, "Venice" (1882), in *Italian Hours*, pp. 7, 16, 22. Cited as *IH* throughout the notes.

evokes all its more familiar associations. "Venetian life, in the large old sense, has long since come to an end, and the essential present character of the most melancholy of cities resides simply in its being the most beautiful of tombs," James wrote in 1892.[19] The very style and tone of the city depend upon its decay; the melancholy resonance of its loss becomes the very note of its distinction. As a society in which Eastern and Western cultures meet and mingle, Venice is the perfect setting for Milly's incarnation as "a symbol of differences." As the city of death, it is the appropriate backdrop for Milly's disappearance.

The shift of the action from London to Venice reflects a significant change in authority in the novel. Milly makes herself at home in the Palazzo Leporelli, appropriating its history and beauty for her own role as princess and dove. In Venice Milly becomes the artist of her own composition. Like the Jamesian novelist, she becomes increasingly vague and disembodied until she is finally present only through the interpretative consciousness of others. In her last days she begins to sacrifice herself for the larger life of her creation. Before the Bronzino, Milly had said to Lord Mark, " 'One never knows one's self' " (I, 222). Milly's ontological insecurity is resolved ultimately in the succession of masks and roles she assumes.

The "complete rupture" between poet and man that James saw in Shakespeare is manifest in Milly's assumed role as artist of her own Venetian painting. Writing about *The Tempest*, James wonders:

The man himself, in the Plays, we directly touch, to my consciousness, positively nowhere; we are dealing too perpetually with the artist, the monster and magician of a thousand masks, not one of which we feel him drop long enough to gratify with the breath of an interval that strained attention in us which would be yet, so quickened, ready to become deeper still. . . . The man everywhere, in Shakespeare's work, is so effectually locked up and imprisoned in the artist that we but hover at the base of thick walls for a sense

19. "The Grand Canal" (1892), *IH*, p. 44.

of him; while, in addition, the artist is so steeped in the abysmal objectivity of his characters and situations that the great billows of the medium itself play with him, to our vision, very much as, over a ship's side, in certain waters, we catch, through transparent tides, the flash of strange sea-creatures.[20]

Shakespeare's very identity for the critical eye is woven into the flow of the poet's language. He is "nowhere" but "everywhere" hidden in "the figured tapestry, the long arras" of the pattern and design he has created.[21] In a similar fashion, Milly fulfills Sir Luke Strett's command "to live"—in that disappearance which implicates all the characters, in their interpretation of her life and death. Milly remains hidden in her own embroidery, for to be is to do, and the function of consciousness demands such a creative dispersal.

Milly's climactic appearance in the novel is her incarnation as "a symbol of differences," placing all the characters in a new relation to the expanding frame of her composition. When Densher arrives at Milly's dinner party, Mrs. Stringham acts as a kind of interpreter. She sums up the splendor of the party by comparing it to one of Paolo Veronese's great crowded canvases: " 'It's a Veronese picture, as near as can be—with me as the inevitable dwarf, the small blackamoor, put into a corner of the foreground for effect' " (*WD*, II, 206). In his brilliant analysis of this chapter, Laurence Holland has related Milly's dinner party to two characteristic paintings by Veronese: "The Supper in the House of Levi" and "The Marriage Feast at Cana."[22] Veronese, the last of the great painters of the Venetian school, betrays a decadent treatment of scriptural subjects in his enormous canvases, filled with historical figures, dwarfs, and other secular elements. His trial by the Inquisition was caused by just such an overly secular treatment of divine themes.

In *Italian Hours* James contrasts Veronese's "Marriage Feast

20. James, *"The Tempest,"* in *Selected Literary Criticism*, p. 300.
21. Ibid., p. 310.
22. Holland, *Expense of Vision*, pp. 307 ff.

at Cana" with Tintoretto's "Marriage of Cana." He contrasts the "absence of a total character" in the "scattered variety and brilliancy" of Veronese with the "poignant, almost startling completeness of Tintoret's illustration of the theme at the Salute Church." James finds that Tintoretto resolves "the eternal problem of the conflict between idealism and realism. . . . In his genius the problem is practically solved, the alternatives are so harmoniously interfused that I defy the keenest critic to say where one begins and the other ends. The homeliest prose melts into the most ethereal poetry—the literal and the imaginative fairly confound their identity."[23] Milly's dinner party proceeds without her, without the divine centrality of Christ who presides over the two feast pictures of Veronese. More poignantly than Veronese's, James's composition assumes the "scattered variety and brilliancy" of a society without a central authority, without the presence of the host. Densher is " 'in the picture,' " as the young man who " 'holds up his head and the wine-cup' " for the sanctifying communion of the feast, but he recognizes that "the Veronese painting . . . was not quite constituted" (*WD*, II, 207, 213). Neither Milly nor Sir Luke Strett, the doctor of her soul, appears until the revels after dinner, refusing the communion of the feast intended to consecrate this new "court life." In the very incompleteness of the scene James captures the crowded human image that Veronese evokes.

Milly's descent into the society that has feasted in her absence, in a sense feasting *on* her absence, completes the painting. It is not Milly who descends but her symbolic power, which assumes its central position in her composition. Her change of dress from the familiar black to the dove's white dramatizes the shift in roles. No longer mourning, she becomes the source of this society's vitality: "Milly, let loose among them in a wonderful white dress, brought them somehow into relation with something that made them more finely genial" (213). Bringing the Veronese painting

23. "Venice: an Early Impression" (1872), *IH*, pp. 80, 79.

into a final harmony of realism and idealism, Milly's symbolic presence echoes the "most ethereal poetry" of Tintoretto in the "embodied poetry" Densher reads into her every aspect (217). The entire tone and style of the scene resolve in a "kind of beatific mildness," reflecting Milly's "supreme idea, an inspiration which was half her nerves and half an inevitable harmony" (213, 214). In the bright inward-darting moment of Milly's revealing art, the "value of her presence" is embodied in her new difference as "younger, fairer." Densher sees her as if for the first time.

It is in the relations and differences constituted in this particular picture that Densher reads for himself the significance of Milly as dove. Whereas Kate is "under the impression of that element of wealth" in Milly "which was a power," Densher reads Milly as dove as a sign of the covering protection of her wings: "It even came to him dimly that such wings could in a given case—*had*, truly, in the case with which he was concerned— spread themselves for protection. Hadn't they, for that matter, lately taken an inordinate reach, and weren't Kate and Mrs. Lowder, weren't Susan Shepherd and he, wasn't *he* in particular, nestling under them to a greater increase of immediate ease?" (II, 218). It is, however, in her appearance that Kate by comparison looks small to Densher. By the very power of her descent, Milly discloses to Densher the distance separating him from Kate and her dreams of wealth and power.

The final meaning of Milly's protection remains ambiguous, open to the various interpretations of the characters. Seen through "a brighter blur in the general light," Milly's distance from Kate and Densher emphasizes the ambiguity of the picture as a whole. In Veronese's "Marriage Feast of Cana" Christ, his halo vaguely traced, sits in the center of the painting behind a group of musicians in the immediate central foreground. The four musicians are portraits of the Venetian painters Tintoretto, Titian, Jacopo Bassano, and Veronese himself. They surround a table, in the center of which is an hourglass, probably a musical timer. What the mediation of these artists serves in our apprehension of the central figure of Christ is precisely analogous to our oblique understanding of Milly as dove. Her incarnation does not reveal divine wisdom and truth, it rather places the world around her in a conscious relation. "Meaning" can be read only through the mediating form of art and thus always remains ambiguous, in part artificial or contrived. The musicians' hourglass reveals that Christ's divinity can be known only through the shifting medium of human time and in terms of our limited discourse. Like Veronese's Christ, James's dove demands interpretation in the mediating "readings" of Kate, Merton, Susie, and Maud as the final meaning of her immanence.

Milly's descent as the dove is final, her fluttering wings remain to "cover" the society that has sought to appropriate her. What the dove brings is an awareness of the limitations of human language and the perpetual need for interpretation in a world of time. Milly dies when she totally diffuses herself in this creative effort. Unlike Christ, she does not promise any transcendental salvation, but rather bequeaths her "fortune" as the consciousness of differences. It is a new kind of Christmas on which Densher receives Milly's letter and love. Many critics have suggested that Densher is redeemed by Milly's grace, while Kate is damned to bear the burden of their lies. He is saved only as he becomes aware of his present, compelled to struggle with the mystery of his being and the lies of his life. Milly may have flown to a new "temple of love" around which Densher now circles, but her presence there reveals the impossibility of his entrance.

As a critique of language and its aesthetic form, *The Wings of the Dove* deals with two conceptions of the relation between our discourse and reality. W. M. Urban has suggested that there can be no immediate correlation of language and reality, no final transparency of the sign that will reveal its total meaning: "Language is *not* 'moulded on reality,' to use Bergson's terms. It is either a veil that has been woven by practice between us and reality, and which must be torn away, or else it is a distortion of

reality which must be corrected by the invention of other instruments and symbolisms."[24] The art of Kate Croy or Maud Lowder, which seeks to transform complex realities into simple meanings, expresses a yearning for a world beyond the perpetual
demands of definition. In a world of time and consciousness such
a utopian vision is a lie, a rending of the delicate embroidery
that successively gives color and form to life. Milly's art and that
of *The Wings of the Dove* follow the creative and vital impulse
to incarnate meaning in the repeated interpretations called forth
by their forms and symbolisms.

In a prophetic moment of insight Milly defines her life and
death to Susan Stringham: " 'Since I've lived all these years as
if I were dead, I shall die, no doubt, as if I were alive—which
will happen to be as you want me. So, you see,' she wound up,
'you'll never really know where I am. Except indeed when I'm
gone; and then you'll only know where I'm not' " (*WD*, I, 199–
200). Milly's symbolic absence places her in the stream of life
and consciousness itself. She becomes the symbol of the mystery
at the heart of our language and our art. All the characters at
the end are condemned to circle about this mysterious meaning
now within their own being. Yet in the very circling of their
approaches and withdrawals the presence of that meaning
blossoms forth in the truth of Milly's sacrifice.

" 'She died for you then that you might understand her,' "
Kate tells Densher in the final moment of the novel. " 'From that
hour you *did*,' " and in Kate's words we recognize that we have
entered a new consciousness of time, a new awareness of the
fullness of the present (II, 403). Kate and Densher have left
the garden of their temple and live in the light of that "symbol
of differences." " 'I'll marry you, mind you, in an hour,' " Densher lies. Yet within an hour the "you" that Densher would have
has vanished. Kate's "headshake was now the end," and in her
recognition she completes the unfinished sentence of her history:
" 'We shall never be again as we were!' " (405).

24. W. M. Urban, *Language and Reality*, p. 51.

In Hawthorne's *The Marble Faun* the sculptor Kenyon finds the disappearance of Hilda dramatically expressed in the flight of the doves she had so patiently tended, as he haunts her tower for some trace of her. He reads their departure as symbolic of his own troubled state. The last lingering dove is the final "clew," which poses a question as unanswerable for Kenyon as Milly's letter is for Merton Densher: "Only a single dove remained and brooded drearily beneath the shrine. The flock that had departed were like the many hopes that had vanished from Kenyon's heart; the one that still lingered, and looked so wretched—was it a Hope, or already a Despair?"[25] Hilda, of course, reappears and Kenyon finds his answer in their own land and in the light of their domestic fireside. Hilda descends from her old tower to be freed by Kenyon's loving embrace, but Milly has flown her tower on the ascending wings of her dove. For Densher the question remains poignant and insistent—itself the significant end. In the modern world of Lancaster Gate, Milly's transformation must remain incomplete.

25. Hawthorne, *The Marble Faun*, II, 286.

7   The Deceptive Symmetry of Art in *The Golden Bowl*

> There it was—her picture. Yes, with all its greens and blues, its lines running up and across, its attempt at something. It would be hung in the attics, she thought; it would be destroyed. But what did that matter? she asked herself, taking up her brush again. She looked at the steps; they were empty; she looked at the canvas; it was blurred. With a sudden intensity, as if she saw it clear for a second, she drew a line there, in the centre. It was done; it was finished. Yes, she thought, laying down her brush in extreme fatigue, I have had my vision.
> —Virginia Woolf, *To the Lighthouse,* 1927*

As expressions of the symbolic imagination of James's later phase, *The Wings of the Dove* and *The Golden Bowl* have more affinity with the unfinished *Ivory Tower* than with *The Ambassadors.* J. A. Ward has suggested that the grouping of the novels of the Major Phase as a thematic or ideological trilogy "has tended to blur some important formal differences among the three novels."[1] Milly's sacrifice and Maggie's careful plan leave us with a sense of society become conscious of itself, recognizing its own contrived nature and the art that must constantly be exercised to sustain human relations. Lambert Strether sums up his own role as an observer of life: " 'That, you see, is my only logic. Not, out of the whole affair, to have got anything for myself.' "[2] *The Ambassadors* ends primarily in the past tense of

---

1. J. A. Ward, *The Search for Form,* p. 165.
2. James, *The Ambassadors,* II, 326. Hereafter cited in the text as *Amb.*

what might have been had Strether really lived all he could. The lost youth he seeks throughout the novel assumes a radically different form in the figure of Milly as dove and in Maggie Verver's will to power. Strether's late education in Paris may shatter the narrow world of the Woollett consciousness, but it also leads to his personal vision of the fragmentation of all social relations. As with the narrator of *The Sacred Fount*, his knowledge leaves him "altogether nowhere," and his final desire is simply to "get away."

Strether's flight hardly promises even the "illusion of freedom" he so desperately presses Little Bilham to preserve (*Amb.*, I, 218). Our vision of what Strether sees focuses on the hollow modernity of the twentieth century, the absence of history and the loss of discrimination and taste. Madame de Vionnet and Maria Gostrey are the last representatives of a grace and humanity being swept away by the Newsomes and the Pococks. The Chad Newsome whom Strether had fashioned in his imagination ought to have fulfilled a nineteenth-century ideal. Strether's final denial of spiritual paternity is a recognition of Chad's fundamental association with the leveling forces of the modern age. When Maria Gostrey remarks in the last scene of the novel, " 'Marie said to me the other day that she felt him to have the making of an immense man of business,' " Strether may return, " 'There it is. He's the son of his father!' " Maria's " 'But *such* a father!' " clarifies which tradition Chad would fulfill in his "advertising art" (II, 321). In part, Strether's inability to save his ideas of youth reflects the general failure of American idealism.

The future is a blank wall to Strether, the gray wash of the modern age. He goes home to "a great difference," which defines his lack of relation to any social world. Strether struggles half-heartedly to maintain his optimism: " 'Yet I shall see what I can make of it' " (II, 325). Strether's new consciousness of the difference between his past and present, of the violence his transatlantic crossing has done to the continuity of his private history, informs the future he hopes to make. There is a world-weariness in Strether's " 'There will always be something,' " rather than the determined rebellion of the traditional American *isolato* who cries " 'No! in thunder.' " Strether has excluded himself from the complex relations of his Parisian world, and he returns to face the reckoning of Mrs. Newsome's moral accounting and still another social expulsion. In a sense his final renunciations are payments for his knowledge.[3] He virtually pays with his life, condemned to wander between a lost past and an unfathomable future. He is the true prisoner of the modern crisis.

In the end Strether inadvertently succeeds in his original ambassadorial function. His sacrifices finally have value only for himself. He first defined his problem to Maria Gostrey in existential terms: " 'I'm always considering something else; something else, I mean, than the thing of the moment. The obsession of the other thing is the terror' " (I, 19). It is Strether himself who is "other" at the end of the novel. As James wrote in his "Project for *The Ambassadors*": "He must go back as he came —or rather, really so quite other that, in comparison, marrying Miss Gostrey would be almost of the old order. Yes, he goes back other and to other things. We see him on the eve of his departure, with whatever awaits him *là-bas,* and their lingering, ripe separation is the last note."[4] Strether's disconnection is both the success and the failure of his central consciousness in the novel. The freedom he discovers condemns him to wander on the periphery of social relations. Like Michel Foucault's passenger on the *stultifera navis,* Strether becomes the prisoner of his own passage. In Foucault's terms, "The land he will come to is unknown—as is, once he disembarks, the land from which he comes. He has his truth and his homeland only in that fruitless expanse between two countries that cannot belong to him."[5]

3. Holland, *Expense of Vision,* p. 281.
4. James, "Project for *The Ambassadors*," in *The Notebooks,* p. 415.
5. Foucault, *Madness and Civilization,* p. 21.

Formally and philosophically the symbols in *The Wings of the Dove* and *The Golden Bowl* take the place of Strether's consciousness in *The Ambassadors*. In the Prefaces James makes explicit that Milly is to be "known" only through the "successive centers" of the other characters and that the relations in *The Golden Bowl* are to be focused in the juxtaposition of "Book First: The Prince" and "Book Second: The Princess" (*AN*, 296, 301–2; 330). The golden bowl, the wings of the dove, and the ivory tower are the incarnations of the meanings for social relations in the novels. They are wrought by a curious and lost art, whose intricate process demands successive interpretations in order to be unlayered. But the crack in the bowl, the disappearance of the dove, and the incriminating letter locked in the ivory tower deny the possibility of any completed meaning for the worlds of these novels. It is Milly's own imagination that brings the dove into the crowded hall of the Palazzo Leporelli, Maggie's art that gathers together the shattered fragments of the golden bowl, and Graham Fielder's act that fills the empty drawer of Rosanna Gaw's gift, the ivory tower. All three methods of symbolization may be said to reflect the architecture of the Jamesian novel, but they also express the function and relation of those "high intelligences" who are most often James's subjects.

The symbolic imagination of the later novels shines forth in the high mandarin style of the narrative voice. The late Jamesian sentence is the presentation of discrete but related verbal images, which syntactically compose a complex of meaning. This is neither an *accumulation* of descriptive signs nor a *progression* of elements toward a fixed end. James's style is more a layered structure of verbal atoms, framed in the circle of the author's own intentional geometry. The sentence mirrors the wayward and circling approach of consciousness to the source of its own meaning. The focus of interest is the activity of definition, which is the true figure in the carpet. Unlike Eliot's "still point" beyond language and time, James's "sacred fount" blossoms in the midst of language itself, in the very interchange of diverse signs.[6] James's language attempts to encompass the varied perspectives in the House of Fiction, condemned to the incompleteness of its form. In the very grammar of his fiction, James must present the "one seeing more where the other sees less, one seeing black where the other sees white, one seeing big where the other sees small, one seeing coarse where the other sees fine" (*AN*, 46).

James's style reflects the intention of the symbolism in the later novels. The reader is impressed by James's unwillingness to define conclusively a personality, a system of ethics, a social relationship. Each character's choices are weighed carefully by the other characters in the novel. The narrative voice emphasizes the multiple significances of an action and its motivations. Just as every word in James's syntax is qualified by what precedes and follows it, so every character finds himself responsible for and defined by others. Those individuals who dream of a world free from such ambiguity usually withdraw into a narrow self-consciousness. Aunt Maud or Kate Croy struggles to remake the world in her own image, most often dehumanizing others in the process. In their insistence upon positive knowledge, such characters violate the complexity of human relations and the integrity of "another man's truth." James himself refuses to provide answers, and his protean style demands the continuing acts of the reader's

6. T. S. Eliot, "Burnt Norton," in *Four Quartets*, p. 19:
    Words move, music moves
    Only in time; but that which is only living
    Can only die. Words after speech, reach
    Into the silence. Only by the form, the pattern,
    Can words or music reach
    The stillness, as a Chinese jar still
    Moves perpetually in its stillness.   [From *Four Quartets* (Harcourt, Brace) and *Collected Poems 1909–1962* (Faber and Faber). Copyright 1943, 1963 by T. S. Eliot. Reprinted by permission of Harcourt, Brace, Jovanovich, Inc. and Faber and Faber, Ltd.]
To James Eliot's stillness would simply reflect the emptiness of the Bronzino portrait in *Wings of the Dove*. It is "only in time" that the Jamesian symbol ever assumes its form.

interpretation and judgment. At the same time the golden bowl promises a perfect form and the ivory tower a sacred space these symbols reveal the impossibility of fulfilling such hopes in a world of time and change. James's later symbols dramatize the destructive element they appear to hide: the human desire to escape the responsibilities of interpretation. In these symbols James suggests that man, in his longing for the ideal, profanes the fundamental difference on which life is founded. As Milly's response to the Bronzino portrait implies, the desire for perfect form requires the loss of vital human relations. *The Wings of the Dove, The Golden Bowl,* and *The Ivory Tower* are basically concerned with the folly of man's longing to escape time, change, and human limitations. And the explicit symbols of these novels reveal only the silence of the infinite and the ambiguity of man's meanings.

In marriage James finds the confrontation of differences ritualized. Not only is marriage the primal social institution, but it is also a familiar Jamesian metaphor for the relation of consciousness to the world. As Geoffrey Hartman recognizes, "A Jamesian marriage, or an analogous contract, is what principally generates as well as imposes form on consciousness."[7] In its best sense, marriage suggests a form that is flexible and open, capable of growth and adaptation. Whether social or aesthetic, values in James depend upon the form one chooses to understand relations with others. And yet form often threatens to violate the plurality of experience. The struggle to maintain a precarious balance between formal definition and the free play of consciousness is a basic problem for James's characters from Isabel Archer to Maggie Verver.

The Golden Bowl concentrates on the conflicts resulting from the contrived marriages, which are basic to the dramatic action. The novel raises questions not only about the value of highly formalized social institutions, but also about the impact of such

7. Geoffrey Hartman, *Beyond Formalism,* p. 55.

values on individual freedom and social responsibility. James considered entitling the novel "The Marriages," but rejected the idea because he had used the same title for a short story (1891). There is also a hint in the *Notebooks* that James had considered "Mystification" for the title.[8] The ambiguity of the true meaning of marital relations in this novel is of primary importance. Maggie's attempt to preserve social propriety in the marriages is an example of the misuse of imagination and creative power. The lies she attempts to hide and then sustains— symbolized in her effort to put the shattered bowl together again—reflect the destructive and subversive qualities of her art.

The personal difficulties in the novel originate in Adam and Maggie Verver's misinterpretation of the meaning of marriage. They understand it as primarily a social form rather than an intersubjective relation. J. A. Ward sees this blindness as fundamental to their modern American personalities: "To both Maggie and her father, the content of marriage is the same as its form. Paradoxically this fallacy springs not from an exaggeration of the importance of form, but from a total ignorance of form. To the Americans, social forms—all surfaces and appearances— are 'European,' something alien and apart from themselves which they admire and wish to acquire. But their gravest mistake is their notion that form can somehow be possessed, even bought, without its being allowed to interfere with one's life."[9] The desire to acquire a European sense of form in part motivates their purchase of the Prince. Amerigo's sense of isolation in the opening pages of the novel reflects how rigorously the Ververs

8. See the *Notebooks*, pp. 233, 194: "2⁰ *The Marriages* (what a pity I've used that name!): the Father and Daughter, with a husband of the one and the wife of the other entangled in a mutual passion and intrigue." The other reference is more tenuous as a possible title for the novel. In a list of names, James writes: "Bender (American—might do for the Father and daughter in the novel of the *Mystification*—even if written Benda). . . ." According to the editors' footnote, "James may conceivably have referred thus to the theme of *The Golden Bowl*."

9. Ward, *Search for Form,* p. 210.

have dealt only with his public role. They fail to relate to him on the basis of his own personality. Adam Verver is one more figure in a long line of American collectors who believe that art and history may be purchased. As long as Maggie remains her father's daughter, she shares Adam's peculiarly destructive innocence and his moral absolutism.

The mystification in the marriages really involves a conflict of moral perspectives. In conversation with Fanny Assingham, Prince Amerigo contrasts his Old World ethics with the Puritan moral sense of the Ververs. In his attempt to engage the alien and closed world of their romantic idealism, the Prince has an " 'honest fear of being "off" some day, of being wrong, *without* knowing it. That's what I shall always trust you for—to tell me when I am. No—with you people it's a sense. We haven't got it —not as you have!' " (*GB*, I, 30). His fear of unknowingly erring emphasizes how much this American moral sense transcends rational intelligence and depends on an inbred intuition. The Prince finds the lack of this kind of sense in his own national character:

"I should be interested," she presently remarked, "to see some sense *you* don't possess."
Well, he produced one on the spot. "The moral, dear Mrs. Assingham. I mean always as you others consider it. I've of course something that in our poor dear backward old Rome sufficiently passes for it. But it's no more like yours than the tortuous stone staircase— half-ruined into the bargain!—in some castle of our *quattrocento* is like the 'lightning elevator' in one of Mr. Verver's fifteen-storey buildings. Your moral sense works by steam—it sends you up like a rocket. Ours is slow and steep and unlighted, with so many of the steps missing that—well, that it's as short in almost any case, to turn round and come down again." [I, 31]

The Prince is declaring his lack of a moral sense only in relation to the Ververs' judgment, as is made clear in his distinction between the staircase and the elevator. The morality of Adam and Maggie is based on an a priori set of values that defines and encloses the events and accidents of their lives. Despite their occasional Catholicism, they are direct heirs of a Puritan world view. The very idea of supralapsarian election implies a transcendental system of ethics for judging fallen man. Appropriately enough the Puritan conscience is associated with the science and machinery of the age—the impersonal forces dehumanizing society in the name of progress. Like the mechanical determinism of the elevator, Adam's and Maggie's sense of right and wrong propels them upward as if unconsciously. Action and thought are evaluated on the basis of absolute values, and life is edited to fit an ideal vision. On the other hand, Amerigo's morality depends upon the creative and aesthetic act of consciousness, implying the free will of the critical individual. The "tortuous" and "half-ruined" stone staircase of the *quattrocento* castle is not simply a means to an end, but a repeated challenge to the constructing intelligence, which must make a sense every step of the way. The staircase reflects the possibility of value and meaning implicit in James's own idea of tradition and history. In the "slow and steep and unlighted" ascent, the individual needs the torch of his intelligence to light the way, using the past to make a meaningful present.

Adam Verver's failure as both father and patron of the arts indicates the inadequacy of his moral system. In his quest for perfection in all things, he chooses carefully what he will recognize or ignore. He is driven by the singleness of his vision, the ideal that informs his life with meaning and order. He imagines himself at a height, "the apex of which was a platform looking down, if one would, on the kingdoms of the earth and with standing-room for but half a dozen others" (I, 131). Unlike Milly Theale, Adam never chooses to descend into the ambiguity of a world of time and change. His mount becomes the legendary " 'peak in Darien,' " whence he discovers new worlds to rifle and possess: worlds of "Genius, or at least of Taste" (141). Adam's vision has the fervor of a religious creed. His "House of Civilization" is "set down by his hands as a house on a rock—a house from whose open doors and windows, open to grateful, to thirsty millions, the higher, the highest knowledge would shine out to bless the land" (145). Both in his vision and his name he is associated with the Biblical Adam, but in a highly ironic manner. Adam Verver aspires to the simplicity of meaning implied in the Edenic condition. In exile, the fallen Adam finds his vocation as father of a race and originator of historical time. Adam Verver merely collects; he lacks the imaginative powers of a true creator.

Adam Verver is an ironic spiritual father for twentieth-century America. His character is a curious mixture of nineteenth-century idealism and modern economic practicality. He prefigures a similar clash of values in the more meretricious Jay Gatsby, both characters revealing the collapse of old systems of order: "The truth was that Jay Gatsby of West Egg, Long Island, sprang from his Platonic conception of himself. He was a son of God—a phrase which, if it meant anything, means just that—and he must be about his Father's business, the service of a vast, vulgar and meretricious beauty. So he invented just the sort of Jay Gatsby that a seventeen-year-old boy would be likely to invent, and to this conception he was faithful to the end."[10] Like James Gatz's creation, "Great Gatsby," Adam Verver's "Patron of the Arts" is a demigod of his own creation, as blind as the sightless eyes of Dr. T. J. Eckleburg. Adam lives in the autotelic world of his own religion of "perfection at any price" (*GB*, I, 146). Like Gatsby, he distorts all experience to fit his solipsistic world: "*His* real friend, in all the business, was to have been his own mind, with which nobody had put him in relation. He had knocked at the door of that essentially private house, and his call, in truth, had not been immediately answered; so that when, after waiting and coming back, he had at last got in, it was, twirling his hat, as an embarrassed stranger, or, trying his keys, as a thief in the night. He had gained confidence only with time, *but when he had taken real possession of the place it had been never again to come away*" (149; italics mine). Adam's isolation in this inner

10. F. Scott Fitzgerald, *The Great Gatsby*, p. 99.

Eden explains his failure to come into the foreground of the novel's action. His childlike nature is not the innocence of the babe, but the selfishness of his dreams.

Adam's failure as a father is the original flaw in the relations of *The Golden Bowl*. As a potential source for social and personal meaning, Adam's judgment violates the variety of human relations for the sake of his ideal vision. Maggie comes to consciousness on her own terms by profaning the sacred ties of filial devotion. In order to save her father from the knowledge that would corrupt his hermetic system of values, she must cut herself off from his authority. Her awareness that Adam needs to be saved defines her distance from him, explaining why Maggie must become an independent source of will and power. Only when she escapes the narrow vision of her father's religion of perfection may she begin to bear her own responsibility for life. Maggie's education involves the destruction of her past for the chance of her own present. As she recognizes in the final movement of the novel, liberation and capitation are inseparable facts in any revolution (II, 341–2).

Adam Verver's "power of purchase" dominates the first book. His power is his wealth, a force that can effect exchanges but that without high intelligence, can generate no changes. Like Cortez and Alexander, Adam might conquer and despoil kingdoms but knows nothing of ruling them. His proposal to Charlotte parallels his negotiations for Mr. Gutermann-Seuss's tiles. His approval of Prince Amerigo requires the same judgment as that of "the Bernardo Luini he had happened to come to knowledge of at the time he was consenting to the announcement of his daughter's betrothal" (I, 197). The singleness of his vision and judgment is imaged in the "one little glass" from which he tastes life. It is no coincidence that this glass is expressly related to the flawed golden bowl itself: "It was as if he had always carried in his pocket, like a tool of his trade, this receptacle, a little glass cut with a fineness of which the art had long since been lost, and kept in an old morocco case stamped in uneffaceable gilt with the arms of a deposed dynasty" (196)'. The flaw implicit in his vision of perfection controls and encloses the characters in the first book.

Acting as her father's daughter, Maggie has to bring Amerigo and Charlotte intimately together by the very demands of her " 'feverish little sense of justice.' " Her goodness initiates the vicious circle of real relations, which shatters the deathly calm of Adam's order in the closing moments of the first book (396, 395)'. If as Fanny says the " 'forms . . . are two-thirds of conduct,' " without passion and intelligence they are monstrous and empty.[11] The fate pursuing and condemning Amerigo and Charlotte originates in the rigor of Adam's and Maggie's insistence upon social order. True humanity comes only with a recognition of the necessary mutability of social forms. Custom and ritual ought to symbolize the more vital interpersonal relations of individuals. Maggie's determination to save the marriages rather than the people involved causes her to become a moral force of the most destructive sort.

If Amerigo and Charlotte are the "passive victims" of Maggie's and Adam's dehumanizing arrangement, just this passivity is at the heart of their "great betrayal." Amerigo is as hollow as Adam, incapable of acting except in his role as *gentiluomo*. His "perfect manners" and lightly ironic wit are reflex actions, as inbred and automatic as Adam's moral sense. He relies on instinct and even superstition rather than reason and analysis. In most instances the Prince chooses the path of least resistance, submitting himself to the stream of life without a struggle. At first he sees his marriage to Maggie in the light of new possibilities: "What was this so important step he had just taken but the desire for some new history that should, so far as possible, contradict and even if need be flatly dishonour, the old? If what had come to him wouldn't do he must *make* something different" (I, 16). His will to create, however, degenerates into his pathetic

11. Holland, *Expense of Vision,* pp. 356–7.

attempt to recapture the past in the affair with Charlotte. Instead of using the Verver millions to create a new order and identity, Amerigo submits himself to the artifices of such balanced and imposed relations as are involved in the marriages.[12]

In his affair with Charlotte, Amerigo does *not* act in defiance of a paralyzing social world, as if rebelling against Adam's and Maggie's false gods. Their intimacy simply reminds them of what they have lost—a love they were not strong enough to preserve. Like Merton and Kate, Amerigo and Charlotte futilely hope that sexual passion may revive their original sense of romance. When they sacrificed their love for financial reasons, they chose social appearances over personal relations. As Fanny Assingham describes their dilemma to her husband: " 'He *had* to have money—it was a question of life and death. It wouldn't have been a bit amusing, either, to marry him as a pauper—I mean leaving him one. That was what she had—as he had—the reason to see.' " In his own inimitable fashion the Colonel makes the Jamesian pun: " 'And their reason is what you call their romance?' " (71)'. By paying deference to the social gods of taste and form, Amerigo sacrifices his individual will along with Charlotte's love. They begin to accept their social situation as a necessary burden, like the Prince's title.

Charlotte and Amerigo feel victimized by their poverty, and they resign themselves to the power of wealth. They stubbornly refuse to accept any responsibility for their awkward situation in the marriages. Aware of the limitations of the Ververs' sense of propriety, they submit to it for want of any more vital interpretation of their mutual relations. Rather than objecting to the almost unnatural preoccupation of Maggie and Adam with each other, they accept the conditions of their servitude. As the Prince tells Fanny: " 'We're certainly not, with the relation of our

12. Dorothea Krook, *The Ordeal of Consciousness in Henry James*, p. 276, emphasizes how much Amerigo's taste, like his wit and manners, is the reflex of a conditioned public personality. Amerigo lacks the imagination or creative power to make things new.

respective *sposi,* simply formal acquaintances. We're in the same boat' " (267). Charlotte and Amerigo remain, nevertheless, " 'a good deal tied up at the dock, or anchored, if you like, out in the stream' " (270). Although Amerigo relates his own journey into Anglo-American life to the more primordial voyage of Poe's Arthur Gordon Pym, he refuses to seize the helm and begin discoveries of his own.[13] The Prince accepts either an imposed social order or his own private blankness, thus denying his original ambition to *"make* something different" of his life. Although his "illustrious ancestor" gave his name to the New World, the modern Amerigo fails to map or name his world. He remains simply another item in the Ververs' extensive collections.

The hollow form of the marriages suggests the absence of creative effort to change the fixed conventions of an artificial social order. Despite the prevalence of metaphors and images relating to the arts, none of the characters demonstrates much imagination in the first book. Yet, in different ways, all four characters dream of the perfection of form and the completion of meaning reflected in the surface of the golden bowl. Long after Fanny has shattered it, Maggie still yearns for " 'the golden bowl —as it *was* to have been. . . . The bowl with all our happiness in it. The bowl without the crack' " (II, 217). Amerigo, Charlotte, Maggie, and Adam all desire that presence of grace implied in the unbroken bowl of Ecclesiastes: "Remember now thy Creator in the days of thy youth, while the evil days come not . . . Or even the silver cord be loosed, or the golden bowl be broken, or the pitcher be broken at the fountain, or the wheel broken at the cistern" (12:1, 6). In Solomon's warning the breaking of the golden bowl is associated with the disappearance of spiritual immanence for fallen man. In James's novel the golden bowl is broken *from the beginning,* and the absence of the spirit is manifest in the ambiguity of human language and

13. Both Adam and Amerigo are related to the dominant images of exploration and discovery in the novel. See Stephen L. Mooney, "James, Keats, and the Religion of Consciousness," p. 399.

thought. Milly's symbolization in *The Wings of the Dove* fore-shadows the function of the golden bowl as the focal point for relations in this novel. As a symbol of differences, the absence of the dove calls for a new consciousness of time and change; the flawed bowl, shattered on Italian marble, discloses the impossibility of either aesthetic or moral perfection in a fallen world.[14]

The bowl symbolizes both the possibilities and limitations of the creative mind to define and order its world. Amerigo recognizes the flaw in the bowl from the beginning, just as he secretly seems to be conscious of the fiction of all social and historical systems of order. Such an absolute sense of relativity frustrates his inquiring mind, forcing him into a cynical stoicism. The Old World of his Italy may be in ruins, but the society of modern England is inscrutable and chaotic. Just prior to his departure for Gloucester with Charlotte, he faces the failure of his ambition to make a sense of his world: "The enquiring mind, in these present conditions, might, it was true, be more sharply challenged; but the result of its attention and its ingenuity, it had unluckily learned to know, was too often to be confronted with a mere dead wall, a lapse of logic, a confirmed bewilderment. And moreover above all nothing mattered, in the relation of the enclosing scene to his own consciousness, but its very most direct bearings" (I, 354–5). At the heart of the new world Amerigo repeatedly comes up against the "lapse of logic" and the "confirmed bewilderment" he had first imaged in the "great white curtain" at the end of Gordon Pym's voyage.

The blankness of the "mere dead wall" stands for some final, fulfilled meaning, out of time and space. The bowl itself symbolizes the inadequacy of any such teleology. Rather than exploit

14. Holland, *Expense of Vision,* p. 348: "The symbol of the bowl helps govern the novel because the bowl and the act of buying it or possessing it, of breaking it and salvaging it later, inform each other, and the bowl does not stand as a merely referential or imposed symbol but serves as part of a profoundly creative act to constitute a field of form, a formal nexus."

the freedom suggested by the emptiness of the bowl, the characters experience the absence as threatening or terrifying. Fearing the failure of her marriage, Maggie tries to save it by preserving its form. Repeatedly, the characters choose the security of social appearance over the difficulties of personal relations. For Maggie, the impossibility of any perfect form is the destructive element: the flaw in the bowl. Therefore she seeks to mask it, protecting her family from the horror of her vision. As her imagination unfolds in the second book, Maggie uses her new art and power to hide this ugly truth. But her contrivance of relations effects the real collapse of personal relations in the novel. Unlike Milly, Maggie tries to *protect* others from a consciousness of time and change, from man's alien condition in "phantasmagoric life." Drawing back from the discovery of new worlds, Maggie ends by affirming the values of the old order.

The process of Maggie's aesthetic education in the second book is a systematic destruction of the idea of perfection imaged in the bowl without a flaw. In the first chapter Maggie waits for Amerigo to return. She is virtually waiting, like Kate Croy in the opening chapter of *The Wings of the Dove,* in the void between two worlds. Isolated in the space of her own changing consciousness, Maggie begins to fulfill Fanny's earlier prophecy of an awakened imagination: " 'She's like an old woman who has taken to "painting" and who has to lay it on thicker, to carry it off with a greater audacity, with a greater impudence even, the older she grows. . . . I like the idea of Maggie audacious and impudent—learning to be so to gloss things over. She could —she even will, yet, I believe—learn it, for that sacred purpose, consummately, diabolically' " (396–7). Maggie's art does grow diabolical in her struggle to maintain the sacred forms of marriage. The thick texture of Maggie's modern picture is designed not to build up the depth and richness of a new, original meaning, but to hide the blankness at the center of her canvas.

Nevertheless, Maggie's imaginative power is unique in *The Golden Bowl.* Throughout the first book the characters assume their positions in the glass cases of Adam Verver's collection. Amerigo is described variously as a Palladian church, a round and perfect crystal, and the "name" of his illustrious ancestor. Maggie herself is a Vatican or Capitoline antique, a statue of Diana or the Muse off its pedestal, a figure in a worn relief around an ancient vase. Even the Principino is treated like an *objet d'art,* another gimcrack in the cabinets of Eaton Square. Fanny's description of Maggie as a painter, learning "to gloss things over," is one of the few descriptions of the creative process in the first book. The emergence and application of Maggie's artistic abilities are the subject of the second book. Not unlike Kate Croy and Aunt Maud, Maggie's creative powers end in a contrived artistry.

Maggie's imagination blooms in the opening chapters of the second book as if released from some old repression. Like Isabel Archer's fireside contemplation, Maggie's vigil involves the struggle of her own consciousness to assume an independent form and meaning. In the garden of her imagination, Maggie confronts the mystery at the heart of the two arranged marriages:

This situation had been occupying for months and months the very centre of the garden of her life, but it had reared itself there like some strange tall tower of ivory, or perhaps rather some wonderful beautiful but outlandish pagoda, a structure plated with hard bright porcelain, coloured and figured and adorned at the overhanging eaves with silver bells that tinkled ever so charmingly when stirred by chance airs. She had walked round and round it—that was what she felt; she had carried on her existence in the space left her for circulation, a space that sometimes seemed ample and sometimes narrow: looking up all the while at the fair structure that spread itself so amply and rose so high, but never quite making out as yet where she might have entered had she wished. She hadn't wished till now—such was the odd case; and what was doubtless equally odd besides was that though her raised eyes seemed to distinguish places that must serve from within, and especially far aloft, as apertures and outlooks, no door appeared to give access from her convenient garden level. The great decorated surface had remained consistently impenetrable and inscrutable. [II, 3–4]

Like Kate's and Merton's temple of love, the "outlandish pagoda" is inaccessible and mysterious. In her desire to enter, Maggie recognizes the distance separating her in the "garden of life" from the sacred space of the temple. Most alluring are those "apertures and outlooks," which offer such an elevated view of the human scene. The detachment of such outlooks is characteristic of the idealism of both Adam and Maggie.[15] And Maggie herself interprets the temple in terms of that equilibrium of relations that defined social and marital order in the first book: "The pagoda in her blooming garden figured the arrangement— how otherwise was it to be named?—by which, so strikingly, she had been able to marry without breaking, as she liked to put it, with her past. She had surrendered herself to her husband without the shadow of a reserve or a condition and yet hadn't all the while given up her father by the least little inch" (5). Like Daniel Touchett, Adam and Maggie have arranged things to try to preserve time and construct a perverse Eden. The temple symbolizes the deathly quality of their plan. As empty as Adam's House of Civilization, the pagoda suggests the "wasted ingenuity" involved in maintaining such art at the cost of vitality, imagination, or human passion.

As Maggie waits, she sees her imaginative awakening in terms that contrast sharply with the aesthetic symmetry of the ivory pagoda:

Something of this kind was the question that Maggie, while the absentees still delayed, asked of the appearance she was endeavouring to present; but with the result repeatedly again that it only went and lost itself in the thick air that had begun more and more to hang, for our young woman, over her accumulations of the unanswered. They were *there,* these accumulations; they were like a roomful of confused objects, never as yet "sorted," which for some time now she had been passing and re-passing, along the corridor

15. Adam Verver is associated explicitly with the ivory tower much later in the novel. Maggie catches "the polished old ivory of her father's inattackable surface" (*GB,* II, 299).

of her life. She passed it when she could without opening the door; then, on occasion, she turned the key to throw in a fresh contribution. [14]

Maggie's view of relations now assumes the form of a disordered room, heaped with the furniture of the "unanswered," not unlike the confusion in the antiquarian's shop in Bloomsbury. Like that "heterogeneous back-shop of the mind" where the artist is "a wary dealer in precious odds and ends," so Maggie's odds and ends suggest her ambiguity and need (*AN*, 47). Her work is now defined as sorting what she has collected into some new order, a furnished space more livable than the cold interior of the pagoda. In the subtle turns of the narrative, Maggie has rejected the distant ideal of the temple for the creative possibilities of her own imagination.

The more she studies the intricacies of her new problem, the more Maggie distances herself from the other characters. With artistic care Maggie tries to develop herself as a substitute for the empty authority of her father. Watching "the family coach pass," with Amerigo and Charlotte providing the motive power "while she and her father were not so much as pushing," Maggie sees herself "in the picture she was studying, suddenly jump from the coach" (23–4). She is not simply fleeing from the responsibilities of her situation, but leaping out of the relations set in the first book. From her new vantage, Maggie may use her art to protect others from what she has seen. The ugly picture of the bondage of Charlotte and Amerigo would destroy Adam's proud idealism. Maggie intends to save her father from experiencing the guilt of their selfishness in the marriages. And yet Maggie's new detachment resembles that offered by her pagoda. Maggie's design involves a false idealism, which seeks to suppress the truth to preserve her father's dream of order "without a flaw."

In the waiting stillness of these opening chapters, Maggie begins to assume her crucial role for the rest of the narrative. Her power eventually will invade the narrator's own tale: the reader will see the characters increasingly through Maggie's eyes. A great deal of dialogue is replaced by the imaginative speeches Maggie reads out of Amerigo's gestures, Adam's smiles, and Charlotte's tone. For James, however, the artistic consciousness relies on a vital interchange with others. The artist is never an authority, but simply one who makes communication and dialogue possible. In her attempt to preserve a dream of perfect form, Maggie leaves the "blooming garden" of life and begins to construct her own sacred temple. By struggling to contrive and order human relations for the sake of her dream, Maggie sacrifices the diversity of the real for an artificial symmetry. She reminds herself of "an actress who had been studying a part and rehearsing it, but who suddenly, on the stage, before the footlights, had begun to improvise, to speak lines not in the text" (33). Maggie may recognize the ambiguity involved in all moral judgments, but she responds by simplifying and defining ethical categories for others. Acknowledging the absence of any absolute moral values, Maggie bears the burden of such knowledge for Adam, Amerigo, and Charlotte. Thus she strives to relieve the others of the need to choose.

The golden bowl reveals to Maggie the inherent flaw in these arranged marriages. She is terrified by the ambiguity that results from the breakdown of her secure moral categories. When Fanny shatters the bowl on the floor of Maggie's room, she tries to destroy Maggie's idea of it: " 'Whatever you meant by it—and I don't want to know *now*—has ceased to exist' " (179). The golden bowl represents the various meanings characters read out of it. Fanny's act is a partial answer to the dealer's original riddle about the supposed crack in the bowl: " 'But if it's something you can't find out isn't that as good as if it were nothing?' " (I, 114). Every form reveals its essential flaw with the pressures of time and change. As soon as it is broken, the bowl represents the imperfection of any order and the continuing interpretation demanded by this awareness. Mrs. Assingham tries to smash the betrayal that Maggie sees in the bowl. She merely succeeds, however, in suggesting to Maggie the futility of her dreams for happiness and innocence.

Maggie confronts the Prince by struggling to "pick up the pieces" of the bowl and hold them in her hands. In her ritual of stooping and gathering what has been destroyed, Maggie betrays her own sense of sacrifice for the salvation of the marriages. But Maggie can "carry but two of the fragments at once." She cannot save both father and husband; she cannot continue to be both daughter and wife. She must choose and thereby accept the sacrifices her situation demands. In her futile attempt to hold all the pieces of the shattered bowl together, Maggie symbolizes her own intention to preserve *both* marriages and thus the lies on which they are founded.

By replacing the central support of the bowl with her own hands, Maggie dramatizes her will to power and the need she feels to compensate for the weakness of the others. In the twists and turns of the Prince's own "enquiring mind," he has always come up against the "blank wall," that "lapse of logic," which has left him passive and hollow. Maggie's recognition of his moral ambiguity allows her to play upon his desire for order and security:

Hadn't she fairly got into his labyrinth with him?—wasn't she indeed in the very act of placing herself there for him at its centre and core, whence, on that definite orientation and by an instinct all her own, she might securely lead him out of it? She offered him thus assuredly a kind of support that was not to have been imagined in advance and that moreover required—ah most truly!—some close looking at before it could be believed and pronounced void of treachery. "Yes, look, look," she seemed to see him hear her say. . . . "There *is* something for you if you don't too blindly spoil your chance for it."   [II, 187–8]

By a promethean act Maggie places herself at the heart of Amerigo's labyrinth. She makes herself the ineluctable end of his efforts to understand, attempting to make him see her presence as the only source of order for his world. The object of Maggie's art, however, is the preservation of the marriages rather than the rekindling of human passions. If Amerigo is like Theseus in Minos's labyrinth, Maggie acts like Ariadne, lending him that "clew of thread" to wend his way into *her* light of day.[16] Maggie makes herself the mystery at the end of Amerigo's quest. At the close of their interview she makes it clear that she has ceased to be as she was. In the final challenge, " 'Find out for yourself!' " Maggie begins to reorder the marriages in relation to her own central power.

The difference in the marriages made by this scene serves as a preface to the trip to Fawns, where Fanny and the Colonel arrive to practice their customary diplomacy. The drama is focused in the more restricted circle of the country house. In London the Portland Place and Eaton Square houses enabled characters to escape and evade one another. At Fawns the couples must confront each other. Maggie says to the Prince of the shattered golden bowl, " 'We can easily take the pieces with us to Fawns' " (II, 189). The free space of the country is limited by the house itself, another one of Adam Verver's museums. Maggie's power must encircle this space, operating from the outside, as if weaving a mystic circle around her father's world. Her triumph is complete only when the furnishings of Fawns are packed in Adam's ubiquitous crates and the house is left deserted. Only then will Amerigo be forced to see Maggie alone in his long, winding labyrinth. Fond as Maggie is of mythological references, she fails to see that this is hardly the role of Ariadne. Her art transforms her into the minotaur—the destructive element itself.

The circling passage of Maggie's imagination assumes its final form at Fawns.[17] Maggie's power may be seen most clearly during

16. As Theseus performs his serial labors, he serves as an archetypal voyager, wanderer—a role suggested both by Amerigo's name and the images associated with him.

17. See Alan Rose, "The Spatial Form of *The Golden Bowl*," p. 116: "*The Golden Bowl* is constructed on spatial principles. By relating scenes,

the bridge game at the country house. The Prince and Charlotte are paired against Adam and Fanny, while the Colonel sits writing letters at the far end of the room. Maggie tries to nap on a sofa, "much in the mood of a tired actress who had the good fortune to be 'off,' while her mates are on" (II, 231). Instead of sleeping, Maggie leafs through a French review, able to "lend herself to none of those refinements of the higher criticism with which its pages bristled" (232). She reads her own higher criticism into the stiff scene at the card table. Maggie has become the sole interpreter of the text of social relations, while the others mask their uneasiness with the formal moves of bridge. In this game all the other images of the play of relations in the novel as card games, circus acrobatics, and stage drama come together.[18] It is as if the complex game of the novel has been condensed in Maggie's reflective imagination, caught and composed at a distance. The behavior of the players conforms "in the matter of gravity and propriety, to the stiff standard of the house" (233). In this artificial scene Maggie feels the "fascination" of her power growing into a "monstrous temptation" to shatter the superficial calm with a single word (233).

Maggie's obsession drives her out to the darkness of the terrace, where she passes around the house to the windows of the empty drawing room: "Spacious and splendid, like a stage again awaiting a drama, it was a scene she might people, by the press of her spring, either with serenities and dignities and decencies, or with terrors and shames and ruins, things as ugly as those formless fragments of her golden bowl she was trying so hard to pick up" (236). The true terror lurks in the "dignities and decencies" Maggie wants to preserve. Her art attempts to restore the fiction of the bowl without a flaw, the illusion of perfect form. She cannot accept the freedom demanded by the symbolic shattering

---

symbols and images in space, and by employing a prose style that abounds in double grammatical focuses, James has succeeded in concreting the narrative flow."

18. Matthiessen, *Henry James: The Major Phase*, p. 98.

of the bowl. It is in the drawing room she plans to enact her drama, in that space where social appearances are all-important.

While Maggie wanders on the terrace, Charlotte walks into her picture. As they retrace Maggie's earlier walk around the house, Charlotte stops her "within range of the smoking-room window" and they take in the scene: "Side by side for three minutes they fixed this picture of quiet harmonies, the positive charm of it and, as might have been said, the full significance— which, as was now brought home to Maggie, could be no more after all than a matter of interpretation, differing always for a different interpreter" (243–4). Maggie responds to the free play of interpretation with the instinctive dread of her Puritan background. She longs for some total order to resolve the apparent relativity of experience. She sees in the other characters an appeal for her to end the ambiguity, to give their relations a secure foundation. But the only frame Maggie can provide for her picture is as confining as the walls of Adam's House of Civilization. Her meeting with Charlotte seems to promise "a new basis and something like a new system" (241). But Maggie's new order is based on the same flaw that lurked in the golden bowl. Charlotte finally asks the question that will bring the entire "picture of quiet harmonies" crumbling down in the truth of Maggie's answer: " 'Have you any ground of complaint of me? Is there any wrong you consider I've done you?' " Maggie dodges the lie she must utter, " 'What in the world *should* it be?' " and " 'All I can say is that you've received a false impression.' " Finally, Maggie brings it out with a quaver of hesitation: " 'I accuse you—I accuse you of nothing.' " In the "richness, almost . . . gaiety" of her final lie, Maggie submits to the destructive element of her art (247, 250).

Maggie's triumph in preserving the illusion of order requires a redefinition of her moral categories: "The heart of the Princess swelled accordingly even in her abasement; she had kept in tune with the right, and something certainly, something that might be like a rare flower snatched from an impossible ledge, would,

and possibly soon, come out of it for her. The right, the right—
yes, it took this extraordinary form of her humbugging, as she
had called it, to the end. It was only a question of not by a hair's
breadth deflecting into the truth" (250-1). Maggie's sense of
rightness is now a conscious denial of the truth. In order to
preserve the marriages, her moral sense must always diverge
from a truth that declares both human frailty and individual
responsibility. Sustaining this fiction while recognizing the deception is far more of a betrayal than Amerigo's and Charlotte's
moment of weakness. The final kiss consummates Charlotte's
deception and Maggie's lie. Unlike the Judas kiss, however, it is
a *mutual* betrayal of communion. In the moral ambiguity of *The
Golden Bowl* neither betrayer nor betrayed, Judas nor Christ,
may be distinguished easily. Yet as Charlotte acknowledges her
own weakness in the kiss, Maggie asserts her strength through
the lie.

Maggie's art manipulates the psychology of others in subtle
ways. She begins to dominate the consciousness of the other
characters, forcing them to act in accord with her plan, even
though they appear to make their own decisions. Adam tells his
daughter that he wants to return home. Charlotte begs Maggie
to let her take Adam back to America. Maggie knows that her
father is afraid to confront the failure of his marriage, which he
dimly senses. She is equally certain that Amerigo and Charlotte
lack the strength to admit their infidelity and thus sacrifice their
social security. In a curious way, Maggie does what the others
want her to do by substituting her own power for their equivoca-
tion and weakness. Nevertheless, Maggie's acceptance of this
burden results in the sacrifice of authentic love and feeling among
the four characters. Milly's sacrifice brings the world of Lancaster
Gate to a consciousness of itself, Maggie's power is used to
restrict the imagination of others.

When Mr. and Mrs. Verver have finally departed from her
world, the Prince sees the Princess in a world full of *her* meaning,
"everything now, as she vaguely moved about, struck her as

meaning so much that the unheard chorus swelled" (367). At the end of his labyrinth the Prince finally sees only the Princess. In the midst of this empty space, each sees the other looking from an impossible distance. Only terror can be lurking in such vision, the horror of the "thing behind," that lie on which their isolation depends. Marriage assumes its final form in their embrace, a communion of fear and mutual duplicity: "He tried, too clearly, to please her—to meet her in her own way; but with the result only that, close to her, her face kept before him, his hands holding her shoulders, his whole act enclosing her, he presently echoed: ' "See"? I see nothing but *you*.' And the truth of it had with this force after a moment so strangely lighted his eyes that as for pity and dread of them she buried her own in his breast" (368–9). The singleness of Amerigo's final vision contrasts sharply with Maggie's refusal to look. Desire remains unfulfilled. Enclosed in his "whole act," Maggie recognizes that redemption has been brought about at a horrible cost. In this very last moment she seems to give up her power, only to awaken to the reality of her nightmare. The marriages have been preserved by emptying them of all possible meaning.

As the creator of her own romance, Maggie destroys the reality that she and Amerigo might have been able to create together. She denies the freedom implicit in her role as the "American Girl," and uses her imagination to turn herself into the "Princess." Like a figure in a fairy tale, she traps herself in a tower of her own making. For James, the artist must revel in the freedom of his condition. Knowledge is the process of becoming conscious of others. James would have agreed with Nietzsche that "knowing means: 'to place one's self in relation with something,' to feel one's self conditioned by something and one's self conditioning it."[19] None of the characters in *The Golden Bowl* understands such intersubjectivity.

In Kafka's *The Trial*, when Joseph K.'s attorney lies ex-

19. Friedrich Nietzsche, *The Will to Power, Complete Works*, XV, 64.

hausted and dying in an enormous bed in his darkened room, he whispers advice to his clients concerning the law and his interpretation of its justice. Lawyer Huld, whose name means "grace," at first suggests a Christ-like figure bearing the immense burden of man's collective guilt. And yet his clients, like the submissive Herr Block, find themselves repeating endlessly their primal dilemma, eternally doomed to the tangles of their cases. Like Maggie Verver, Huld is a false savior by the very nature of his sacrifice. By consenting to bear the responsibility for his clients, Huld relieves them of the lonely need to examine and interpret their own lives. He offers them a paradoxical kind of consolation. Subjecting themselves to his authority, they never confront the ambiguity of their condition. For Kafka, Law exists because man desires to escape the constant demands of individual interpretation and responsibility. Neither Huld nor Maggie is really diabolical, for their attempts to save their fellows are sincerely motivated. In the modern worlds of James and Kafka, however, any such "salvation" directs man away from his need to become his own messiah, his own interpreter. As Kafka wrote in "The Coming of the Messiah": "The Messiah will come as soon as the most unbridled individualism of faith becomes possible—when there is no one to destroy this possibility and no one to suffer its destruction; . . . The Messiah will come only when he is no longer necessary; he will come only on the day after his arrival; he will come, not on the last day, but on the very last."[20]

All the characters at the end of *The Golden Bowl* share the guilt for their failure: Amerigo lacks imagination and the will to act; Maggie uses her intelligence to control others; Charlotte is doomed to live out the lies of her life; and Adam must struggle to preserve his "innocence." Maggie's failure, however, remains the most significant, for it has taken the greatest expense of potential vitality and imagination. Her conscious refusal to accept the incompletion of man's knowledge and a human frailty that

20. Franz Kafka, "The Coming of the Messiah," in *Parables and Paradoxes*, p. 81.

needs love suggests how the artistic possibilities open to man may be perverted. Maggie may break with her father's naive idealism, but she uses her knowledge to preserve the illusion of order. In her misuse of creative power, she demonstrates how the symmetry of art can do violence to the real.

8 Henry Adams and Henry James in the Context of Modern Literature

A consciousness disjunct
Being but this overblotted
Series
Of intermittences
—Ezra Pound, *Hugh Selwyn Mauberley*, 1920*

The young, dispossessed Isabel Archer dreams of a realm where truth is beauty, beauty truth. Kate Croy and Merton Densher manipulate the world for the sake of an ideal love beyond time, "like a temple without an avenue." Maggie Verver yearns for the golden bowl "without the crack," in the subjunctive of "as it *was* to have been." And Graham Fielder sees his detachment from the corruptions of the world imaged in Rosanna's ivory tower with its protective doors and hidden compartments. Their arts attempt to achieve the symbolic shape of perfect form, completed meaning, and full presence. The language they use ought to be redemptive, prophetic of new, unfallen worlds. They are all on the track of laws, keys, and answers to their fundamental alienation. For them the world is full of meaning only awaiting the proper vision, the correct method of discovery. For the romantic imagination in James's fiction, there must be an inherent order in things.

From such a perspective, the intention of language is to unite, to resolve the differences and contradictions of man in time. Linguistic activity may be interpreted as primarily metaphoric, a means of uncovering relations and similarities between ap-

* From *Personae*. Copyright 1926 by Ezra Pound. Reprinted by permission of New Directions Publishing Corp. and Faber and Faber, Ltd.

parently discordant terms.[1] In the most general sense, such a metaphoric function intends the concordance of consciousness and the world. Metaphor involves a transcendence of self and other and thus embodies an attempt to express the inexpressible. Through his language man ought to discover his true situation and begin to decipher a cosmic order. History becomes the progressive accumulation of meanings; individual identity a problem of shaping experience to fit a dream for order. Consciousness struggles for its justification and the verification of its discoveries. Such an outlook always involves a redemptive vision: that man's alienation might be resolved, his loneliness cured, his thirst for knowledge satisfied.

For Henry Adams eight hundred years of Western civilization seemed to rely on the conception that "in literary language, Thought was God;—Energy in abstract and absolute form;— the ultimate Substance;—*das Ding an sich*. Most philosophy rested on this idea that Thought is the highest or subtlest energy of nature."[2] Adams involved himself in the ancient effort to relate human consciousness and its language to natural force, as in his late scientific essays. If consciousness could be defined in relation to either natural energy or a primal Will, as Schopenhauer had argued, then man might find his place in a general cosmic design.[3] For James's artist and Adams's historian, the

1. See Roman Jakobson, "Two Aspects of Language and Two Types of Aphasic Disturbances," *Selected Writings,* II, 258: "Similarity in meaning connects the symbols of a metalanguage with the symbols of the language referred to. Similarity connects a metaphorical term with the term for which it is substituted."

2. Adams, "A Letter to American Teachers of History," *Degradation of Democratic Dogma,* pp. 219–20.

3. Ibid., p. 194: "For the historian, Schopenhauer's method had the double merit of logically merging the two great historical schools of thought. The old idea of Form, which ruled the philosophy of Aristotle and Thomas Aquinas, slipped readily over the idea of Energy, taught by Kelvin and Clausius, . . . the logic of 'Will' or 'Energetik' imperatively required that every conception whatever, involving a potential, obliged ontologists to regard the will-power of every stem as the source of var-

question remains simple and insistent: "The mind either was an independent energy or it was not."[4]

For the Norman architects of Mont-Saint-Michel and the medieval Schoolmen who structured the Church Intellectual, their arts pointed toward the truth of God, the hidden order of nature. The desire and intention are not so different from the idealism of Isabel Archer or Maggie Verver. For both Adams and James the expression of man's *desire* for unity is what ultimately describes both his art and history. Man's rituals and forms celebrate the presence of an absence, the silence at the center that necessitates the dance. Words present their own significances in a world otherwise devoid of meaning. For Adams and James language affirms the separation of man from the world. A sign is not a transcendent third term through which man may approach the reality of his condition. The need to speak or write is a constant reminder of an external world which man can neither know nor have. In a sense, all writing seems to share the longing implicit in the *Education* for a silence beyond the constant needs of interpretation. Like the narrator of *The Sacred Fount*, the modern writer recognizes with mixed emotions that his activity has itself as its object, that the end of his task uncovers only the need for him to have written.[5] The necessity of interpretation is founded on the absurdity inherent in the irredeemable divorce of man from the world. Camus's expression of the problem reflects the ambiguity with which both Adams and James had to struggle: "The absurd is born of this confronta-

iation in the branches, and to admit, as a physical necessity, that the branch which has lost the power of variation should be regarded as an example of enfeebled energy falling under the second law of thermodynamics."

4. Ibid., p. 221.

5. Roland Barthes, "To Write: An Intransitive Verb?" in *The Languages of Criticism and the Sciences of Man*, p. 144: "The field of the writer is nothing but writing itself, not as the pure 'form' conceived by an aesthetic of art for art's sake, but much more radically, as the only area [*espace*] for the one who writes."

tion between the human need and the unreasonable silence of the world."[6]

Such an outlook involves a language founded on metonymy rather than on metaphor, whose very function affirms the difference between word and thing, consciousness and the world. In his study of aphasic disturbances Roman Jakobson has distinguished two distinct and apparently exclusive linguistic impairments. Whereas speech disturbances in some patients affect their abilities to select and substitute various signs (similarity disorder), in others the functions of combination and contexture are affected (contiguity disorder). These two bipolar characteristics of language ordinarily function together, although one aspect tends to predominate in a particular form of discourse. Jakobson suggests that metaphor is most characteristic of the similarity function, metonymy most appropriate for describing signification through contiguity.[7] In the final section of his study Jakobson speculates on the application of his findings to literary interpretation:

The primacy of the metaphoric process in the literary schools of romanticism and symbolism has been repeatedly acknowledged, but it is still insufficiently realized that it is the predominance of metonymy which underlies and actually predetermines the so-called "realistic" trend, which belongs to an intermediary stage between the decline of romanticism and the rise of symbolism and is opposed to both. Following the path of contiguous relationships, the realist author metonymically digresses from the plot to the atmosphere and from the characters to the setting in space and time. He is fond of synecdochic details.[8]

The prose narratives of Adams and James seem to participate in both this general realistic mode and the phase of literary transition noted by Jakobson. His remarks, however, seem to have certain implications for the epistemology of these writers. The primary intention of such a realism is neither an ultimate meaning nor a

6. Albert Camus, *The Myth of Sisyphus and Other Essays*, p. 21.
7. Jakobson, "Two Aspects of Language," pp. 243, 254.
8. Ibid., p. 255.

central symbol, but that process of signifying which is the perpetual "change of name" of a metonymic mode.

Thus the late Jamesian sentence is less the "refinement of sensibility" than an active variation, the continuing play of contextual and syntactic combinations. Henry James seems to agree with his brother that consciousness is known only through its experienced relations. In his fiction we come to know characters as they are defined through the contiguous relations of the narrative style. The last paragraph of *The Golden Bowl*, the final confrontation of Maggie and Amerigo, illustrates the technique: "He tried, too clearly, to please her—to meet her in her own way; but with the result only that, close to her, her face kept before him, his hands holding her shoulders, his whole act enclosing her, he presently echoed: ' "See"? I see nothing but *you*' " (*GB*, II, 368–9). The syntax of the sentence and the general context of the novel make the elements of James's narrative and dialogue reflect the tension and moral ambiguity of this last encounter. The simple interpretation that Amerigo finally "tried . . . to please her" is undercut by the adverbial modification "too clearly." Amerigo is trying "to please her," but only "to meet her in her own way." The subsequent series indicates how both Amerigo and Maggie are playing their respective games of deception and manipulation to the very last. On the one hand, Amerigo is "close to her" only because her face is "kept before him"; but on the other hand, "his hands holding her shoulders" and "his whole act enclosing her" suggest Maggie's entrapment. Even Amerigo's dialogue echoes Maggie's word "See" and ends with his mocking reference to her control over him: " 'I see nothing but *you*.' " Syntactic contiguity demonstrates the impossibility of speaking any final word concerning the complex moral issues in *The Golden Bowl*. The narrator thus dramatizes the tension between Amerigo and Maggie with the qualification and modification built into our grammar.

In James's works more than masterful technique is involved: an implicit attitude toward language and consciousness. Truth is not the end of the process nor is significance the completion of signification. James speaks of "drawing relations" or "dramatizing a scene"—technical phrases, they involve the recognition that words bear value only in their active relations within a particular context. James's incomplete novels also indicate the limitations of language and the writer's need repeatedly to replace old terms with new signs. No other turn-of-the-century writer demonstrates as clearly as James what Roland Barthes calls "an unfulfilled technique of meaning": "It means that the writer is concerned to multiply significations without filling or closing them, and that he uses language to constitute a world which is emphatically signifying but never finally signified."[9] James finds a homologous relation between consciousness and its defining language. To recognize the differences and ambiguity that compose man's world is a moral imperative in James's later fiction. This attitude refuses absolute truth, completed meaning, and dogmatic tone. Geoffrey Hartman succinctly characterizes James's modern epistemology: "James obstacles himself; he refuses simply to know. Every mind tends to be viewed through another, and the desire to know positively (and can even the artist escape it?) is always presented as a vampirish act."[10]

Adams struggled with his own desire "to know positively." The last chapters of the *Education* suggest, however, that it was a need Adams recognized could not be fulfilled. Adams's dynamics of failure suggests a fundamentally existential mode of survival. At its most lucid Adams's desire to know is not unlike the Sartrean *projet,* which allows man to live into the future: "Fundamentally man is *the desire to be,* and the existence of this desire is not to be established by an empirical induction; it is the result of an *a priori* description of the being of the for-itself [*être pour-soi*], since desire is a lack and since the for-itself is the being which is to itself its own lack of being."[11] For Adams as

9. Barthes, "Literature and Signification," in *Critical Essays,* p. 268.
10. Hartman, *Beyond Formalism,* p. 70.
11. Jean-Paul Sartre, *Being and Nothingness,* p. 565.

well, consciousness recognizes itself through failure and lack, both of which have a metaphysical intention. *Mont-Saint-Michel and Chartres* celebrates man's desire to know God in both the thirteenth and twentieth centuries. Adams regards God as Unity, which ought to be the relation of man to his world, the concordance of self and other. But the failure to know God declares the separation of man from his world, and it is this alienation that is the foundation of man's desire. Sartre's expression of man's desire is no more explicit than Adams's in *Chartres* or the *Education:*

> The best way to conceive of the fundamental project of human reality is to say that man is the being whose project is to be God. Whatever may be the myths and rites of the religion considered, God is first "sensible to the heart" of man as the one who identifies and defines him in his ultimate and fundamental project. If man possesses a pre-ontological comprehension of the being of God, it is not the great wonders of nature nor the power of society which have conferred it upon him. God, value and supreme end of transcendence, represents the permanent limit in terms of which man makes known to himself what he is. To be man means to reach toward being God. Or, if you prefer, man fundamentally is the desire to be God.[12]

What Sartre terms the "pre-ontological comprehension" of God seems to clarify Adams's repeated insistence that unity is the fundamental *instinct* of man. The loss of that instinct is experienced in the attempt to bring God or Unity to consciousness, to conceptualize one's desire for order. Thus Adams argues in *Chartres* that the logic of the Schools marked the decline of the Virgin's power for medieval man. To become conscious is to ask an ontological question that involves its own answer. To question one's being is to miss it, to lack its presence. Consciousness is made necessary because I do not have the world, just as language is demanded by my separation from that for which I must substitute a sign. Consciousness itself is a lack of being, and

12. Ibid., p. 566.

to recognize this is to give up positive knowledge and commit oneself to the phenomenology of knowing. In his later works Adams begins to redefine conventional notions of unity as the desire for unity itself. The authenticity of Henry Adams in the *Education* is based on precisely this notion, and his anguished failures to achieve it are recognitions of a burdensome freedom.

"The desire to know positively" is not the primary focus of Adams's and James's later works alone but is fundamental to modern fiction from Kafka to Camus. The man who refuses to recognize his alienation and accept responsibility for his world is the prisoner of the modern situation. In "The Beast in the Jungle" (1903) John Marcher claims an ironic heroism when he tells May Bartram, " 'I'm only afraid of ignorance to-day— I'm not afraid of knowing.' "[13] Marcher's insistence upon knowing is a denial of his own independence, a commitment to a world that preserves a secret or hides a truth. "The Beast in the Jungle" dramatizes the fact that the truth of man's relation to his world involves a negation. Like Kafka's Joseph K., Marcher is the man who relinquishes his responsibility and thus projects an external fate for himself. The law courts in *The Trial* appear to K. external and inscrutable because he refuses to recognize the need for an internal court in perpetual session. In a similar sense, Marcher's evasive "beast" externalizes his own denial of individual consciousness and his insistence upon an authority outside himself. Like so many other victims of modern anguish, Marcher refuses that choice which is consciousness: " 'It isn't a matter as to which I can *choose,* I can decide for a change. It isn't one as to which there *can* be a change. It's in the lap of the gods. One's in the hands of one's law—there one is. As to the form the law will take, the way it will operate, that's its own affair' " (*B*, 85). James wrote in his *Notebooks* that "the wasting of life is the implication of death."[14] Marcher's wasted life is

13. James, "The Beast in the Jungle," p. 102. Hereafter cited in the text as *B*.

14. James, *Notebooks,* p. 183.

related proportionately to his refusal to accept the necessity of his human situation.

The beast Marcher imagines lurking outside is really devouring him from within. James is especially careful to give Marcher full credit for the image: "Something or other lay in wait for him, amid the twists and turns of the months and years, like a crouching beast in the jungle. Such was the image under which he had ended by figuring his life" (*B*, 79). The entire story and perhaps James's symbolic mode in the later novels as well rely upon Marcher's responsibility for the image of the beast. James regards Marcher as attempting to symbolize nothingness, the "sounded void" at the heart of his desire for the identity the beast ought to bring. Both Marcher and May Bartram come to view it as " 'the real truth' about him"; and the irony is that Marcher does express his impoverished self in his attempt to name that which is silent. Marcher's beast symbolizes his refusal to acknowledge the nothingness on which consciousness and life are founded. In one of his aphorisms, Kafka has described man's refusal of such a condition as his true original sin: "Original sin, the ancient wrong that man has committed, consists in the reproach that man makes and from which he never desists: that a wrong has been done to him, that original sin was committed against him."[15]

Marcher's desire for the "truth of his life" is the destructive element symbolized by his beast. James makes it clear that the desire ends by burdening and deforming man's spirit: "Such a feature in one's outlook was really like a hump on one's back" (*B*, 79). Marcher suffers from pride of detachment from the world, a confidence Puritanical in its insistence on his election to a place of privilege. In the beginning of their long wait for Marcher's "beast" to spring, May Bartram appears as a sympathetic character, whose feelings for another are perverted by Marcher's obsession. In their initial relationship, however, May is no less guilty than Marcher for avoiding life. She views her

15. Kafka, *Beschreibung eines Kampfes,* pp. 295–6; translation mine.

involvement in his special fate as her only access to the inter-personal communication that she has missed in her life. Like Isabel Archer in the early chapters of *Portrait of a Lady*, how-ever, May's desire for romantic love distorts reality. Like the self-destructive characters in *The Sacred Fount*, May and John live each through an other who is little more than a projection of their respective needs. May's submission to John is contrived. Both May and John increasingly withdraw from a wider social world, each fearing any intrusion of the real that might threaten the closed world they have created.

When May finally recognizes that Marcher's "beast" is his means of avoiding life, she lies to protect him and her idea of love from the terrible truth. When Marcher guesses that she knows his secret, she insists that he go on as he is. She fears that Marcher's recognition of his empty life will destroy the one bond that holds them together, as well as the chance for love that March-er represents for her. Thus May lies to avoid confronting the true emptiness that she knows lurks beneath the surface of her own wasted life.

Initially May struggles like Maggie Verver to preserve an artificial relationship, but at the very end she imitates Milly Theale in her sacrifice. Aware that she is dying, May attempts to renew Marcher, to bring him to recognize what he has for-saken for his "unhappy perversion." Perhaps the "deep disorder in her blood" reflects not only her mortality, but her growing awareness that in deluding Marcher she has lost her own integrity. She learns what Maggie avoids in her final embrace with Ameri-go: love must come from the confrontation of two different and independent individuals. Thus she uses her death as Milly uses hers, struggling to destroy illusions in an act of true love: "She showed how she wished to leave their business in order. 'I'm not sure you understood. You've nothing to wait for more. It *has* come' " (*B*, 109–10). May tries to make it possible for Marcher to come to his own understanding of the emptiness she has seen in both their lives. In the climactic scene of the tale May silently offers herself to Marcher, offering him a chance to act in his own way to put them in some new relation. In this moment she transcends the repetitive dialectic of master and slave (or "author" and "victim" of the sacrifice) and offers herself as a sign to Marcher: " 'It's never too late.' She had, with her gliding steps, diminished the distance between them, and she stood nearer to him, close to him, a minute, as if still charged with the unspoken. Her movement might have been for some finer emphasis of what she was at once hesitating and deciding to say" (*B*, 105). Like Milly in her descent to the party in the Palazzo Leporelli, May has transformed herself into a text for interpretation. She recognizes that she alone cannot bring Marcher to understand his wasted life, she can only provide the opportunity for him to see his own truth. Maggie Verver is compelled to "awaken" Charlotte and Amerigo to *her* truth, so that they will see her alone at the center of their labyrinths. But May "only kept him waiting, however; that is he only waited" (*B*, 106) Marcher's hesitation is the sign of her failure. May sees that only in her absence will he learn to see his beast. She has given all she has, and by using her death to lead Marcher to confront his own illusions, May expresses a vital love.

May's absence finally symbolizes Marcher's own emptiness, which he has all too well made for himself. Like the wings of the dove or the ugly text of the golden bowl, the beast in the jungle symbolizes a primal lack, that nothingness which ought to compel man to interpret his world. In the figure of the beast Marcher attempted to give a shape and a name to his own existential predicament. Its beastliness comes to represent Marcher's own resignation of consciousness, his own choice *not to choose*. Marcher resigns his humanity in his refusal to try to "live without appeal" or to preserve "the illusion of freedom" Lambert Strether clings to.[16]

16. See Camus, *Myth of Sisyphus*, p. 39: The absurd man "wants to find out if it's possible to live *without appeal*." James, *Ambassadors*, p.

Marcher has missed not simply romantic love, but more important, the experience of another as other. For James love springs from the awareness of human suffering and loneliness. Even as May is dying, Marcher feels her pain only as *his* loss. Man's ontological anguish has meaning for James only when one can say, You too must be suffering. The experience of nothingness symbolized by the beast ought to suggest a human communion, an intersubjective experience of another's strangeness and alienation. This is what Marcher recognizes he has missed when he watches the mourning widower in the cemetery: "No passion had ever touched him, for this was what passion meant; he had survived and maundered and pined, but where had been *his* deep ravage? He had been *outside* of his life, not learned it from within, the way a woman was mourned when she had been loved for herself" (*B*, 124–5).

Like Maggie terrified at the end of *The Golden Bowl* or Merton and Kate at the end of *Wings of the Dove*, Marcher confronts at last the negative principle that has informed his life. There remains the hint of redemption in such knowledge, as if what he now knows might enable him to re-enter the stream of life: "This horror of waking—*this* was knowledge, knowledge under the breath of which the very tears in his eyes seemed to freeze. Through them, none the less, he tried to fix it and hold it; he kept it there before him so that he might feel the pain. That at least, belated and bitter, had something of the taste of life" (*B*, 126). But Marcher cannot rise to the occasion of this last chance; he still refuses to confront his knowledge. Like Maggie, who hides her face "for pity and dread" of what she sees of herself in Amerigo's eyes, Marcher seeks to avoid his bitter truth: "His eyes darkened—it was close; and, instinctively turning, in his hallucination, to avoid it, he flung himself, face down, on the tomb" (*B*, 126–7). Marcher's final denial seems

---

218: " 'Still, one has the illusion of freedom; therefore don't be, like me, without the memory of that illusion.' "

238 Henry Adams and Henry James

to foreshadow Joseph K.'s summary of his ignorance and death:
" 'Like a dog!' he said; it was as if the shame of it must outlive
him."[17]

John Marcher creates his beast in order to avoid the necessity
of interpretation. James's use of the symbol is designed to destroy
the illusions on which Marcher has built his waiting life. The
symbolic modes of Adams and James seem to attempt a similar
disillusionment. The central symbols in the later works of both
authors reveal through negation. They disclose man's responsibility as they signify their own essential emptiness. And yet the
world is full of signs, man always willing to be betrayed into the
truth. The act of disclosure reveals the nature of such truth to
the interpreter, who only then may recognize the fragile quality
of his translations and creations. The sacred fount offers clues
to a little law, only to reveal the absence of any principle of order
except in the constructing imagination. The wings of the dove
offer the hope of redemption, but in Milly's art bring Merton
and Kate to confront the lie on which they have based their
lives. The golden bowl promises a sacred marriage, only to show
in its flaw the fundamental tensions on which human relations
are founded and sustained. The beast in the jungle threatens a
destiny beyond man's control, but reveals at last the burdensome
freedom of man's alienation.

Adams longs for the absent Virgin, his own personal symbol of
a unity destructive of conventional notions of law or similarity.
The Dynamo announces the degradation of social and even
individual mental forces, as well as man's subservience to natural
force. The Saint-Gaudens sculpture at Rock Creek celebrates a
dream of peace: silence, beyond the continuous need for interpretation. "A Dynamic Theory of History" begins with scientific
confidence and ends in philosophic doubt. In his own dream of
unity Adams recognizes that order itself is perhaps one more
illusion in a universal entropy: "The degradationist replies . . .

17. Kafka, *The Trial*, p. 229.

that the impression of Order is an illusion consequent on the dissolution of the higher Order which had supplied, by lowering its inequalities, all the useful energies that caused progress. The reality behind the illusion, is, therefore, the absence of the power to do useful work,—or what man knows in his finite sensibilities as death."[18] *Pteraspis* serves to symbolize for the degradationist the hopelessness of uniformity, continuity, or progress in either natural or human sequences. Adams's consistent deconstruction of a metaphysics of unity is an attempt to open up the dead categories and illegible signs of the nineteenth century and make it possible for the interpreter to engage his modern situation: "The teacher of 1900, if foolhardy, might stimulate; if foolish, might resist; if intelligent, might balance, as wise and foolish have often tried to do from the beginning; but the forces would continue to educate, and the mind would continue to react. All the teacher could hope was to teach reaction" (*EHA*, 497).

James's and Adams's symbolic modes mediate the silence behind man's existence without hiding it. Their symbolisms actively sustain the tension between nothingness and interpretation that makes it possible for meaning to come into being. But the interpreter's activity consists of more than simply naming his world, for there is always the problem of the fullness of meaning. As Geoffrey Hartman has suggested, "Meaning is everywhere; the problem is that of fullness rather than emptiness, of redundancy and insignificant signification. Things come to us preinterpreted."[19] The languages of James and Adams are designed not only to deconstruct the conventional and "preinterpreted," but also to displace their own signs with new ones, suggesting the *play* rather than the *accretion* of meaning. For James, of course, such a process best reflects the psychology of human relations. The necessity of interpretation demanded by the works of Adams and James gives priority to the act of present vision and its construction of a past relation and future possibility. Man does

18. Adams, "Letter to American Teachers," pp. 256–7.
19. Hartman, *Beyond Formalism*, p. 353.

not cut himself off from his history, but revises and informs it through such an active knowledge. The freedom of the interpreter has a moral content, since the silence that compels his art requires him to accept responsibility for his meanings.

The later works of Adams and James seem to indicate two related tendencies for twentieth-century fiction. The dynamics of failure described in the *Education* suggests the impossibility of man transcending the limits of his own consciousness. The futile effort of Henry Adams to give a formal structure to history from the *History* to *Chartres* and the *Education* implies the fundamental incompletion of human knowledge in a constantly changing universe. Existential fiction, such as Rilke's *Notebooks of Malte Laurids Brigge,* Svevo's *Confessions of Zeno,* and Sartre's *Nausea,* stresses the conflict between man's desire to know positively and the limits of his rational faculties. The paralysis of such a latter-day nihilist as John Barth's Jacob Horner in *The End of the Road* is caused by a similar frustration with man's reason and the contingent nature of reality. The notion that reason can discover only its own reflection in its dealings with a blind universe of force seems central to both Adams's thought and later literature concerned with an absurd reality. Adams's fear that "man created nothing" (EHA, 484) is at the heart of the dark terror in the works of Céline, Sartre, and Beckett.

The "literature of exhaustion," however, also offers the possibility of new and vital art.[20] The free play of interpretation necessitated by man's alienation offers the freedom of signification employed by many modern artists. Jorge Luis Borges, John Barth, and Vladimir Nabokov, seeming to "invent alternatives to the world," are responding to questions about man's knowledge and being posed by the existentialists. Acknowledging

20. See John Barth, "The Literature of Exhaustion," p. 32. Barth uses Borges to demonstrate "how an artist may paradoxically turn the felt ultimacies of our time into material and means for his work—*paradoxically* because by doing so he transcends what had appeared to be his refutation, in the same way that the mystic who transcends finitude is said to be enabled to live, spiritually and physically, in the finite world."

existential literature's commitment to express absurdity, they use the open possibilities of language to create endless myths of what Camus terms man's "difficult wisdom and . . . ephemeral passion."[21] David Foster sees in such literature an openness that "both its multiplicity and its creative vitality bespeak, in the last analysis, its relativeness and its inadequacy ever to attain the 'final' word."[22] These counterrealists seem to give up the need for a truth beyond man's limits, and they commit themselves to the "unreality" of consciousness. Borges writes: "Let us admit what all idealists admit: the hallucinatory nature of the world. Let us do what no idealist has done: seek unrealities which confirm that nature."[23]

James's later works reveal both the potential exhaustion and the vitality of human consciousness. Man may do little but repeat endlessly fundamental questions of being, time, and knowledge. Freud is no more eloquent than Sophocles in dealing with the problems of fathers and sons, Schopenhauer no more syncretic than St. Thomas in expressing man's longing for the security of being. In far more than a mere rhetorical sense, the *style* describes the originality of the artist. In James's fiction the constant interchange of man's conflicting interpretations of his situation reflects the harmony of James's stylistic and philosophic attitudes. The play of relations itself in James's language makes meaning possible.

I do not mean to suggest simply that Adams prefigures an existential literary tradition, whereas James's later novels suggest the possibility of a modern counterrealism. Such distinctions would falsify the complexity of both authors. Adams and James acknowledge the nothingness on which man must found his social, aesthetic, and interpersonal structures. They recognize the need for man to give over false gods and authorities, and to

21. Camus, *Myth of Sisyphus,* p. 87.
22. David Foster, "Borges and Structuralism: Toward an Implied Poetics," p. 346.
23. Jorge Luis Borges, "Avatars of the Tortoise," in *Labyrinths,* p. 208.

accept the responsibilities implicit in individual interpretation and communication. James may seem more capable of sustaining such a tenuous view of human existence and continuing his own creative endeavors, but he also experiences the horror of man's alienation. The game is treacherous and tragic, but perhaps some beauty and nobility lurk in the anguished burden of human consciousness. And Adams himself does not remain paralyzed by his failure to reconcile the conflicting forces of modern life. He complains loudly of man's limitations, and still insists upon multiplying those structures that he knows as the finest and subtlest art. The art of Henry Adams and Henry James uses its artifice to question the nature of all signification, thus returning us at last to the human dialogue we ought to be renewing.

Works Cited

I. GENERAL STUDIES

St. Augustine. *Confessions*. Trans. R. S. Pine-Coffin. Baltimore: Penguin Books, 1961.

Barth, John. "The Literature of Exhaustion." *The Atlantic,* August 1967, 29–34.

Barthes, Roland. *Critical Essays*. Trans. Richard Howard. Evanston, Ill.: Northwestern Univ. Press, 1972.

Borges, Jorge Luis. *Labyrinths*. Ed. Donald Yates and James Irby. New York: New Directions, 1964.

Camus, Albert. *The Myth of Sisyphus and Other Essays*. Trans. Justin O'Brien. New York: Vintage Books, 1955.

Carlyle, Thomas. *Sartor Resartus*. Intro. W. H. Hudson. New York: Dutton, 1965.

Conrad, Joseph. *Lord Jim, A Romance*. Garden City, N.Y.: Doubleday, Doran and Co., 1921.

Cooper, James Fenimore. *The Deerslayer: Or, the First War-Path, A Tale*, 2 vols. Philadelphia: Lea and Blanchard, 1841.

Derrida, Jacques. *L'écriture et la différence*. Paris: Éditions du Seuil, 1967.

Eliot, T[homas] S[tearns]. *Four Quartets*. New York: Harcourt, Brace and World, 1943.

Feidelson, Charles, Jr. *Symbolism and American Literature*. Chicago: Univ. of Chicago Press, 1953.

Fitzgerald, F[rancis] Scott. *The Great Gatsby*. New York: Charles Scribner's Sons, 1925.

Foster, David. "Borges and Structuralism: Toward an Implied Poetics." *Modern Fiction Studies,* XIX (Autumn 1973), 341–51.

Foucault, Michel. *Madness and Civilization: A History of Insanity in the Age of Reason*. Trans. Richard Howard. New York: New American Library, 1965.

Franklin, Benjamin. *Benjamin Franklin's Autobiography and Selected Writings*. Ed. Larzer Ziff. New York: Holt, Rinehart, and Winston, 1967.

Gibbon, Edward. *The Autobiography of Edward Gibbon*. Ed. Lord Sheffield. London: Oxford Univ. Press, 1907.

Goldmann, Lucien. *The Hidden God: A Study of Tragic Vision in the "Pensées" of Pascal and the Tragedies of Racine*. Trans. Philip Thody. New York: Humanities Press, 1964.

Hartman, Geoffrey. *Beyond Formalism: Literary Essays, 1958–1970*. New Haven: Yale Univ. Press, 1970.

Hawthorne, Nathaniel. *The English Notebooks*. Ed. Randall Stewart. New York: Russell and Russell, Inc., 1962.

——. *The Marble Faun*, vols. IX–X in *The Complete Writings of Nathaniel Hawthorne*. 22 vols. Boston: Houghton Mifflin and Co., 1900.

Holton, Milne. *Cylinder of Vision: The Fiction and Journalistic Writings of Stephen Crane*. Baton Rouge: Louisiana State Univ. Press, 1972.

Jakobson, Roman. *Selected Writings*. The Hague: Mouton, 1971.

James, William. *Essays in Radical Empiricism and A Pluralistic Universe*. Ed. Ralph Barton Perry. Gloucester, Mass.: Peter Smith, 1967.

——. *Some Problems of Philosophy*. New York: Longmans, Green and Co., 1911.

Jean-Aubry, G. *Joseph Conrad: Life and Letters*. 2 vols. Garden City, N.Y.: Doubleday, Page and Co., 1927.

Kafka, Franz. *Beschreibung eines Kampfes: Novellen, Skizzen, Aphorismen aus dem Nachlass*. New York: Schocken Books, 1946.

——. *Parables and Paradoxes*. New York: Schocken Books, 1958.

——. *The Trial*. Trans. Willa and Edwin Muir. New York: Schocken Books, 1964.

Lévi-Strauss, Claude. *The Savage Mind*. Trans. George Weidenfeld and Nicolson, Ltd. Chicago: Univ. of Chicago Press, 1966.

——. *Tristes Tropiques: An Anthropological Study of Primitive Societies in Brazil*. Trans. John Russell. New York: Atheneum, 1964.

Macksey, Richard and Donato, Eugenio, eds. *The Languages of*

Criticism and the Sciences of Man: The Structuralist Controversy. Baltimore: The Johns Hopkins Press, 1970.

Malraux, André. *The Voices of Silence.* Trans. Stuart Gilbert. Garden City, N.Y.: Doubleday and Co., 1956.

Man, Paul de. "Literary History and Literary Modernity." Ed. Morton W. Bloomfield, *In Search of Literary Theory* (Ithaca: Cornell University Press, 1972), pp. 237–67.

Melville, Herman. *Clarel: A Poem and Pilgrimage in the Holy Land.* Ed. Walter E. Bezanson. New York: Hendricks House, 1960.

——. *The Letters of Herman Melville.* Ed. Merrell R. Davis and William H. Gilman. New Haven: Yale Univ. Press, 1960.

——. *Moby-Dick or, the Whale.* Ed. Luther S. Mansfield and Howard P. Vincent. New York: Hendricks House, 1952.

——. *The Portable Melville.* Ed. Jay Leyda. New York: Viking Press, 1952.

——. *White Jacket: or the World in a Man-of-War.* Intro. William Plomer. New York: Grove Press, 1956.

Miller, J[oseph] Hillis. *The Form of Victorian Fiction.* Notre Dame, Ind.: Univ. of Notre Dame Press, 1968.

Nietzsche, Friedrich. *The Will to Power,* vols. XIV–XV in *The Complete Works of Friedrich Nietzsche.* Trans. Antony M. Ludovici. New York: Russell and Russell, Inc., 1964.

Ortega y Gasset, José. *The Dehumanization of Art and Other Essays on Art, Culture, and Literature.* Princeton: Princeton Univ. Press, 1968.

——. *History as a System and Other Essays toward a Philosophy of History.* New York: W. W. Norton, 1961.

Pearce, Roy Harvey. *The Continuity of American Poetry.* Princeton: Princeton Univ. Press, 1961.

——. "Whitman: The Poet in 1860." *Historicism Once More: Problems and Occasions for the American Scholar.* Princeton: Princeton Univ. Press, 1969.

Pound, Ezra. *Literary Essays of Ezra Pound.* Ed. T. S. Eliot. London: Faber and Faber, 1960.

Ruskin, John. *The Seven Lamps of Architecture.* London: Smith, Elder, and Co., 1849.

Sartre, Jean-Paul. *Being and Nothingness: An Essay on Phenomeno-*

logical Ontology. Trans. Hazel E. Barnes. New York: Philosophical Library, 1956.

Saussure, Ferdinand de. *Course in General Linguistics.* Ed. Charles Bally and Albert Sechehaye, in collab. with Albert Reidlinger. Trans. Wade Baskin. New York: McGraw-Hill, 1966.

Spiller, Robert E., ed. *The American Literary Revolution: 1783–1837.* Garden City, N.Y.: Doubleday and Co., 1967.

Tanner, Tony. *City of Words: American Fiction 1950–1970.* New York: Harper and Row, 1971.

Thompson, Lawrance. *Melville's Quarrel with God.* Princeton: Princeton Univ. Press, 1952.

Thoreau, Henry David. *The Variorum Walden.* Ed. Walter Harding. New York: Twayne Publishers, 1962.

——. *A Week on the Concord and Merrimack Rivers.* New York: New American Library, 1961.

Urban, W[ilbur] M[arshall]. *Language and Reality.* London: Allen and Unwin, 1939.

Vincent, Howard P. *The Tailoring of Melville's "White-Jacket."* Evanston, Ill.: Northwestern Univ. Press, 1970.

Vodička, Felix. "The Integrity of the Literary Process: Notes on the Development of Theoretical Thought in J. Mukařovský's Work." *Poetics,* IV (1972), 5–16.

Whitman, Walt. *Leaves of Grass.* Ed. Sculley Bradley and Harold Blodgett. New York: W. W. Norton, 1973.

Wild, John. *The Radical Empiricism of William James.* New York: Anchor Books, 1970.

Wilden, Anthony. "Death, Desire and Repetition in Svevo's *Zeno.*" *Modern Language Notes,* LXXXIV (1969), 98–119.

II. HENRY ADAMS

The Degradation of the Democratic Dogma. New York: Macmillan, 1919.

Democracy: An American Novel. London: Macmillan and Co., 1882.

The Education of Henry Adams. Boston: Houghton Mifflin Co., 1918.

Esther: A Novel. By Franc[e]s Snow Compton [pseud.]. 1884.

Reprint, intro. Robert E. Spiller. New York: Scholars' Facsimiles and Reprints, 1938.

The History of the United States During the Administrations of Jefferson and Madison. 9 vols. New York: Charles Scribner's Sons, 1889–1891.

Letters of Henry Adams (1858–1891). Ed. Worthington Chauncey Ford. Boston: Houghton Mifflin Co., 1930.

Letters of Henry Adams (1892–1918). Ed. Worthington Chauncey Ford. Boston: Houghton Mifflin, 1938.

Letters to a Niece and Prayer to the Virgin of Chartres. With a niece's memories by Mabel La Farge. Boston: Houghton Mifflin Co., 1920.

Mont-Saint-Michel and Chartres. Boston: Houghton Mifflin Co., 1913.

Tahiti: Memoirs of Arii Taimai e Marama of Eimeo, Teriirere of Tooarai, Terrinui of Tahiti, Tauraatua i Amo, Memoirs of Marau Toaroa, Last Queen of Tahiti. 1901. Reprint, ed. Robert Spiller. New York: Scholars' Facsimiles and Reprints, 1947.

Adams, Mrs. Henry. *The Letters of Mrs. Henry Adams 1865–1883.* Ed. Ward Thoron. Boston: Little, Brown, and Co., 1936.

Aiken, Henry David. "Foreword" to *Democracy.* New York: New American Library, 1961.

Baym, Max I. *The French Education of Henry Adams.* 1951. Reprint, New York: Columbia Univ. Press, 1969.

Bell, Millicent. "Adams's *Esther:* the Morality of Taste." *New England Quarterly,* XXXV (June 1962), 147–61.

Blackmur, R. P. "The Harmony of True Liberalism: Henry Adams's *Mont-Saint-Michel and Chartres.*" *Sewanee Review,* LX (1952), 1–27.

Branner, Robert, ed. *Chartres Cathedral.* Norton Critical Study in Art History. New York: W. W. Norton and Co., 1969.

Cater, Harold Dean. *Henry Adams and His Friends: A Collection of His Unpublished Letters.* Boston: Houghton Mifflin Co., 1947.

Colacurcio, Michael. "The Dynamo and the Angelic Doctor: The Bias of Henry Adams' Medievalism." *American Quarterly,* XVII (1965), 696–712.

Conder, John. *A Formula of His Own: Henry Adams's Literary Experiment*. Chicago: Univ. of Chicago Press, 1970.

Hochfield, George. *Henry Adams: An Introduction and Interpretation*. New York: Barnes and Noble, 1962.

Hume, Robert A. *Runaway Star: An Appreciation of Henry Adams*. Ithaca, N.Y.: Cornell Univ. Press, 1951.

Jordy, William H. *Henry Adams, Scientific Historian*. New Haven: Yale Univ. Press, 1952.

Koretz, Gene H. "Augustine's *Confessions* and *The Education of Henry Adams*," *Comparative Literature*, XII (Summer 1960), 193–206.

Levenson, J. C. *The Mind and Art of Henry Adams*. Boston: Houghton Mifflin Co., 1957.

Lyon, Melvin. *Symbol and Idea in Henry Adams*. Lincoln: Univ. of Nebraska Press, 1970.

Mane, Robert. *Henry Adams on the Road to Chartres*. Cambridge: Harvard Univ. Press, 1971.

Minter, David L. *The Interpreted Design as a Structural Principle in American Prose*. New Haven: Yale Univ. Press, 1969.

Samuels, Ernest. *Henry Adams: The Middle Years*. Cambridge: Harvard Univ. Press, 1958.

——. *Henry Adams: The Major Phase*. Cambridge: Harvard Univ. Press, 1964.

Sayre, Robert F. *The Examined Self: Benjamin Franklin, Henry Adams, Henry James*. Princeton: Princeton Univ. Press, 1964.

Scheyer, Ernst. *The Circle of Henry Adams: Art and Artists*. Detroit: Wayne State Univ. Press, 1970.

Wagner, Vern. *The Suspension of Henry Adams: A Study of Manner and Matter*. Detroit: Wayne State Univ. Press, 1969.

White, Lynn, Jr. "Dynamo and Virgin Reconsidered." *American Scholar*, XXVII (Spring 1958), 183–94.

III. HENRY JAMES

The American Scene. Bloomington, Ind.: Indiana Univ. Press, 1968.

The Art of the Novel: Critical Prefaces. Ed. R. P. Blackmur. New York: Charles Scribner's Sons, 1934.

The Complete Tales of Henry James. 12 vols. Ed. Leon Edel. Philadelphia: J. B. Lippincott Co., 1964.

Italian Hours. New York: Horizon Press, 1968.

The Letters of Henry James. 2 vols. Ed. Percy Lubbock. New York: Charles Scribner's Sons, 1920.

The Notebooks of Henry James. Ed. F. O. Matthiessen and Kenneth B. Murdock. New York: Oxford Univ. Press, 1947.

Notes of a Son and Brother. London: Macmillan and Co., 1914.

The Novels and Tales of Henry James. The New York Edition. 26 vols. New York: Charles Scribner's Sons, 1907–1917.

    The Portrait of a Lady, vols. III–IV. 1908.

    The Altar of the Dead, The Beast in the Jungle, The Birthplace, and Other Tales, vol. XVII. 1909.

    The Wings of the Dove, vols. XIX–XX. 1909.

    The Ambassadors, vols. XXI–XXII. 1909.

    The Golden Bowl, vols. XXIII–XXIV. 1909.

Partial Portraits. 1888. Reprint. Ann Arbor: Univ. of Michigan Press, 1970.

The Sacred Fount. New York: Charles Scribner's Sons, 1901.

Selected Literary Criticism of Henry James. Ed. Morris Shapira. London: William Heinemann, 1963.

A Small Boy and Others. New York: Charles Scribner's Sons, 1913.

Allott, Miriam. "The Bronzino Portrait in Henry James's *The Wings of the Dove." Modern Language Notes,* LXVIII (January 1953), 23–5.

Bell, Millicent. "The Dream of Being Possessed and Possessing: Henry James's *The Wings of the Dove." Massachusetts Review,* X (1969), 97–114.

Buitenhuis, Peter. *The Grasping Imagination: The American Writings of Henry James.* Toronto: Univ. of Toronto Press, 1970.

Edel, Leon. *Henry James: The Master, 1901–1916.* Philadelphia: J. B. Lippincott Co., 1972.

Holland, Laurence. *The Expense of Vision: Essays on the Craft of Henry James.* Princeton: Princeton Univ. Press, 1964.

Krook, Dorothea. *The Ordeal of Consciousness in Henry James.* Cambridge: Cambridge Univ. Press, 1967.

Matthiessen, F[rancis] O[tto]. *Henry James: The Major Phase*. New York: Oxford Univ. Press, 1963.

——. *The James Family*. New York: Alfred Knopf, 1961.

McComb, Arthur. *Agnolo Bronzino: His Life and Works*. Cambridge: Harvard Univ. Press, 1928.

Michel, André and Migeon, Gaston. *Le musée du louvre, sculptures et objets d'art*. . . . Paris: Librairie Renouard, 1912.

Morris, Wright. *The Territory Ahead*. New York: Atheneum, 1963.

Poulet, Georges. *Studies in Human Time*. Trans. Elliott Coleman. Baltimore: The Johns Hopkins Press, 1956.

Rose, Alan. "The Spatial Form of *The Golden Bowl*." *Modern Fiction Studies*, XII (Spring 1966), 103–16.

Ward, J[oseph] A. *The Search for Form: Studies in the Structure of James's Fiction*. Chapel Hill: Univ. of North Carolina Press, 1967.

Wegelin, Christof. *The Image of Europe in Henry James*. Dallas, Tex.: Southern Methodist Univ. Press, 1958.

Winner, Viola Hopkins. *Henry James and the Visual Arts*. Charlottesville: Univ. of Virginia Press, 1970.

Index